Theory and Credibility

Theory and Credibility

INTEGRATING THEORETICAL AND
EMPIRICAL SOCIAL SCIENCE

SCOTT ASHWORTH

CHRISTOPHER R. BERRY

ETHAN BUENO DE MESQUITA

PRINCETON UNIVERSITY PRESS
PRINCETON & OXFORD

Published by Princeton University Press
41 William Street, Princeton, New Jersey 08540
6 Oxford Street, Woodstock, Oxfordshire OX20 1TR

press.princeton.edu

Library of Congress Cataloging-in-Publication Data

Names: Ashworth, Scott, 1972- author. | Berry, Christopher R., author. |
    Bueno de Mesquita, Ethan, 1974- author.
Title: Theory and credibility : integrating theoretical and empirical
    social science / Scott Ashworth, Christopher R. Berry, Ethan Bueno de
    Mesquita.
Description: Princeton : Princeton University Press, [2021] | Includes
    bibliographical references and index.
Identifiers: LCCN 2021004843 (print) | LCCN 2021004844 (ebook) | ISBN
    9780691213835 (hardback) | ISBN 9780691213828 (paperback) | ISBN
    9780691215006 (ebook)
Subjects: LCSH: Social sciences—Research—Philosophy. | Quantitative
    research. | Mathematical models. | Empiricism.
Classification: LCC H62 .A693 2021 (print) | LCC H62 (ebook) | DDC
    300.72—dc23
LC record available at https://lccn.loc.gov/2021004843
LC ebook record available at https://lccn.loc.gov/2021004844

British Library Cataloging-in-Publication Data is available

Editorial: Bridget Flannery-McCoy and Alena Chekanov
Production Editorial: Nathan Carr
Jacket/Cover Design: Karl Spurzem
Production: Erin Suydam
Publicity: Kate Hensley and Kathryn Stevens

This book has been composed in Arno and Helvetica Neue LT Std

10 9 8 7 6 5 4 3 2 1

For Mom and Dad
SA

For Ané
CB

For Rebecca
EBdM

CONTENTS

PREFACE

We first started thinking systematically about the themes in this book when we had the opportunity to direct the Empirical Implications of Theoretical Models (EITM) Summer Institute in 2011. When we joined the EITM team, we thought we had a pretty good understanding of how theory and empirics fit together. As you can see from the publication date of this book, that turned out not to be the case.

Writing down our ideas, and especially trying to teach them to a group of truly outstanding students, forced us to confront the many ways in which they were incomplete, ill formed, and often wrong. It also set us on a path whereby we were given frequent opportunities to write, think, and debate about these issues with colleagues around the world. Those conversations were essential for straightening out our thinking.

Some of the most important conversations took place at our home institution, the Harris School at the University of Chicago. At the same time we were starting to grapple with these difficult intellectual issues, we and a core group of colleagues were working to build a research group at Harris whose animating idea was to foster a robust dialogue between theory and empirics. Our experiences as part of this intellectual community—in seminars, through co-authorships, and by training graduate students together—helped us learn what a fruitful interaction between theory and empirics looks like.

A decade on, we certainly do not have all of the issues figured out. But we have learned some lessons along the way that not only clarified our thinking but changed the way we do our research. We hope they might be of similar value to other scholars.

Who Is This Book For?

First and foremost, we wrote this book for PhD students who are thinking about how they can contribute to substantive literatures that are important to them and about how the kind of work they want to do fits into the larger enterprise of political science. It is easy to lose the forest for the trees during graduate training. In the midst of a formal theory or methods class, it can be hard to see how either enterprise connects to the other, much less how the two together relate to the research questions that animate you. We hope that reading this book alongside that training will help you gain perspective on why you are learning what you are learning and how you will ultimately put it to use.

Graduate students are not, however, our only target audience. Our own experience suggests that gaining new perspective on these issues can be valuable, even post-tenure. So we hope this book will also be read by colleagues who are interested in exploring or revisiting questions about how theory and empirics work together to advance our disciplinary goals.

And, of course, it would make a nice stocking stuffer for anyone on your list with an interest in formal theory and causal inference.

How to Use This Book

There are two ways to think about using this book. One is as a book to read. If that's your plan, we recommend starting at the beginning and going to the end. The other is as a classroom text. In that case, there are a few options.

We think this book could make a useful contribution to several different kinds of classes offered in political science PhD programs. The most straightforward use is in a class designed to introduce students to the logic of social scientific inquiry.

A second use is as a supplementary reading in a formal theory or causal inference course. In the former, Chapter 4 may be particularly useful for helping students think about the value of simple models and abstraction. And in the latter, Chapter 5 is designed to help students think conceptually about issues of substantive identification without getting lost in the technical details that are covered in their textbooks. In both cases, showing how the technical work of the course will pay off in terms of substance may be motivating for many students.

A third use is as an early context-setting reading in a more applied course or field seminar. The book provides several tools that will be useful to students as they read particular research contributions or work to make sense of literatures. For instance, both the framework presented in Figure 2.1 of Chapter 2 and the tool we call the ERD in Chapter 5 can be applied to almost any paper. We think doing so will be a clarifying exercise for many students.

Finally, at the Harris School, we teach a graduate course specifically about the interaction of theory and empirics. Part I of this book, along with a subset of the papers we discuss in Part II, constitute the syllabus of that course. For such a course, it is important to note how Part II is organized. In each chapter, we describe one of the ways in which theory and empirics interact. We then discuss several papers that illustrate the idea. Each paper adds something new. But an instructor could nonetheless pick and choose one or two sections from each of these chapters along with their introductions and conclusions. And, indeed, there are certain substantive threads that run across chapters (e.g., the role of parties in congress, the relationship between the economy and civil conflict, electoral accountability). So the picking and choosing can be done in a way that creates substantive coherence.

One final note concerns technicality, which we've tried to keep to a minimum. Our focus is on conceptual understanding. This book is intended as a complement for textbooks in formal theory or causal inference, not a substitute. We believe reading this book will be most valuable to those who are concurrently learning those topics or have had at least some prior exposure.

ACKNOWLEDGMENTS

We are indebted to Skip Lupia for inviting us to join the EITM team and to Skip and the other co-PIs and organizers—Brandice Canes-Wrone, Scott de Marchi, Sean Gailmard, Kosuke Imai, and Adam Meirowitz—for many thoughtful and stimulating discussions. We also appreciate feedback from the participants and other instructors at several EITM Summer Institutes where we presented some of this material, including 2011 in Chicago, 2012 in Princeton, 2014 in Mannheim, and 2017 in Berkeley. The wonderful team of mentoring faculty in residence—Daniel Berger, Laurel Harbridge-Yong, Bethany Lacina, Michael Peress, Margaret Peters, and Dustin Tingley—at the Chicago EITM deserve special recognition.

We are truly grateful to Chris Blattman and Will Howell, who went well above and beyond the obligations of collegiality, reading and rereading drafts of our early chapters in a desperate attempt to help us write better.

We received incredibly detailed and thoughtful feedback from the participants in book conferences held at the University of Chicago and Stanford. They include Avi Acharya, Dan Black, Chris Blattman, Peter Buisseret, Steve Callander, Katherine Casey, Emilee Chapman, Daniel Diermeier, Jesse Driscoll, Oeindrila Dube, Steven Durlauf, James Fearon, Dana Foarta, Alex Fouirnaies, Anthony Fowler, Sean Gailmard, Josh Gottlieb, Justin Grimmer, Jens Hainmueller, Will Howell, Ryan Kellogg, Keith Krehbiel, Andrew Little, Greg Martin, Daniel Moskowitz, Jack Paine, Soledad Artiz Prillaman, Mehdi Shadmehr, Ken Shotts, Austin Wright, and Adam Zelizer. We are especially grateful to Andy Hall, who organized the Stanford conference for us, and to Nolan McCarty, whose efforts to organize one for us at Princeton were undermined by a global pandemic.

Dimitri Landa, Sandy Gordon, and Stephane Wolton generously provided detailed comments on large parts of the manuscript, which we enormously appreciate.

In addition, we have benefited from conversations with and comments by David Baron, David Brockman, Professor Ed Doob, Matthew Gentzkow, Mathias Iaryczower, Kris Ramsay, Cyrus Samii, Dustin Tingley, Rocio Titiunik, Scott Tyson, participants in the Emory Institute for Quantitative Theory and Method's conference on "Research Design is Not Enough" including Chuck Cameron, Tom Clark, Adam Glynn, Pablo Montagnes, Nolan McCarty, Betsy Sinclair, Jeff Staton, participants in the Warwick Festschrift Conference in honour of Ken Shepsle including Bruce Bueno de Mesquita, Torun Dewan, John Eguia, John Ferejohn, Abhinay Muthoo, John Patty, Maggie Penn, Ken Shepsle, and Barry Weingast, and participants in the APSA and MPSA roundtables on "Causal Inference, Big Data, and Theory" organized by Matt Golder and Bill Clark, and including Sean Gailmard, Justin Grimmer, Luke Keele, John Patty, Maggie Penn, Rocio Titiunik, and Josh Tucker. Mike Cheng and Xiaoyan Wang provided excellent research assistance.

It was a pleasure to work with the team at Princeton University Press. We are thankful to Bridget Flannery-McCoy for her support of our work and to several anonymous referees whose feedback made a huge difference in the quality of our argument.

Finally, our greatest debt is to our families. Georgia, Ané, Diego, Alondra, Rebecca, Abe, and Hannah offered support and patience, even while quarantined with us for months as we put the finishing touches on this project. We hope it is some solace that, having endured so many close-quarters, out loud manuscript readings, they'll be under no obligation to actually read the final product.

Theory and Credibility

1

Introduction

The rise of formal theory and the credibility revolution are two of the great developments in social science over the past half century. With these advances, the potential for productive dialogue between theory and empirics has never been greater.

So it is distressing that, in political science, theory and empirics appear to be drifting apart. Ironically, these two developments, which should be drawing scholars together, have instead been dividing them.

The credibility revolution has sensitized social scientists to the challenges of separating correlation from causation and forced us to reckon with the plausibility of the causal interpretations routinely given to empirical estimates (Angrist and Pischke, 2010; Samii, 2016). But it has also opened up a schism.

On one side are scholars concerned that the pursuit of credible causal estimates is displacing the canonical goal of understanding important political phenomena. The papers we write, they argue, seem no longer to be about the questions that motivate us. "Why does this important thing happen?" has been replaced by "What is the effect of x on y?" Scholars with this worry might agree with some of the credibility revolution's critique of prior practice. But they fear it has gone too far. They see adherents of the credibility revolution as dismissive of what can be, and indeed what has been, learned by empirical scholars employing other approaches. The credibility revolution, they hold, unnecessarily limits the scope of evidence that is considered legitimate. We have let a fetish for a particular kind of credibility distract us from our true goals. Political scientists have expressed these worries in various ways. Clark and Golder (2015) describe the rise of "radical empiricism" divorced from theory. Huber (2013) laments that, because "good causal identification is not always possible on questions of central importance," the credibility revolution has led political scientists to "excessively narrow the range of questions we ask." And Binder (2019, p. 419) warns that "prioritizing identification strategies risks losing sight of the theoretical and analytical interests that motivate the research."

On the other side are scholars who have embraced the credibility revolution, arguing that much of the canonical quantitative work in political science offered only what Gerber, Green, and Kaplan (2014) call "the illusion of learning." For these scholars, there is no point in tackling questions that cannot be answered well. We should instead focus on questions accessible to credible research designs. Samii (2016, p. 941) describes the "prevailing convention in political science" prior to the credibility revolution as "what we might call mass production of quantitative 'pseudo-general pseudo-facts' through multiple regression." And Sekhon (2009, p. 503) argues that "without an experiment, a natural experiment, a discontinuity, or some other strong design, no amount of econometric or statistical modeling can make the move from correlation to causation persuasive. This conclusion has implications for the kind of causal questions we are able to answer with some rigor."

This schism recalls the earlier divide opened up by the rise of formal theory and its increased focus on model building (Green and Shapiro, 1994; Friedman, 1996; Walt, 1999). Like the adherents of the credibility revolution, early rational choice theorists, as Green and Shapiro (1994, p. 3) describe, "[did] not contend that traditional political scientists have studied the wrong phenomena," but rather that they "have studied the right phenomena in the wrong ways."

In the role of today's critics of the credibility revolution were those worried that a fetishization of mathematical elegance was distracting political scientists from the goal of generating insights that were genuinely useful for explanation or suitable for empirical assessment. Green and Shapiro (1996, p. 54) lamented that "empirical progress has been retarded by what may be termed method-driven, as opposed to problem-driven, research." What is interesting or useful, critics asked, about narrow models built on assumptions that bear, at best, only a distant relationship to reality? For instance, in his critique of formal models in international relations, Walt (1999, p. 9) argued that "[a] consistent, precise yet trivial argument is of less value than a bold new conjecture that helps us understand some important real-world problem . . . a logically consistent but empirically false theory is of little value."

Lined up to oppose such critics were those arguing that formalization allows scholars to avoid errors of logic and achieve greater transparency. Responding to Walt, Powell (1999, p. 98) argued, "[e]ven if tightening the connections between assumptions and conclusions were all that formal theory had to offer, this would be a very important contribution." Cameron and Morton (2002) point to three virtues of formalization: seeing with clarity which assumptions drive which results, avoiding mistakes of logic through rigor, and achieving a kind of unity or coherence by eschewing hypotheses that depend on contradictory assumptions.

These two schisms foreshadowed today's deepening divide between theorists and empiricists. While, in principle, nearly everyone agrees that theory and empirics ought to work together, in practice, each side feels the other often doesn't hold up its end of the bargain. On the one hand, a group of theoretically minded scholars is baffled and dismayed by the empirical turn toward research designs for credibly answering narrow causal questions. Why, they wonder, are empiricists obsessed with carefully answering uninteresting questions, rather than doing work that speaks to theoretical questions? On the other hand, a group of empirically minded scholars is similarly baffled and dismayed by theorists' focus on abstract models built on, from their perspective, demonstrably false assumptions. Of what use, they wonder, can such models be for explaining the world or guiding empirical inquiry?

As a result of this mutual puzzlement and dissatisfaction, these two groups are pulling apart—going about their own business and viewing the other with increasing skepticism. This widening gap threatens the link between theory and empirics that is essential to the social scientific enterprise.

The moment is ripe to draw these two groups back together. Formal theory and the credibility revolution are natural partners that, together, can support a richer and more productive dialogue between theory and empirics than has ever before been possible in political science.

However, as a discipline, we are not currently prepared to realize this potential. Empiricists and theorists alike are too quick to dismiss one another's enterprise. We all need a better framework for thinking about how the two fit together. Each side needs to better understand what kind of knowledge the other is trying to create, and how they go about it. Only with this understanding will theorists see how to make their models genuinely useful to empirical inquiry and empiricists see how to structure their research in ways that speak to theoretically meaningful questions.

This book provides such a framework. We explain to empiricists why theorists build the sorts of models they do, the kind of understanding such models provide, and how such models generate insight that is vital for interpreting empirical evidence. We explain to theorists why empiricists use the sorts of research designs they do, the kind of quantities credible research designs estimate, and why those quantities are exactly what is needed to speak to theoretical questions. And we give both sides a way of thinking about how these two activities together underpin the accumulation of social scientific knowledge.

We do this through both conceptual analysis and detailed examples. Some of the ideas may be familiar. Others will be new. We organize and synthesize them in ways we believe are conceptually clarifying. One payoff of this book, then, is to help scholars better understand how their own research fits into the overall enterprise of political science and what that enterprise entails. This is the work of Part I.

But conceptual understanding, though important, is not our end goal. We want this conceptual understanding to have a practical payoff for research. We believe this book will give scholars, from first-year PhD students to seasoned veterans, a lens that brings into focus opportunities for substantively important contributions that might otherwise be missed. More than anything else, understanding and pursuing these intellectually exciting opportunities for real synergy will bring us back together and improve our discipline. This is the work of Part II.

Our argument starts with the observation that theoretical implications are always all-else-equal claims. This means holding all else equal in empirics is important, for two reasons. First, if the empirical analysis has not held all else equal, we don't know whether the reason for disagreement between a theoretical implication and an empirical estimate is that the theoretical mechanism is not at work or that the empirical estimate and theoretical implication are about different quantities. Second, an empirical finding is a better guide for theorizing when it is about the sort of all-else-equal relationship theoretical models produce as implications.

For an example of how holding all else equal is important for assessing theory, consider the empirical finding that members of the House Appropriations Committee secure more pork than those not on the committee (e.g., Lazarus, 2010). This finding is often taken as confirmatory evidence for the theoretical claim that congressional rules grant committee members outsized influence (Shepsle and Weingast, 1987). But that finding is actually not very informative about the theory. The theoretical implication is an all-else-equal one. But the empirical comparison fails to hold all else equal—for instance, we might worry that the sort of member who can secure a coveted seat on Appropriations might also be the sort of member who would have captured more federal funding regardless. When we use the tools of the credibility revolution to take the all-else-equal caveat more seriously, things don't look as good for the theory. For instance, Berry and Fowler (2016) compare the spending garnered by the same member before and after gaining a seat on Appropriations and find the bump from joining Appropriations is negligible.

For an example of how formal theory is particularly useful for interpreting empirical findings that hold all else equal, consider the empirical literature showing that exogenous events outside of the control of incumbent politicians (e.g., natural disasters) affect electoral fortunes. These all-else-equal results are often interpreted as evidence of voter irrationality (Wolfers, 2002; Achen and Bartels, 2004; Leigh, 2009; Healy, Malhotra, and Mo, 2010). But an implication of Ashworth, Bueno de Mesquita, and Friedenberg's (2018) formal model of electoral accountability is that, all else equal, even when voters are rational, incumbent electoral fortunes are responsive to natural disasters. A natural disaster gives voters an extra opportunity to learn about an incumbent's quality (e.g., how well they responded to a global pandemic). If, absent new information, most incumbents expect to win reelection, this new information will create more downside than upside risk. Hence, the empirical fact that, all else equal, disasters hurt incumbent electoral fortunes on average, does not necessarily mean that voters are irrational.

These two examples show how formal theory and credible empirical research work together, whether for assessing a particular theoretical implication or interpreting a particular empirical finding. Even greater progress can occur when this partnership is sustained in a back-and-forth over time, as illustrated by the literature on the economic causes of civil war.

Theorists of civil conflict have long argued that grievance drives rebellion and that a thriving economy, by alleviating grievance, might reduce conflict (Gurr, 1970). In an important early quantitative contribution, Fearon and Laitin (2003) provide cross-country evidence that per capita income is negatively correlated with the onset of civil war. But they also found that other factors thought to affect grievance (e.g., ethnic divisions, lack of democracy) are not correlated with the onset of civil war. Hence, they argue that a different theoretical interpretation is needed. They suggest that governments in wealthier countries have greater capacity to control territory, which limits the conditions conducive to insurgency.

Scholars working in the tradition of the credibility revolution question how informative these empirical findings are about any of the theories. Theoretical implications about the relationship between the economy and civil conflict are all-else-equal claims. But these cross-country comparisons do not plausibly hold all else equal (Miguel, Satyanath, and Sergenti, 2004). For instance, perhaps a high risk of civil conflict harms the economy by causing capital flight or deterring foreign investment. And, indeed, findings from research that takes the all-else-equal caveat more seriously don't look as good for the theories. For example, Bazzi and Blattman (2014) find no relationship between plausibly exogenous shocks to the world prices of a country's commodity exports and civil conflict in that country.

The story doesn't end there. One plausible interpretation of Bazzi and Blattman's null finding is that economic mechanisms are unimportant. But theory suggests both a reinterpretation and a path forward for empirical scholarship. The reinterpretation comes from observing that, while commodity-bundle price shocks might hold all else equal, their effect also likely reflects competing mechanisms. For instance, in addition to the grievance mechanism, Grossman (1991) models a predation mechanism that works in the opposite direction—all else equal, positive economic shocks might exacerbate conflict by increasing the value of the territory over which the rebels are fighting. The path forward is suggested by Dal Bó and Dal Bó's (2011) theoretical model that differentiates two types of commodities. Shocks to the price of labor-intensive goods should affect wages and thus primarily activate grievance-type mechanisms. Shocks to the price of capital-intensive goods should instead primarily activate predation-like mechanisms. Dube and Vargas (2013) take up this idea empirically in the context of conflict in Colombia. They estimate how conflict changes differentially in coffee-producing and oil-producing municipalities in response to shocks to world coffee and oil prices. Their results agree with the theoretical implications—all else equal, negative shocks to the price of labor-intensive coffee increase conflict in municipalities that produce coffee relative to those that don't and negative shocks to the price of capital-intensive oil decrease conflict in municipalities that produce oil relative to those that don't.

For all the progress made over the course of this exchange between theory and empirics, it also exemplifies a common lament among critics of the credibility revolution. The literature seems to have been diverted from studying broad questions about the sources of civil conflict to narrow questions about the sources of civil conflict in the municipalities of Colombia. But this worry is misplaced. The narrowing of focus allowed for greater clarity of thought, a tighter link between theoretical implications and empirical estimates, and a disentangling of mechanisms. Moreover, with these insights in

place, scholars were then able to again broaden the scope, but without sacrificing the deeper connection between theory and empirics. For instance, several
subsequent studies use research designs similar to Dube and Vargas's to
analyze the same mechanisms, using data on economic and conflict activity
measured at the level of fifty square kilometer grid cells spanning multiple countries, and produce similar findings (Berman and Couttenier, 2015;
Berman et al., 2017).

Looking across these examples we see why the credibility revolution and
formal theory are natural complements. The essence of formal theory is the
crafting of models that embody mechanisms and reveal the all else equal
implications of those mechanisms. The essence of the credibility revolution
is the crafting of research designs that make credible the claim to have held
all else equal, at least on average—exactly what is needed to assess and guide
theory.

A major theme of this book is that such exciting opportunities for a deeper
connection between theory and empirics lie waiting throughout political science, on topics ranging from elections to civil war to bureaucratic politics to
international organizations. Our ambition is that this book, itself a joint effort
by empirical and theoretical researchers, will better equip readers to discover
these opportunities. And, along the way, we hope it helps both groups gain a
deeper appreciation for what their colleagues are up to, and why it matters.

PART I
Foundations

2

The Framework

If we are going to learn to spot opportunities for a deeper connection between theory and empirics, we have to spend some time on details. Details about why theorists write the kinds of models they do, and how those models can be made more useful to empiricists. Details about why empiricists use the kinds of research designs they do, and how those research designs can be made to speak better to theoretically meaningful questions. Details about how exactly the connection between them works, and what makes that connection informative.

But it would be a mistake to start there. We worry that if we dove right into the details, you would have no context for understanding why we emphasize some issues and downplay others. Or how our discussion of the details fits into the big picture—creating the robust dialogue between theory and empirics that is necessary for a thriving political science. In short, we'd miss the forest for the trees.

So, in this chapter, we look at the connection between theory and empirics from thirty thousand feet. We provide a conceptual framework for thinking about how the entire enterprise fits together. Broadly, how do theoretical models and empirical research designs relate to the world and to each other? When we compare a theoretical implication to an empirical finding, what kinds of scientific claims are we learning about? How can we make such comparisons maximally informative about the questions that motivate us—that is, questions about how the social world works?

The framework we provide will not be wholly new. It would be worrying if it were. After all, political scientists have been going about the business of accumulating knowledge by combining theory and empirics for generations. And we all have at least some inchoate sense of how this works. But some of the ideas are new and, perhaps more importantly, we believe the synthesis is clarifying. We hope that after reading this chapter you will have a clearer vision of how the whole enterprise holds together and where your work fits into that enterprise.

Indeed, this conceptual work will have some intellectual payoffs even before we get to the details in the coming chapters. After presenting the framework, we jump right into an extended example, drawn from the literature on women's underrepresentation in electoral politics. There, we will see how viewing the dialogue between theory and empirics through the lens we suggest can change our thinking about what we learn from various kinds of theoretical and empirical contributions and can highlight opportunities for new research by suggesting questions that we might not have previously thought to ask.

After that, we compare and contrast our framework to two other prominent approaches to linking theory and empirics, namely structural modeling and causal mediation analysis. That comparison leads us into a discussion of our framework's perspective on extrapolation. This is particularly important in light of the argument, advanced by some critics, that an unintended consequence of the credibility revolution has been to push scholars to focus on data from very localized settings, limiting our ability to learn about more general principles.

2.1 The View from Thirty Thousand Feet

Figure 2.1 summarizes our framework for linking theory and empirics. It is centered on a target of inquiry in the world, or *target* for short. A target is the part of the real world we are trying to learn about, whether with theory or empirics. A model of committee power takes real-world legislatures as its target, as does an empirical study relating committee membership to legislative outcomes. Likewise, theoretical or empirical research about economic shocks and civil war has the behavior of people in actual countries as a target.

Theoretical models and empirical research designs, of course, are distinct from the target. But they each, in their own way, attempt to represent the target. So our view from thirty thousand feet is going to clarify a bit about what it means for theoretical models and empirical research designs to represent real-world targets. Once we can see more clearly how models and research designs relate to the world, we'll also gain some clarity on how they relate to one another.

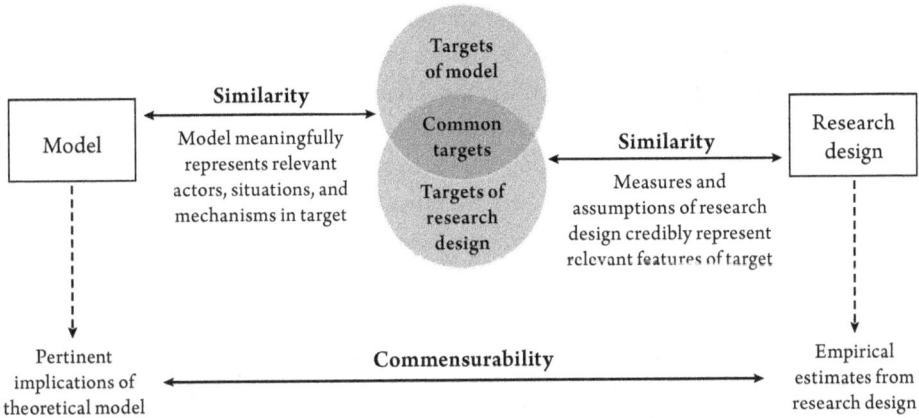

FIGURE 2.1. Our framework for linking theory and empirics.

We begin with models and the idea of *similarity* (Giere, 1988). Theoretical inquiry involves trying to explain a real-world target by representing some features of that target. To do that, the model must be, in a sense to be clarified in what follows, similar to the target. The word *model* calls to mind formal rational choice models, and those are a paradigmatic instance of the idea. But the notions of representation and similarity apply more broadly. They can be applied to other formalizations, including both computational models and conceptual schemas for formalizing causal relationships, such as those of Pearl (2009) and Imbens and Rubin (2015).[1] And they apply to a variety of approaches to informal theorizing, for instance, Zaller's (1992) Receive–Accept–Sample model of public opinion.

Models are always simplifications, ignoring much of what is going on in the target. They often make assumptions that are demonstrably false as descriptions of the world. So how could they be useful for explanation? The answer comes from fleshing out the notion of similarity. A model is meant to be similar to the target in a very particular way. Certain actors, situations, and mechanisms in the model must meaningfully represent analogous actors, situations, and mechanisms in the target. We call those the *representational features* of the model. Not everything in the model is meant to be representational. Any theoretical model has *auxiliary features* that are not descriptive of the target but help with tractability or simplification. Claims about representational features define the scope conditions of the model.

1. Blair et al. (2019) treat such schemas as theoretical models.

Consider, for example, a simple model of crisis bargaining. An attacker receives a noisy signal of the defender's military strength and makes an appeasement offer to the defender; the defender compares the offer to the expected payoff from war (which depends on its military strength) and then either accepts the offer (resulting in peace) or rejects the offer (resulting in war). Some features of this model are intended to be representational. For instance, the model treats the states as purposive—having beliefs and preferences. So the states in the real world to which the model is applied must have sufficiently strong leaders or other domestic processes that make this meaningful. And military strength in the model should meaningfully represent some actual feature of states that affects their likelihood of success in war. Other features of such a model might be auxiliary. For instance, it might facilitate analysis to assume a specific functional form (say, the natural log) to describe how military strength translates into military success or a specific distribution (say, a uniform distribution) to describe the attacker's beliefs about the defender's military strength. But it would be absurd to think the relevant features of the world are actually characterized by the natural log function or uniform distribution. These are auxiliary features of the model.

Analysis of a model yields implications about relationships between objects in the model. Some of those implications depend on the representational features but are robust to changes in the auxiliary features. Those implications are suitable for assessing similarity of the model and the target. We call these the *pertinent implications*. The key thought is that, if similarity is true, then the pertinent implications of the model should be reflected in the target. If, by contrast, the theoretical implication depends crucially on an auxiliary feature of the model that is not plausibly similar to the world, then there is no reason to expect to see the implication reflected in the world.

In our model of crisis bargaining, we might find that the stronger the defender is militarily, the more likely the dispute is to end in war. This implication is pertinent if it follows from representational features of the model—say, from the fact that the defender's payoff from war is increasing in its military capacity—but doesn't depend crucially on auxiliary features—say, the specific function mapping military capacity to war payoffs or the specific distribution of military capacities. Suppose this implication does indeed follow from representational features of the model. If the model is similar to the target, then we should expect to see the implication reflected in the target—all else equal, defender states should reject appeasement offers more often when they are militarily stronger.

It is not only theoretical models that are linked to the world through similarity. Empirical inquiry involves a research design, also linked to a real-world target through a relationship of similarity. The research design uses various measures and statistical procedures to estimate some relationship of interest. Similarity of the research design to the world has two aspects. First, the measures used should meaningfully represent the relevant features of the target—that is, they should have what Adcock and Collier (2001) call *measurement validity*. Second, the research design provides good estimates of the relationship of interest only under certain assumptions. Those assumptions should plausibly describe the target. If both of these aspects of the similarity relationship are true, then the estimates generated by the research design reflect the specified relationship between the relevant features of the world.

In our crisis bargaining example, a research design needs valid measures of military strength and whether war occurred. With such measures in hand, one thing we might try to do is simply estimate the correlation between a defender's military strength and war. All we would need to assume for this procedure to credibly estimate the correlation is that our sample is representative. But to estimate the all-else-equal relationship between a defender's military strength and the likelihood of war, we'd need to make stronger assumptions— for instance, that conflicts involving stronger and weaker defenders aren't systematically different in ways that matter for the generosity of appeasement offers and war. Finding a research design to make that assumption plausible is a difficult task.[2] But if these assumptions aren't plausible, then the research design is not similar to the target.

We can link theory and empirics to one another when there is some overlap in the set of targets they point to. In such a case, we can learn about similarity by comparing the implications generated by theoretical models to the estimates generated by empirical research designs. If a theoretical model is similar to a real-world target, then the pertinent implications of the model should be reflected in the target. If an empirical research design is similar to a real-world target, then the estimates that come out of the research design reflect relationships between the relevant features of the target. So if both similarity relationships hold, we have reason to expect agreement between the theoretical implications and empirical estimates. And conversely, disagreement gives us some reason to doubt the combination of those similarity claims.

---

2. See Morgan and Moriarty (1995) for a related empirical exercise.

But how informative agreement or disagreement is depends on whether the theoretical implication and the empirical estimate are *commensurable*— that is, whether the relationship in the target being described by the theory and the relationship in the target being described by the empirics are the same relationship. For instance, our argument in Chapter 1 suggests that the correlation between per capita income and civil conflict is not commensurable with the implications of a grievance-based theory of conflict. Nor is the correlation between a membership on Appropriations and federal spending commensurable with the implications of a theory of committee power. The theoretical implications are about all-else-equal relationships, while the empirical findings are not.

Failure to respect all-else-equal conditions is the most important source of incommensurability. As we will argue in Chapter 3, and as others have argued before us, the implications of theoretical models are always all else equal. As such, commensurability says that empirical findings are maximally informative about similarity when research designs deliver empirical estimates of analogous all-else-equal relationships.[3]

Returning to our crisis bargaining example, suppose we found that there is a negative, rather than positive, correlation between a defender's military strength and the probability of war. This finding disagrees with our theoretical implication. But it is not terribly informative about whether the mechanisms embodied in the model are at work in the world, because the theoretical implication and the empirical finding are not commensurable. Perhaps, for instance, only strong attackers with reliable allies get involved in conflicts with strong defenders in the first place. Then the negative correlation we find in the data need not mean the mechanisms in our model are not at work. It might instead reflect the fact that all else is not held equal in this comparison. By contrast, suppose we found a research design that involved defenders' military capacities being subjected to random shocks after a dispute had begun, but before the appeasement offer was made. Agreement or disagreement between the relationship estimated from that research design and our

---

3. As we will discuss in greater detail, the "all" in all else equal should not be taken literally. A theoretical model might have an implication that says that, when a parameter changes, some behavior changes that then changes some outcome. None of these three variables is held constant in the analysis. Similarly, in empirical work, the all-else-equal relationship between, say, a treatment and an outcome might run through a mediator, which is not intended to be held equal. We'll have more to say on these issues in subsequent chapters.

theoretical implication would be considerably more informative about the similarity of our model and the world.

2.2 Learning from Agreement or Disagreement

Our goal is to accumulate knowledge of mechanisms that explain important political phenomena. As such, what we really want to learn about is the similarity relationship between theoretical models and the real world.[4]

This process starts by studying models that we already have good reasons to believe might be similar to the target of inquiry. If the actors, situations, and mechanisms embodied in the model don't plausibly represent analogous actors, situations, and mechanisms in the world, even agreement between the implications of the model and empirical findings won't do much to convince us that we have a good explanation of what's going on.

But even with a plausible model in hand, there is much work to do. We don't directly observe whether mechanisms are at work, nor can we directly test the similarity between a model and the target. Instead, we proceed indirectly, seeking evidence for or against similarity by comparing the implications of a model embodying the mechanisms believed to be at work to empirical estimates from a research design with the same target.

Here, we confront a challenge for learning about theoretical mechanisms. Agreement or disagreement between a pertinent theoretical implication and an empirical finding is informative about the joint claim that the two similarity conditions plus commensurability all hold. That is, it is informative about the chain of connections represented in Figure 2.1, and a chain is only as strong as its weakest link. If a theoretical implication and an empirical finding don't agree, maybe it means the model is not similar to the target, maybe it means the research design's measures are invalid or its assumptions are not plausible, or maybe it means the theoretical implications and empirical estimates are not commensurable.

Thus, how much we learn about what mechanisms are at work depends critically on how strong our reasons are for believing both that the research design is similar to the target and that the theoretical implications and empirical estimates are commensurable. If the research design uses good measures and plausible assumptions to estimate a highly commensurable quantity, then

---

4. Recall that one instance of a theoretical model in our framework is the causal models of Pearl (2009) and Imbens and Rubin (2015).

agreement or disagreement is very informative about mechanisms. But as the quality of the measures, the plausibility of the assumptions, or the commensurability of the empirical estimates and theoretical implications diminish, so too does how much we can learn about the mechanisms embodied in the model.

This is why the credibility revolution is so important for forging a productive link between theory and empirics. It is focused on research designs that make credible the claim to have estimated the kind of quantities that are commensurable with theoretical implications—in particular, all-else-equal relationships.

That said, our framework does not suggest we must let the great be the enemy of the good. It allows that we learn things from imperfect models or research designs. But the tighter we can make each of the connections—the similarity of the model or research design to the target and the commensurability of the theoretical implications and the empirical estimates—the more we learn. Thus, progress in a research agenda can take the form of strengthening the reasons for believing any of these claims.[5]

In this way, a research agenda progresses through a back-and-forth between theory and empirics. In one direction, theoretical models can guide empirical inquiry. If a theoretical model implies some relationship, then you might proceed by looking for a credible research design for estimating a commensurable quantity in order to assess the similarity of the theoretical model to the target. In the other direction, empirical findings can guide theorizing. If a research design has estimated some relationship in data, you might proceed by looking for a plausibly similar model with a commensurable implication to explain the empirical finding.

These steps occur in an iterative process. Figure 2.1 describes the relationship of one theoretical model and one empirical research design to a target and to one another. But in any given target, there may be many mechanisms at work and, so, many theoretical models may have some explanatory value. And, for any given target, different research designs estimate different quantities of interest. Knowledge about any particular target thus accumulates through the back-and-forth. That process may encompass multiple research designs and models of many mechanisms. And it will involve criticism and response—whereby weaknesses in claims of similarity and commensurability motivate future research. This iterative process is the subject of Part II.

5. Little and Pepinsky (2019) make a closely related argument.

We turn now to an example of a dialogue between theory and empirics that illustrates our framework. This example, focused on women's underrepresentation in electoral politics, shows how the approach we advocate advances the canonical goals of political science—explicating and assessing the mechanisms that explain important political phenomena—while also providing conceptual clarity on how this works.

2.3   Women's Underrepresentation in Electoral Politics

A central question in American politics is why so few women hold elected office. In 2020, for instance, women made up only about one-quarter of the House of Representatives and Senate. Comparable proportions of women occupy other elected offices in the United States, and women are significantly underrepresented in most other countries as well (Lawless, 2015).

Broadly speaking, the literature has identified several mechanisms that might explain this fact. We will focus on just two of them. For many years, scholars looked to voter discrimination as a likely explanation (e.g., Erskine, 1971; Ferree, 1974). A more recent literature proposes an alternative account based on a perception gap—systematic underestimation by women and over-estimation by men of their personal qualifications for office (Fox and Lawless, 2011).

These mechanisms are compatible, and it is entirely possible for both to be at work. But a significant strand of the literature argues that voter discrimination is not an important part of the explanation for women's underrepresentation in office in contemporary American politics. This conclusion is based on two empirical findings.

First, women are underrepresented not only among elected officials, but also among candidates for office (Fox and Lawless, 2005). Second, a series of studies shows that, when women do run for office, they are just as likely to win as are men (Darcy and Schramm, 1977; Burrell, 1994; Seltzer, Newman, and Leighton, 1997). More precisely, while women candidates win less often than men on average, accounting for the incumbency advantage erases this differential. In other words, conditional on running, women incumbents are as likely to win as men running as incumbents are, and women running in open-seat elections are as likely to win as men running in open-seat elections, although incumbents are more likely to be men. These "startling" findings "surprised even savvy political operatives, and decidedly contradicted the widely held beliefs that women have a tougher time winning office" (Duerst-Lahti, 1998, p. 17).

Why are these findings taken as evidence for the perception gap and against voter discrimination? If voters are biased, the argument goes, then women should win at a lower rate than men. So the fact that women and men win at equal rates suggests voters do not discriminate. Moreover, the argument continues, if women underestimate their qualifications and men overestimate theirs, then women will run at lower rates than men. As such, women will be underrepresented among candidates and elected officials, even though they may perform equally well when they do run. As Lawless and Fox (2013, p. 1) write:

> [W]hen women run for office—regardless of the position they seek—they are just as likely as men to win their races. The large gender disparities in U.S. political institutions, therefore, do not result from systematic discrimination against women candidates. Rather, the fundamental reason for women's under-representation is that women do not run for office.

This argument reflects an important move in the literature. There are two possible mechanisms, both having an implication that agrees with the empirical fact that women are underrepresented among elected officials. As such, that empirical fact doesn't provide any guidance as to whether only one or both of these mechanisms is at work. And so scholars have looked for implications that distinguish the two mechanisms to better assess the evidentiary basis for believing each is at work.

These are not the only empirical facts to which we can compare theoretical implications. Anzia and Berry (2011) find that, once in office, women perform better than men. Comparing men and women who represented the same congressional districts, they show that, on average, women secure more federal funds for their districts, sponsor and co-sponsor more legislation, and garner more co-sponsors for their legislation. Subsequent research has produced additional evidence that women politicians outperform men on average (e.g., Fulton, 2012; Volden, Wiseman, and Wittmer, 2013; Lazarus and Steigerwalt, 2018).

In what follows, we develop a formal model meant to represent the perception gap mechanism. We do so to explore what we learn from the empirical findings about whether the perception gap is at work in the world. Doing so reveals two insights.

First, the empirical finding that the literature has taken as offering the strongest evidence in favor of the perception gap actually does the opposite. Our model of the perception gap mechanism does not predict that women and men win at the same rate, conditional on running. Rather, it predicts that women win at higher rates than men. The perception gap creates positive selection—because women underestimate and men overestimate their quality, the pool of women candidates is better than that of men. Consequently, if voters don't discriminate, women win at higher rates than men.

Second, the literature has not generally argued that the finding that women perform better than men in office is evidence supportive of the perception gap. But we show that, because of the positive selection just described, women's superior performance is in fact an implication of our model embodying the perception gap mechanism. (It also turns out to be an implication of a model embodying voter discrimination.)

With these two results in hand, and guided by our framework, we then take two more steps in relating theory and empirics. First, we ask how much agreement or disagreement between the model's implications and the empirical findings tells us about whether the perception gap is at work in the world. Assessing the similarity of the research design and commensurability is essential for answering this question. We argue that the agreement concerning women's performance in office relative to men's is more informative than the disagreement concerning win rates, because the former comes from a research design that does a better job of holding all else equal. (It would be even more informative if it wasn't also an implication of a model of voter discrimination.)

Second, we use the model to look for other opportunities to assess whether the perception gap is at work. To that end, we directly represent close elections in our model, which allows us to find theoretical implications that are commensurable with the estimates of a regression discontinuity design. The result is surprising. Informal reasoning yields a strong intuition that, if voters do not discriminate, a man and a woman who each won a close election that pitted a man against a woman should have the same expected quality. But this intuition is incorrect. In the presence of a perception gap, women who win such elections have higher expected quality than men who win such elections. And so the model implies that, even in a regression discontinuity design focused on close elections involving a man and a woman, women are expected to perform better in office than men.

2.3.1   The Model

To represent the actual target, US congressional elections, we want a model that allows us to analyze how people decide whether to run for office, their likelihood of winning should they run, and their performance in office should they win.[6] We focus on the idea that potential candidates have characteristics that matter for electability and characteristics that matter for their performance in office, and that these characteristics are positively correlated. Moreover, to focus on the perception gap, we assume everything else about men and women is the same.

There are two equally sized groups of potential candidates, one consisting of men and one of women. Each potential candidate has a cost of running, c. The cost represents any feature of real-world politicians that pulls against running—other career opportunities, dislike of campaigning, time away from family, and so on. Candidates get a benefit B if they win office. This represents real world benefits of holding office, which might include moving policy in a desired direction, prestige, or future earning potential. We assume the benefits of winning are larger than the costs of running, so that if a politician was certain to win, they would run.

Each potential candidate also has a quality θ, which is a real number. Higher numbers represent higher quality. There is a distribution of qualities among potential candidates such that some are better than others. We assume that this distribution is continuous and is the same for men and women. Quality in the model represents any feature of real-world candidates, other than gender, that voters care about and that matters for performance in office.

To capture the perception gap, we assume that a woman of quality θ perceives her quality as $\phi_W(\theta) < \theta$ and that a man of quality θ perceives his quality as $\phi_M(\theta) > \theta$, with ϕ_W and ϕ_M strictly increasing. Candidates' true qualities are correctly observed by other candidates and by the voters.

At the beginning of the game, each potential candidate decides whether to run for office. These candidates are then paired off at random to face each other in elections. A potential candidate runs for office if the expected benefit (equal to the probability he or she wins times the benefit of winning) exceeds the cost of running.

---

6. More details on this model are in Ashworth, Berry, and Bueno de Mesquita (2020).

We assume each election is decided by a representative voter, though the results would hold unchanged in a model with a heterogeneous electorate in which we could identify a pivotal voter. A voter's evaluation of a candidate depends on the candidate's quality and some idiosyncratic noise. To isolate the perception gap mechanism, we assume voters do not care directly about gender. The noise represents anything unanticipated that might happen over the course of campaigning, such as candidate gaffes, partisan swings, or scandals. The voter chooses between candidates by comparing the sum of the candidate's quality and noise. Notice, because of the noise, sometimes the candidate with lower quality will win an election.

The winner of the election generates a level of performance given by a strictly increasing function of quality, $\pi(\theta)$. This reflects the assumption that electability and the factors that lead to good performance are positively correlated.

We study subgame-perfect Nash equilibria (henceforth, *equilibria*). This means that, when deciding whether or not to run for office, potential candidates think about how likely they are to win, which in turn depends on their beliefs about which other potential candidates are going to run. This is the standard solution concept for games like this one.

In equilibrium, there is some threshold of perceived probability of winning such that the expected benefits exactly equal the costs. Since a candidate's probability of winning is increasing in their quality, this implies potential candidates use cutoff rules—entering if and only if their quality is above a threshold.

Candidates with the same quality, whether men or women, have the same actual probability of winning. However, men and women perceive their qualities differently. As a result, a woman of any given true quality perceives her probability of winning as lower than a man of that same quality. Since men and women perceive their probabilities of winning differently, they use different cutoffs. As illustrated in Figure 2.2, women use a more stringent cutoff—because of the perception gap, a woman must have a higher actual quality to be willing to run.

Figure 2.3 shows the implications of the different cutoffs for who runs and the distribution of qualities among potential candidates. The number of women candidates is the area under the curve above the cutoff used by women. The number of men candidates is the area under the curve above the cutoff used by men. So women are underrepresented in the pool of

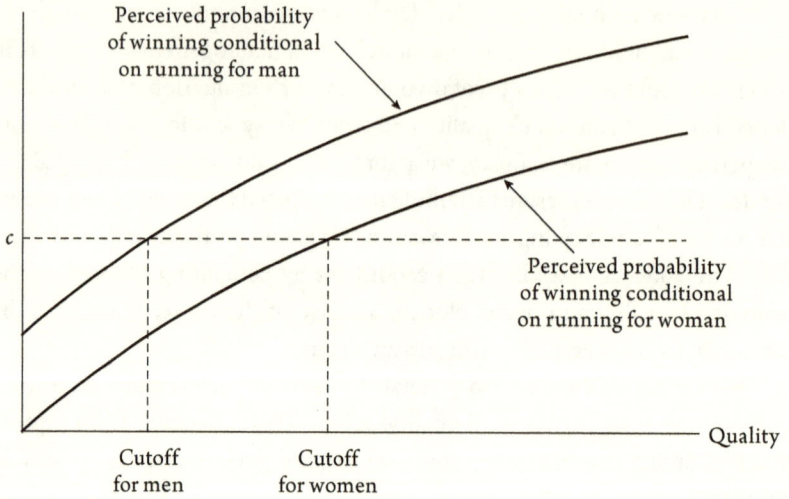

FIGURE 2.2. Cutoff rules when women underestimate and men overestimate their true quality.

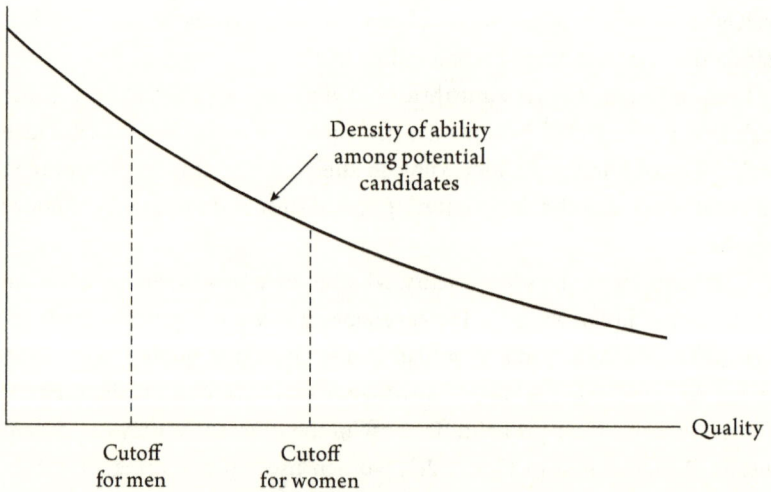

FIGURE 2.3. Density of abilities among men and women in pool of candidates.

candidates—women and men make up equal shares of potential candidates, but women comprise fewer than half of actual candidates running.

More importantly, women are positively selected relative to men. That is, because women use a more stringent cutoff rule, the distribution of quality is better in the pool of women candidates than in the pool of men. There is a group of lower quality men who would not have run had they been women. These lower quality men drag down the overall probability a man wins. Recall, there is no voter bias in this model. Hence, the perception gap implies that women win with higher probability than men, conditional on running. This implication disagrees with the empirical finding in the literature.

Since voters don't discriminate and women candidates start with a better distribution of quality than do men, the distribution of quality among women winners is also better than the distribution of quality among men who win. As a consequence, the perception gap implies that women perform better in office than men, on average. This implication agrees with the empirical finding in the literature.

2.3.2 Learning from Agreement and Disagreement

Our discussion, thus far, followed a familiar course. We explicated the implications of a theoretical model and related it to empirical findings, all in a fairly standard way. It will be helpful, now, to view this example through the lens of our framework for linking theory and empirics, as illustrated in Figure 2.1. Doing so reveals how our framework supports many aspects of conventional social scientific practice while also providing some conceptual clarity on what is being learned through such practice and on some potential stumbling blocks.

The empirical estimates from the literature that we described correspond to the dashed line on the right side of the figure. Our derivation of the implications of our theoretical model correspond to the dashed line on the left. We brought these together by considering whether they agree or disagree with one another. But, as we have emphasized, the interpretation of such agreement or disagreement depends on our reasons for believing the underlying claims of similarity and commensurability. We take these in turn.

Start with the left-hand side of Figure 2.1. What are the reasons (other than the evidence we've just been discussing) to believe the claims of similarity between our model of the perception gap and the target—here, elections for the US Congress? First, for the similarity claim to have even face validity, it is important that the agents in the model make decisions for reasons that are plausibly similar to those of the people they represent in the target. This seems reasonable here. In deciding whether to run, the agents in the model, like real politicians, consider factors such as their likely challengers, the probability of winning, the benefits of holding office, and the costs of running. Second, other existing evidence provides reasons to believe the perception gap mechanism embodied in the model may be at work in the world. For instance, surveys of potential candidates show evidence consistent with a perception gap (Fox and Lawless, 2011; Lawless and Fox, 2013). Third, the model makes a series of auxiliary assumptions that simplify analysis. These assumptions are not intended to be representational. Many such assumptions are innocuous— for example, the continuum of candidates or the representative voter—in the sense that there are good reasons to believe the theoretical implications we've discussed do not depend on them. Others, for instance random pairing of candidates, may not be innocuous and invite further research.

There is an important restriction on the plausibility of this similarity claim. In the model, the two candidates in an election are symmetric, possibly differing only in quality and in gender. But in many real-world congressional elections, there is an additional asymmetry created by incumbency. Incumbents differ from challengers in at least two ways. First, incumbents have already won office, and thus benefit from a process of positive selection for quality. Second, incumbency is widely thought to bring systematic advantages due to perquisites of office such as greater access to campaign resources, gerrymandering, or public attention.[7] As such, the plausibility of the similarity claim is significantly stronger for open-seat elections than for elections with an incumbent.

Next turn to the right-hand side of Figure 2.1. Claims of similarity between the research designs and the target involve consideration of both measurement validity and the plausibility of the assumptions needed to estimate a quantity commensurable with the theoretical implication. Let's take these in turn.

Measurement validity is straightforward with respect to the share of men and women who win conditional on running. It is less straightforward with respect to performance in office. Anzia and Berry focus on two aspects of performance: federal funds secured for the district and bill sponsorship. You might worry that these measures are not valid or encompassing measures of performance. For example, do politicians who achieve better outcomes on these dimensions achieve worse outcomes on other dimensions? One approach to alleviating such concerns is to study other partial measures of performance, such as Volden, Wiseman, and Wittmer's finding that women also perform better on an omnibus measure of legislative effectiveness.

---

7. We will discuss these two aspects of incumbency extensively in Part II.

Next turn to the plausibility of the assumptions for estimating quantities commensurable with the theoretical implications.

To think about commensurability, let's start by asking what is being held equal to derive the theoretical implications. One assumption of the model is that men and women have the same underlying distribution of quality. So, for instance, if men and women in the real world had differential access to education, and education affects electability, these differences should be accounted for by the research design. This is why it was crucial that Lawless and Fox's (2010) *Citizen Political Ambition Studies* survey focused on the "eligibility pool" of women and men who are already well situated to run for office: lawyers, business leaders, educators, and political activists. But a commensurable research design should not hold everything equal. For example, in the model, the perception gap mechanism works through endogenous entry decisions that result in the distribution of quality among women candidates being better than among men. As such, commensurability says that a research design should not control for systematic differences in qualifications among women and men who decide to become candidates.

Regarding the results on probability of election, recall our earlier argument that similarity of the model is most plausible for open-seat elections. So the theoretical implication is really about such open-seat elections, and a maximally commensurable research design is one that focuses on those elections. This is just what we find in, for example, Table 4.3 of Seltzer, Newman, and Leighton (1997).

But the all-else-equal condition for the result that women should win more often than men extends beyond incumbency. For instance, our model assumed that voters are unbiased. We did so to emphasize the literature's focus on the perception gap as an alternative mechanism that operates even when voters are unbiased. But this is an important assumption. Suppose, in the world from which the data are drawn, voters are in fact biased and women are more likely to run in districts where voters are less biased. Then the correlation between gender and electoral fortunes in the data does not respect the same all-else-equal condition as the theoretical implication. The empirical correlation and the theoretical implication are incommensurable. As such, we learn less about whether the perception gap mechanism is at work from the disagreement between our theoretical implication and the empirical findings than we would if we had a more commensurable all-else-equal estimate.

What about the relative performance of women and men in office? Again, the theoretical implication is all else equal. So we might be concerned about differences across districts that affect both whether or not a woman wins in that district and the various measures of performance in office. A research design that does not account for such district characteristics does not credibly yield estimates that are commensurable with the all-else-equal theoretical implication. For instance, we might worry that more urban districts both attract more federal funds and are more likely to elect a woman. To address such concerns, Anzia and Berry use a difference-in-differences research design that holds constant features of a district that are fixed over the time period being considered, such as urbanness. We do, however, still need to worry about characteristics of a district that matter for performance and are not fixed over time. We discuss the specifics of Anzia and Berry's argument in more detail in Chapter 3. But their move toward credibly estimating a commensurable all-else-equal quantity makes the agreement between the empirical finding and the theoretical implication more informative about whether the perception gap mechanism is at work.

2.3.3   Modeling Other Research Designs

We've just explored one of the important roles for a model within our framework—to explicate implications that can be compared with existing empirical findings. But this is not the only role a model can play. Another is to explore whether there are other empirical quantities that might also be used for assessment, especially quantities for which we could imagine a credible research design.

In this section we illustrate this idea, using our model to ask what we could learn from a regression discontinuity design focused on close elections (as in Anzia and Berry, 2011, Appendix B). To do so, we ask what theoretical implication is commensurable with the estimates a regression discontinuity yields.

An informal analysis might seem to suggest that close elections should yield no difference in performance between men and women winners in our model of the perception gap. (At least, that is what we expected to find when we thought about this model informally.) To see the intuition, consider a simplification of the theoretical model in which there is no idiosyncratic noise. Since voters don't discriminate, a tie between a man and a woman occurs only in elections in which the two candidates are in fact of equal quality. As such, women and men have the same distribution of quality conditional on winning such a close election. Intuitive as this argument is, the model reveals it to be knife edged. If there is any idiosyncratic noise, then this implication does not hold.

How does our informal intuition break down? In the presence of noise, a tie between a man and a woman can occur in one of two ways: the woman was higher quality than the man but the noise favored the man, or the woman was lower quality than the man but the noise favored the woman. As we saw in Figure 2.3, the perception gap leads to the distribution of quality among women candidates being better than the distribution of quality among men candidates. This implies that, when a woman and a man tie, it is more likely that the woman was higher quality than the man but that the noise favored the man than it is that the woman was lower quality than the man but that the noise favored the woman. Hence, the perception gap implies that, even conditional on a close election between a man and a woman, the distribution of quality among women who win is better than the distribution of quality among men who win, so women should perform better in office than men, on average.

2.4 A Comparison to Other Approaches

Now that we've given an overview of our vision for linking theory and empirics, and put it to work in an example, it is worth pausing to compare it to some other views. Here, we focus on two: a view that was commonly expressed in the empirical implications of theoretical models (EITM) movement of the early 2000s and the ongoing methodological literature on causal mediation analysis.

Broadly, the EITM movement's vision for linking theory and empirics built on ideas from the structural approach in economics, in which "the mathematical structure of an empirical or statistical model" is derived directly from "the structure of a formal model" (Morton, 1999, p. 101).[8] Writing for a contemporary economics audience, Andrews, Gentzkow, and Shapiro (2020, p. 714, footnote 9) define structural somewhat more expansively, "to include any article that explicitly estimates the parameters of an economic model." This definition of course applies equally well to structural approaches to models of politics.

---

8. Also see Granato, Lo, and Wong (2010) and the report from the initial EITM workshop available at http://eitminstitute.org/EITM_REPORT.pdf.

An appeal of the structural approach is that, once you have estimated the parameters of a theoretical model, you can compute a rich variety of quantities of interest. Moreover, some of those quantities may not be otherwise accessible empirically. But we think there are also a couple of important advantages of the approach we advocate. First, because our approach is unconstrained by the need to estimate model parameters, it often allows for theoretical assumptions that are more general or satisfying. Second, because our approach treats all pertinent implications of the model as suitable for assessment, rather than focusing only on estimating key parameters, it allows the empiricist to focus on those implications for which the most credible research designs are available. As such, a scholar following our approach can typically link theory and empirics more flexibly and under less restrictive assumptions than a scholar working in the structural tradition. That said, we are sympathetic to the structural approach and see important conceptual similarities between it and our framework. Most importantly, the assessment of theoretical models and the interpretation of empirical estimates are deeply intertwined in both. We have more to say about the relationship in Chapter 7.

In the causal mediation literature, identifying and estimating the importance of intermediate causes is the key to linking theory and empirics (Green, Ha, and Bullock, 2010; Imai, Keele, and Tingley, 2010). Indeed, Imai, Keele, and Tingley, (p. 309) argue that "the identification of causal mechanisms is required to test competing theoretical explanations of the same causal effects."

While sharing an emphasis on mechanisms, our framework embraces a more indirect approach. This has the advantage of suggesting ways to assess whether certain mechanisms are at work in the world while avoiding some of the strong assumptions that are necessary for causal mediation analysis. Our basic idea is that models that embody certain mechanisms generate implications. We assess whether those mechanisms are at work by empirically evaluating whether those implications are reflected in the world. Some of those implications may be about intermediate causes, so the two approaches are complementary. But there are many implications of theoretical models that do not require knowledge of intermediate causes. On our approach, such implications constitute equally good opportunities to assess whether the mechanisms embodied in a model are at work in the world. We return to the relationship between our framework and causal mediation analysis in Chapters 4 and 9.

2.5   Extrapolation

One virtue of the structural and causal mediation approaches is that both allow for certain kinds of extrapolation. In this section we consider what our framework has to say about extrapolating.

Doing so allows us to address an important worry, often expressed by critics of the credibility revolution, concerning the opportunistic choice of targets of study. The demands of credibility, the argument goes, lead empirical researchers to study settings amenable to a credible research design, even if those are not the settings of greatest interest. For instance, for the sake of credibility, empirical work may focus on local politics even when scholars are more interested in national politics, variation in behavior within a civil war even when scholars are more interested in interstate conflict, or MTurkers when scholars are actually interested in voters.

We can express this concern in the parlance of Figure 2.1. We can directly link theory and empirics only for those targets that lie in the intersection of the targets of a model and the targets of a research design. But there may be many targets of the model, including perhaps the most interesting ones, that are not in that intersection.

Our framework offers a way to think about extrapolation that clarifies when the critics' worry is warranted and when it can be, at least in part, overcome. Consider a situation in which there are reasons to believe some model is similar to several targets. Not all of those targets, however, are in the overlap with a credible research design that also satisfies commensurability. We can directly assess similarity in a convincing way only for targets that are in the overlap. What can we learn about targets outside the overlap from such an exercise?

Suppose that the estimates from the research design did not agree with the implications of the model. This reduces our confidence in the similarity between the model and the target under study. But it does more than that. If the model and the target are not in fact similar, it means that some of our prior reasons for believing similarity must have been wrong—we missed something important about the target in our thinking. That fact should perhaps also make us reevaluate the strength of our reasons for believing the model is similar to other targets not directly under study. Maybe we missed something analogous in those targets. Indeed, presumably the reasons we thought the model was similar to both targets is because we thought the agents, situations, and mechanisms in the two targets are themselves similar. And so, if those agents, situations, and mechanisms turned out not to be well represented by the model in the target under study, they might turn out not to be well represented by the model in other, similar targets.

If disagreement between the theoretical implications and the empirical estimates in the target under study would reduce our beliefs about similarity to other targets, then agreement must increase our beliefs about similarity to other targets. Thus, evidence in support of the similarity of a model and a target provides at least some warrant for extrapolation—it increases our confidence in similarity to other, similar targets.

Similarity between two targets plays an important role in this argument for extrapolation. If we have reasons to believe two targets are similar, then assessment of similarity of a model to one target is informative about similarity of the model to the other and there are good grounds for extrapolation. But if the reasons for believing the two targets are similar are weaker, then the warrant for extrapolation is also weaker.

To be a little more concrete, return to our example of women's underrepresentation. The evidence we discussed drew on data from relatively recent US congresses. It therefore supports a direct assessment of the similarity of the model to those congresses. We might be interested in whether the same similarity relationship holds in other targets, such as the next congress, presidential elections, or elections in other countries. We have pretty good reasons for believing that recent past congresses and upcoming congresses are similar—they involve many of the same people, elected from the same districts, and holding office in the same institution under the same rules. We have some reasons for believing congressional elections are similar to presidential elections, but they are weaker. And we have even weaker reasons for believing US congressional elections are similar to elections in other countries. For each of these targets, there may be some amount of information that can be drawn from an assessment of similarity of the model to the US Congress. But the amount of information, and thus the warrant for extrapolation, diminishes with the strength of our reasons for believing the targets are similar.

Our notion of extrapolation through similarity also maps neatly onto ongoing debates about the place of experiments, especially lab experiments, in social science (e.g., Hafner-Burton et al., 2017). In a lab experiment, the experimental subjects (be they undergraduates, MTurkers, or what have you) are the target of study. But the target of interest is often real-world political actors such as legislators, bureaucrats, foreign policy elites, or voters. If we want to extrapolate from the lab study, we must ask whether the target of study (in the lab) is similar to the target of interest. The ongoing debate is about how strong the reasons are for believing such similarity, something that varies across different areas of study.

2.6   Conclusion

The remaining chapters in Part I take up each of the three pillars of the framework we developed in this chapter. Chapter 3 focuses on commensurability and its relationship to all-else-equal conditions. Chapter 4 discusses models and their similarity relationship to the world. Chapter 5 turns to research designs, discussing similarity and its relationship to the credibility revolution.

3

All Else Equal

Formal theory and credible research designs are natural complements because their shared attention to all-else-equal conditions strengthens commensurability. But there are important differences in how all-else-equal claims arise in theoretical and empirical work, and a thorough treatment of commensurability requires sensitivity to these differences.

This chapter explains some subtleties of how all-else-equal claims work in each case. We show how these types of claims fit together to achieve commensurability, emphasizing the different obligations the all-else-equal caveat places on theorists and empiricists. Finally, we point out that our analysis of all-else-equal claims in theory and empirics suggests that the tools of the credibility revolution have broader applicability than is often appreciated. Those tools are essential for assessing any all-else-equal claim, whether or not it has a causal interpretation.

3.1   All Else Equal in Theory

Theorizing in the social sciences often involves model building. These models span a wide range of approaches, from mathematical models in the rational choice tradition, to agent-based computational models, to informal models rooted in arguments about Weberian ideal types. What unites these approaches is a strategy of indirect representation (Godfrey-Smith, 2006). You represent some real-world target with an abstract model and try to learn about the target in two steps—developing the logic of the model, on the one hand, and arguing that it is similar to the target, on the other.

While developing the logic of a model, you ask questions about the model itself. For this step, you are not concerned with the model's relationship to the target. You are just trying to figure out the model's implications.

Theoretical models are made up of *primitives* and *endogenous outcomes.* Primitives are the inputs that describe the model. Endogenous outcomes are the outputs of analysis of the model. For instance, the primitives in the previous chapter's model of women's underrepresentation included the distribution of quality among potential candidates, the function mapping quality to performance, the preferences of voters and politicians, and the functions defining the perception gap. The endogenous outcomes included which potential candidates run, men's and women's probability of election conditional on running, and men's and women's expected performance conditional on winning.

You derive implications of a model by fixing primitives and asking about the endogenous outcomes. You might fix all of the primitives. For example, we fixed all the primitives in the model of women's underrepresentation to compare men's and women's probability of winning, conditional on running. You might also fix some primitives and ask what happens as others vary. This is a *comparative statics* question. For instance, we could have asked how the probability a woman is elected changes as the perception gap increases.

This example shows that the "all" in all else equal should not be taken literally. Theoretical implications hold primitives equal, but not endogenous outcomes. When we say that changing the perception gap changes the probability a woman wins office, all else equal, we are holding constant all the primitives of the model other than the perception gap. But we are not holding constant other endogenous outcomes. Indeed, changes to other endogenous outcomes are an important part of the logic of the relationship between the perception gap and women's electoral prospects. When the perception gap changes, the cutoff rules used by women and men (endogenous outcomes) change, which results in a change in the distribution of quality of both women and men candidates (also endogenous outcomes). All of these changes to endogenous outcomes affect how the electoral prospects of women relative to men (our final endogenous outcomes, at least in this paragraph) change as the perception gap changes, holding constant all other primitives of the model.

Finally, we should be clear what we mean when we talk of fixing primitives. We aren't specifying a particular value for the cost of running or a specific function mapping quality to performance. All we mean is that we don't allow the cost of running or the function mapping quality to performance, whatever they may be, to change. We simply hold them constant as we make the comparison. This is the sense in which theoretical implications are all else equal.

It is important that we don't have to specify the values of these primitives. The unit of analysis in our model is a congressional district. And we'd like to claim that our model is similar to many congressional districts. But the cost of running and the relationship between quality and performance surely differ across congressional districts. If we were to commit to specific values for primitives, we might well limit the scope of applicability of our model. Needing to commit only to a positive cost or an increasing function leaves the model sufficiently general that the scope of applicability remains broad.

3.2 All Else Equal in Empirics

The credibility revolution in empirical work is also concerned with all-else-equal claims. The paradigmatic case comes from work on causal inference, as elucidated in the potential outcomes framework (Holland, 1986).

That framework starts with a *unit of analysis*, or *unit*, that might or might not be exposed to some *treatment*. That unit might be an individual but might also be a larger aggregate. In a study of voter behavior, the unit might be an individual voter; in a study of elections, the unit of analysis might be an individual politician or an individual electoral district; in a study of legislative bargaining the unit might be the entire legislature; in a study of interstate war the unit might be a country or dyad of countries.

The outcome for a unit depends on whether or not it is exposed to treatment. This is described by each unit's *potential outcomes* function, which gives the outcome for that unit if it is treated and if it is untreated. The *unit-level causal effect* of the treatment is the difference in the potential outcomes for a particular unit if that unit is treated rather than untreated.

To see the idea, consider the effect of the perception gap on the probability a woman is elected. Take the unit of analysis to be a congressional district. A civic organization might create a training program intended to reduce the perception gap. The outcome might be whether or not the district is represented by a woman. The unit-level causal effect is the difference in whether or not the district is represented by a woman depending on whether or not the training program is deployed.

These causal effects are all-else-equal relationships. The effect is defined at the level of an individual unit. This means that everything about the individual unit that is not a consequence of the treatment is being held equal when we describe the causal effect of the treatment.

But, just as with theory, the "all" in all-else-equal should not be taken literally here. The unit-level causal effect holds constant everything about the individual unit that is not a consequence of the treatment. But it does not hold constant features of a unit that change as a result of the treatment. For instance, suppose that, in some district, a woman is elected if and only if the district experiences the training program. This might occur because the program changes women's perceptions of their electoral prospects. The effect of the training program in this district is not the difference in whether or not a woman is elected, holding constant women's views of their electoral prospects. Rather, it is the difference in whether or not a woman is elected, holding constant everything about the district that is not a consequence of the training program.

An empirical researcher faces a fundamental challenge when investigating a causal relationship—there is no way to observe the same unit under two different treatment statuses at the same time. Thus unit-level effects are never observed. This is the well-known fundamental problem of causal inference. What the researcher may be able to do instead is to observe different units, some treated and some untreated. Comparing the outcomes for these units might inform her about averages of unit-level effects.[1]

Trying to learn about average effects from such comparisons creates its own challenges. The treated and untreated units typically differ in other ways as well. If those differences are *relevant*—that is, matter systematically for outcomes and are not themselves caused by the treatment—then some of the average difference in outcomes between treated and untreated units is the result of these other factors, rather than treatment status. In this event, the average difference in outcomes between treated and untreated units does not correspond to the average of the unit-level effects.

The credibility revolution is about finding ways to make credible claims about averages of unit-level effects. At their core, all of the techniques associated with the credibility revolution generate estimates based on comparisons of subsets of the data where it is hoped all relevant factors are equal on

---

1. Of course, one could also use other statistics, such as a median, or some other quantile. We talk about the average, since, in practice, this is the focus of most empirical work.

average. In this sense, the estimates are credible just to the extent that hope is fulfilled—all else (relevant) is equal (on average).

3.3   Commensurability and All Else Equal

So far, we have developed a sense of what all else equal means in both theoretical and empirical research. Now we can relate all else equal back to the issue of commensurability, as discussed in Chapter 2.

The implications of theoretical models always carry an all-else-equal caveat rooted in the fixing of primitives. As such, commensurability requires research designs that respect analogous all-else-equal conditions. This seems to complete the argument that the credibility revolution plays an important role in making commensurability more achievable. But there is one dangling issue that threatens this argument. What, exactly, is the relationship between fixing primitives in a theoretical model and holding all else equal on average in empirical work?

Suppose you want to empirically assess a theoretical implication that fixes certain primitives. Commensurability requires that the empirical research design hold constant the things represented by those primitives. But when we fix primitives, we are not committing to specific values of those primitives. We are simply saying that, whatever their value, they must be held fixed. So, even if working with data from targets that are in fact similar to the model, the empiricist still faces an all-else-equal challenge. For instance, consider two different congressional districts, both similar to our model of women's underrepresentation. They might well differ from one another by having different perception gaps but also different costs of running. Comparing the probability a woman is elected in places with higher and lower perception gaps using these two districts does not respect the all-else-equal caveat. The cost of running is fixed in deriving the theoretical implication, but not held equal in the research design. Commensurability fails. The lesson is that commensurability requires the research design to hold equal anything held constant when deriving the theoretical implication.

This argument clarifies something else. We can think about theoretical implications, which fix primitives, as operating at the unit level. That might make you worry about a second commensurability problem, having to do with level of analysis. How can we relate theoretical unit-level implications to empirical estimates about aggregates, such as an average?

As a starting point, notice that if an implication of a theoretical model holds for all individual units, then it also holds on average. In this way, unit-level theoretical implications straightforwardly imply analogous aggregate-level implications. Interestingly, this means that we don't need to get too hung up on whether we assess similarity by estimating the average treatment effect for the population, or for some subpopulation (e.g., a local average treatment effect).

Empirical scholars are often directly interested in heterogeneous effects— the possibility that a treatment has different effects for different units. Such heterogeneous effects might appear to contradict our assertion that unit-level theoretical implications map straightforwardly into analogous aggregate-level all-else-equal relationships. This worry is misplaced. We need not interpret a theoretical model as implying that some all-else-equal relationship is identical across units. As we've already noted, the all-else-equal implications of models are often derived without committing to specific values of primitives. As such, theoretical implications generally concern the sign or direction of a relationship, not its quantitative magnitude.

This all becomes clearer in an example. Consider Weingast, Shepsle, and Johnsen's (1981) canonical common-pool model of distributive politics. It implies that, as the size of a legislature increases, total district-level spending increases. The implication is a monotonicity relationship. It does not entail the claim that the magnitude of the relationship is the same across all legislatures represented by the model.

Weingast, Shepsle, and Johnsen derive this implication under minimal assumptions about preferences and functional forms. So their model is consistent with legislatures that differ significantly in, for example, the marginal benefit from pork and, thus, differ in the magnitude of the relationship between the number of legislators and distributive spending. It is, then, ironic that Weingast, Shepsle, and Johnsen give a quantitative name to their qualitative monotonicity implication—"the law of $\frac{1}{N}$."[2]

In a setting like this, the empiricist's averaging preserves the qualitative, directional implication of the theory. And observed heterogeneity in empirical treatment effects is consistent with the theoretical model.

None of this is to say models can't have heterogeneous effects as an implication. A model might well imply that the effect of a change in one parameter varies with the value of a second parameter. It is just to say that the

2. We use the word "ironic" in the sense of Morissette (1995).

mere presence of heterogeneity does not create a problem for the commensurability. In our experience, the average is always informative about the average.[3]

When theory does suggest heterogenous effects, that heterogeneity can be of as much interest for assessing mechanisms as is the average effect. For instance, a natural adaptation of Weingast, Shepsle, and Johnsen's model suggests a moderator for the relationship between the number of districts and distributive spending, namely, district magnitude. The model has two all-else-equal implications—one about the average and the other about heterogeneous effects. First, on average, more legislators implies more distributive spending, all else equal. Second, this relationship between district magnitude and distributive spending is stronger in smaller districts than in larger districts, all else equal. Baqir (2002) studies both implications in the context of city councils. He shows that adding seats to a city council increases spending on average, and more so in councils that are elected by ward rather than at large.

3.4   Theoretical Assumptions, Empirical Challenges

Theoretical models are not intended to explicitly describe the entire process that gives rise to the outcome in question. They are radical simplifications, meant to represent some important features of the target and yield implications useful for assessment.

Importantly, this means that empiricists cannot rely on theoretical models for guidance about what needs to be accounted for in a statistical analysis. After all, much that is held equal in the theoretical implications is only implicit in the model. As such, the standard for whether a variable must be accounted for is not whether that variable was included in the motivating theoretical model nor whether it is part of the process generating the outcome. Rather, the standard is whether failing to account for that variable would violate the all-else-equal requirements of commensurability.

That is not to say that theoretical models never have anything to say about what should be held equal. If a primitive is explicitly held constant when deriving an implication, its analogue must be held constant in empirical analysis.

3. We are indebted to our statistician colleague, Colm O'Muircheartaigh, for this formulation.

And endogenous outcomes should not be held constant. But, for the most part, the empiricist is left unguided by the model about just how to meet the challenge of all else equal.

Return to our example about the effect of the size of a legislature on distributive spending. In his empirical examination of this implication, Baqir (2002) notes that larger cities tend to have larger city councils. They are also more likely to have a strong-mayor form of government, which gives greater budgetary authority to the executive. Independent theoretical reasons suggest that spending outcomes vary with mayoral strength (Coate and Knight, 2011). The theoretical mechanisms underlying the law of $\frac{1}{N}$ and the effect of strong mayors are different. There is no need for theorists interested in one of them to explicitly include the other in their models. But this is certainly not the case for Baqir's attempt to credibly estimate the all-else-equal relationship between city council size and budgets. The absence of mayors from the motivating theoretical model would not justify ignoring differences in mayoral strength in the empirical analysis (and Baqir doesn't).

To summarize: A theoretical model generates an all-else-equal implication. If similarity holds, we expect this relationship to be reflected in the target. An empiricist must generate an estimate of a commensurable all-else-equal relationship from the same target. Once this task is taken up, the empiricist no longer needs to refer to the theoretical model for guidance. Indeed, doing so is unlikely to be particularly helpful, since the model does not make explicit many things that may nonetheless confound the all-else-equal claim empirically.

3.5   All Else Equal Need Not Be Causal

Seeing all-else-equal conditions as essential for commensurability illuminates a way that the credibility revolution's techniques apply more broadly than is suggested by the emphasis on causal inference in discussions of such work. All-else-equal claims from theoretical models need not be causal (though they often are). A theoretical model might predict an association between two endogenous outcomes. In such an implication, neither endogenous outcome causes the other. But empirical assessment of a noncausal theoretical claim still requires commensurability. And that commensurability requires just as much attention to holding all else equal as when estimating causal effects.

Strategies developed for causal inference are often appropriate, even when the goal is not causal inference.

To see the idea, return again to our discussion of the perception gap and women's underrepresentation in electoral politics. That model has causal implications. For instance, all else equal, a change in the perception gap causes a change in the average quality of elected women. This result fixes all primitives but one and describes the causal effect of the primitive (the perception gap) that we allow to move. But some other implications are not causal. For instance, all else equal, elected women perform better on average than elected men. This result fixes all of the primitives and compares two endogenous outcomes. As such, it is not a causal claim. The implication is not that turning an elected official from a man into a woman, holding quality fixed, improves performance.[4] Rather, the implication is that the process by which people decide to run for and win office results in elected women being of higher quality than elected men, on average.

Nonetheless, all of the concerns we raised earlier about the commensurability of the unit-level theoretical implication and an aggregate-level empirical estimate are at play. As such, achieving commensurability for this noncausal implication requires just as much attention to holding all else equal as would estimating a causal effect.

To assess the theoretical implication that, all else equal, women perform better than men in the US Congress, you might be tempted to simply compare the average federal funds received by districts represented by men and women. But this difference is unlikely to hold all else equal in the way required for commensurability. For instance, it might reflect attributes of the districts—for example, that they are poorer, more liberal, or more urban—that are associated both with electing women and attracting more federal spending.

Anzia and Berry (2011) use a difference-in-differences research design to address precisely such concerns. Their design compares the change in performance in districts that switched from having a man to a woman representative

---

4. The lack of a causal interpretation in this example is distinct from the potential conceptual incoherence of talking about causal effects of a nonmanipulable characteristic, like gender. We could have described a model of a perception gap based on any feature of a candidate, including ones that are in principle experimentally manipulable, and derived a similar all-else-equal, but not causal, implication.

(or vice versa) to the change in performance in districts that did not have such a switch. And they further restrict attention to switches that occur within ten-year time blocks, to capture redistricting in the wake of each decennial census.

This approach holds constant features of a district that are fixed over the time period being considered. For instance, as long as we believe urbanness is changing slowly enough that it can be thought of as a fixed characteristic of a district over the course of a decade, Anzia and Berry's approach accounts for it. Holding fixed such district characteristics is essential for commensurability, even though there is no causal inference going on.

Reinforcing the point from the previous section, these specific concerns about district characteristics do not come from the theoretical model. The model is not (and was not intended to be) a complete description of the process by which federal funds are allocated. It is a simplification meant to highlight the impact of the perception gap. As such, it would have been an absurd distraction for the theoretical model to explicitly include district income or urbanness; they were implicitly held equal by not being explicitly represented in the model. Nevertheless, since these variables are in fact correlated with federal spending and with legislator gender, they must be accounted for in the empirical analysis or it will not estimate a commensurable all-else-equal relationship.

We do still need to worry about characteristics of a district that matter for performance and are not fixed over a decade. If there are such characteristics, they must be accounted for to yield estimates that are commensurable with the theoretical implication. Put differently, the key assumption linking the research design to the world is that there are no such characteristics—had districts that do switch the gender of their representative not done so, their change in federal spending would have been the same (in expectation) as the districts that in fact did not switch. Anzia and Berry provide two reasons to believe this assumption is plausible. First, they show that districts that do and don't switch had similar trends in federal spending before the switch occurred, suggesting that there are not differential pre-existing trends. Second, by focusing on ten-year time intervals, they rule out a particular differential trend pointed to by substantive knowledge of Congress. In particular, districts' eligibility for geographically targeted federal programs shifts over time due to demographic changes. And these demographic changes might also be associated with electing women. However, those shifts in eligibility occur only with each census and thus are accounted for by the fact that Anzia and Berry restrict attention to the ten-year time periods between censuses. Of course, there may well be other concerns that lead reasonable people, thinking about the substantive politics, to question this key assumption.

3.6   Conclusion

We have explained how all-else-equal relationships play a central role in the commensurability of theoretical implications and empirical estimates. Commensurability is one of the three pillars supporting the connection between theory and empirics. Chapters 4 and 5 will discuss the other two, similarity of the model to the target and similarity of the research design to the target.

4

Models

The models used in social scientific theorizing are simplifications, representing only a small piece of a larger phenomenon. They leave almost everything out. At first glance, such models look like poor support for a bridge to the world, or to empirics. In this chapter, we argue against that first impression.

We make the argument with two audiences in mind. First, we expect the discussion to resonate with the intuitions of many theorists. Seeing these intuitions more fully articulated will, we hope, facilitate making models that are valuable for empirical social scientists.[1] Second, we hope to reassure empiricists about what their model-building colleagues are up to. Empiricists constantly confront the messiness of the world that generates their data. They might naturally feel skeptical about simplified theoretical models. How could such simplifications provide understanding of such a messy and complicated reality? We want to give such skeptics a look inside the mind of a theorist whose view is the exact opposite—the only path through the mess is simplification. We don't expect the arguments here, on their own, to convert every skeptic. But we hope the foundations laid here will help them read Part II with their minds open to the possibility that we'll convince them more fully there.

Our argument starts from the premise that the primary goal of social scientific theorizing is to explain social phenomena in terms of mechanisms (Elster, 1998; Hedström and Swedberg, 1998). This is not to claim that elucidating explanatory mechanisms is the only goal. Social science can be valuable for forecasting, evaluating policy, and so on. But, in keeping with our focus on the canonical goals of political science, we put explanation front and center.

1. Clarke and Primo (2012), Little and Pepinsky (2016), and Paine and Tyson (2020) draw out these intuitions in related ways.

Mechanisms are answers to *why* questions. A contrast will help illustrate what we mean. In the debate about women's underrepresentation, there is agreement on the answers to some *do* questions—women do run less often and do win less often than men. But there is disagreement on the answer to a *why* question—why do women run and win less often than men? Is it because of voter bias, a perception gap, both? The disagreement is over the mechanisms that explain the phenomena.

We start by laying out a view of the role of models in theorizing. We then discuss how we determine the mechanisms underlying a result by exploring the model's crucial features. Along the way, we compare this approach to the one that comes from the literature on causal mediation analysis. We relate all of this to the question of how models are used to explain social phenomena. We pay particular attention to mechanisms that foreground the intentions of the actors involved. Finally, we offer some guidance about what makes a good model when the goal is to provide understanding. This final section is, at least in part, aimed at empiricists who might sometimes find themselves puzzled by the choices their theoretical colleagues make.

4.1   Models

Theorists study models out of the belief that, precisely because the social world is so complex, making sense of it requires breaking it down into smaller pieces that can be carefully analyzed and understood. Models let us isolate mechanisms in order to learn what they do and what they imply.

We build on Giere's (1988, 2006) model-based view of theorizing. On that view, models operate within theoretical traditions. A theoretical tradition contains principles that constrain and guide the construction of models. This is what Giere (2006, p. 62) has in mind when he argues that fundamental principles in physics, "act as general templates for the construction of more specific models . . . to the principles, one adds what I'm here calling 'specific conditions,' the result being a more specific, but still abstract, object. The principles thus help both to shape and also to constrain the structure of these more specific models." A theoretical tradition's principles reflect commitments to particular kinds of explanation.

We can illustrate this view by reflecting on some of the principles of the rational choice theoretical tradition. The definition of a game creates one of Giere's general templates. A rational choice theorist specifies a game by filling in blanks corresponding to things like players, possible actions, types, beliefs, and payoffs (Myerson, 1991).

We build models on certain principles so we can think about the world through a particular theoretical lens. This process has two steps. Paraphrasing Morgan (2012, p. 31), the first step is "enquiry into the model"—analyzing the model without reference to a target in the world—and the second step is "enquiry with the model"—relating the model to the world for the purpose of explanation and assessment. The second step works because the model is linked to a target through a claim of similarity.

Exactly what similarity amounts to is a question of considerable philosophical interest (Frigg and Nguyen, 2020). We won't try to summarize the debate here. Loosely speaking, an assertion of similarity is a claim that learning about the model provides insight into the target. For this to work, the actors, situations, and mechanisms embodied in the model should meaningfully represent the actors, situations, and mechanisms in the world. The mechanisms piece is important. Mere descriptive similarity between the actors and situations represented in a model and the actors and situations in the world is not enough if the mechanisms are not also representational features of the model.

This approach helps us honestly address the standard critique that models are built on some obviously false assumptions, and does so without giving up on modeling. An honest theorist must concede the central claim of the critique—many modeling assumptions are false if taken as statements about the target. But, we think, a theorist can nonetheless argue that her model is useful for thinking about the target. To do so, she must make plausible the claim that the representational features—the actors, situations, and mechanisms embodied in her model—are similar enough to the target that aspects of the former will be reflected in the latter.

Given the informality of our notion of similarity, it will be useful to flesh out the idea in an example. So let's return to our model of women's underrepresentation.

First, think about how the various actors make decisions. In the model, potential candidates decide whether to run by comparing the cost of running to the expected benefit of running. These expected benefits depend on the benefit of holding office and the probability of winning. Real political candidates do not literally compare mathematically calculated expected benefits and costs. But when potential candidates think about running, they might well consider polling or expert advice to figure out their chance of winning and compare that against the opportunities they'd be giving up to run for office. In this sense, the considerations at work in the model are reflected in the world.

Next, consider the model's assumption that a candidate's electability and performance in office are positively correlated. The positive relationship might reflect voters caring about how well a politician will perform in office. The fact that they aren't one and the same might reflect vote choices being impacted by other observable features of a candidate that have little to do with how a candidate will perform in office. For instance, a candidate's family name or charisma might matter in elections but be relatively unimportant in Congress. It might also reflect the fact that all sorts of idiosyncratic features of the world, having nothing to do with the candidate at all, affect vote choice or success while in office. With respect to vote choice, this might include things like partisan swings or scandals concerning the other candidate. With respect to governing, this might include whether the candidate's party ends up in the majority or minority in Congress.

Finally, consider mechanisms. The key mechanism embodied in the model is the perception gap. The model embodies the idea that women under-estimate and men overestimate their electability. For the model to be similar to the target, it is crucial that women underestimate their own ability, relative to men.

Suppose some model is in fact similar to its target. In this case, the pertinent implications of the model should be reflected in the target. This undergirds two key activities. The first is explanation. If we have reason to believe the similarity relationship holds, we can explain phenomena in the world (e.g., underrepresentation) in terms of the mechanisms embodied in the model. The second is assessment. To evaluate the similarity claim, we can see whether the model's pertinent implications agree with empirical findings.

4.2   Mechanisms

It is not always easy to see exactly what mechanism explains a phenomenon inside a model. As we've said, mechanisms are answers to *why* questions. To figure out the mechanisms behind some endogenous outcome of a model we ask why that outcome occurs. We answer this question by considering nearby models—models that are alike in many respects but differ in others—in an attempt to identify the *crucial features* of the model. This process of exploration helps us determine which features of the model constitute the mechanisms. For instance, suppose we reanalyzed the model of women's underrepresentation, but zeroed out the perception gap. We would find that women run as often, are elected at the same rate, and have the same expected performance as men. The perception gap is crucial for the results that, on average, women run less often, are more likely to win conditional on running, and perform better than men. As such, it is a mechanism underlying them.

We can clarify this process of exploration to uncover a model's crucial features with another example. Many papers studying delegation build on a model of the following sort (Holmström, 1984; Gilligan and Krehbiel, 1989; Epstein and O'Halloran, 1999). There is an uninformed principal and an informed agent. Each has preferences over outcomes given by a quadratic-loss utility function. The principal's payoff from outcome x is $-(x - x_p)^2$, where x_p is the principal's ideal outcome. Similarly, the agent's payoff from outcome x is $-(x - x_a)^2$, where x_a is the agent's ideal outcome. Outcomes depend on two things: the policy chosen (π) and a mean-zero idiosyncratic shock (ε). These components are additively separable: $x = \pi + \varepsilon$. We model the idea that the principal is uninformed and the agent is informed by assuming the principal knows only the distribution of ε, while the agent knows its actual value.

The principal faces a choice: to delegate or not. If the principal delegates, the agent chooses the policy. If the principal does not delegate, she chooses the policy herself. In the former case, the agent will choose the policy so that the final outcome equals his most preferred outcome: $\pi = x_a - \varepsilon$. If the principal does not delegate, she chooses the policy that maximizes her expected utility. Since ε is mean zero and loss is quadratic, this is $\pi^* = x_p$. The principal decides whether to delegate by comparing the expected utility of these two possible choices.

If the principal delegates, the outcome is $x = x_a$ for certain. So her expected utility is

$$-(x_a - x_p)^2.$$

If the principal does not delegate, her expected utility is

$$\mathbb{E}[-(\pi^* + \varepsilon - x_p)^2] = -\operatorname{var}(\varepsilon).$$

Comparing, the principal delegates if

$$(x_a - x_p)^2 < \operatorname{var}(\varepsilon).$$

This has two implications. The principal is more likely to delegate when the agent's ideal outcome and the principal's ideal outcome are closer together (i.e., $x_a - x_p$ is small). This result is often called the ally principle. Second, the principal is more likely to delegate when she faces a lot of uncertainty about how policies translate into outcomes (i.e., var(ε) is big). We call this result the uncertainty effect.

Why is the principal more inclined to delegate when the agent is an ally or when there is more uncertainty? That is, what mechanisms underlie these two implications? Are they the same mechanism or are they different? Epstein and O'Halloran (1999, p. 54) summarize a standard intuition as follows:

> This quadratic loss function has two important implications. First, actors will prefer outcomes that are closer to their ideal point . . . but actors will also be risk-averse . . . Even though actors want outcomes close to their preferred policy, then, they may nonetheless be willing at the margin to accept a system that biases policy away from their preferences if they can simultaneously reduce the uncertainty associated with these outcomes.

Are each of these features of the model—distance aversion and risk aversion—crucial for each of the implications?

Bendor and Meirowitz (2004) show that the answer is no. In fact, both the ally principle and the uncertainty effect hold in a model that includes distance aversion (i.e., the principal values outcomes closer to her ideal point), but that makes no assumptions about risk attitudes. (It also makes no assumptions about a variety of other aspects of the aforementioned model, such as the one-dimensional policy space.)

To see this, let's consider a nearby model that retains some features from our earlier model, but generalizes the principal's utility function. Suppose, given a policy π, that the agent knows the outcome. But the principal doesn't. From the principal's perspective, the outcome is $x = \pi + \varepsilon$, where ε is a mean-zero random variable with probability density function f.

The principal and the agent each have a most preferred outcome and their payoffs from an outcome are decreasing in its distance from their most preferred outcome. But these preferences need not satisfy any particular assumption about risk attitudes. Denote the principal's utility from an outcome x that is distance $\Delta(x)$ from the principal's most preferred policy by $u_p(\Delta(x))$. Finally, continue to assume that the policy space is rich enough that any actor could, if informed, choose a policy that achieved their most preferred outcome.

As before, if the principal does not delegate, she chooses a policy that maximizes her expected utility, taking into account the uncertainty about outcomes. Call this best policy π^*. The expected utility from not delegating is

$$\int u_p(\Delta(\pi^* + \varepsilon))f(\varepsilon)\,d\varepsilon.$$

If the principal does delegate, her payoff is simply $u_p(\Delta(x_a))$, her utility from the agent's most preferred outcome. Thus, she delegates to the agent if and only if

$$u_p(\Delta(x_a)) > \int u_p(\Delta(\pi^* + \varepsilon))f(\varepsilon)\,d\varepsilon. \tag{4.1}$$

Let's first see that the ally principal continues to hold in this model without any assumption about risk aversion. The left-hand side is larger the closer the agent's most preferred outcome is to the principal's most preferred outcome. The right-hand side is unaffected by the agent's preferences. As such, the closer the agent's most preferred outcome is to her own, the more willing the principal is to delegate. This shows that the ally principal has nothing to do with risk aversion—the mechanism explaining the ally principle involves the interplay of a principal who is distance averse and an agent with policy expertise. Risk aversion is not part of the mechanism.

Next let's see that, despite the earlier intuition, the uncertainty effect also continues to hold even if the principal is not risk averse. To get some intuition, consider Figure 4.1. There we've drawn a utility function for the principal that does not correspond to risk-averse preferences. Suppose that ε can only take one of two values, $-\underline{\varepsilon}$ or $\underline{\varepsilon}$, and it takes them with equal probability. No matter which realization of ε occurs, the distance between the final outcome and the principal's most preferred outcome will be $\underline{\varepsilon}$, so the principal's payoff will be $u_p(\underline{\varepsilon})$. Now consider an increase in the principal's uncertainty, which is most naturally represented by a mean preserving spread of the distribution of ε. So, now ε takes the values $-\overline{\varepsilon}$ and $\overline{\varepsilon}$ with equal probability, where $\underline{\varepsilon} < \overline{\varepsilon}$. With that increase in uncertainty, the principal's payoff from delegation is $u_p(\overline{\varepsilon}) < u_p(\underline{\varepsilon})$. Increasing the principal's uncertainty reduced the attractiveness of delegating, without any assumption about risk aversion. What actually matters for the uncertainty effect is that spreading out the distribution of shocks makes it more likely that the final outcome will end up far from the principal's most preferred outcome, which is bad for the principal regardless of her risk preferences. Bendor and Meirowitz show that this result generalizes

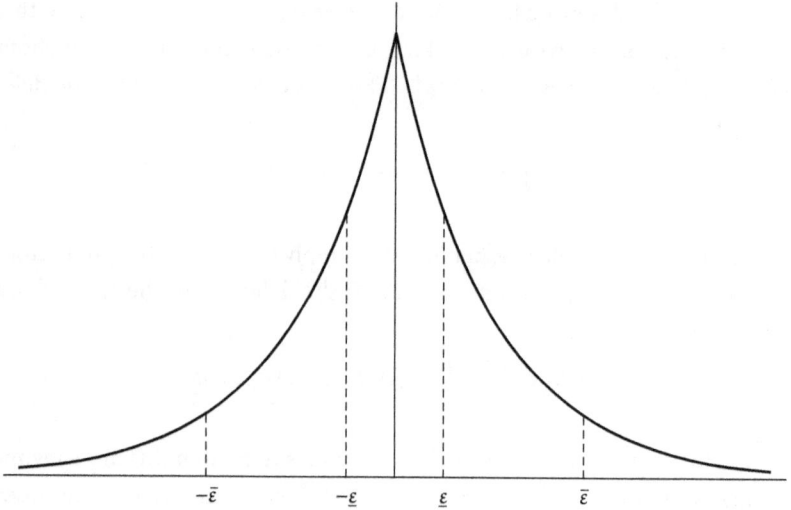

FIGURE 4.1. A mean preserving spread of the distribution of shocks makes delegation less attractive, even if the principal is not risk averse.

well beyond this simple example with only two possible realizations of the noise.

Thinking about mechanisms as answers to *why* questions within a model is different from another important approach to mechanisms in social science. That approach understands mechanisms as intermediate causes, often called *mediators* (Imai, Keele, and Tingley, 2010). Suppose that canvassing prior to an election increases voter turnout. We might wonder why this is the case. Evidence of a mediator—say, that being canvassed makes voters aware of the election and that being aware of the election increases voter turnout—could be part of a satisfactory answer to that *why* question. Why did canvassing cause voters to turn out? Because canvassing increased voter awareness. Increasing voter awareness, on this view, is a mechanism by which canvassing increases turnout.

This notion of a mechanism as an intermediate cause is the impetus behind methodological approaches such as causal mediation analysis. There, the goal is to assess how much of some causal effect is attributable to a particular mediator. For instance, in their work on the political legacy of slavery for contemporary political attitudes, Acharya, Blackwell, and Sen (2016) argue that variation in the extent of slavery in a locale in the nineteenth century might affect contemporary racial attitudes in that locale both through the persistence of political attitudes and through a mediator—the racial composition of that locale today. They use causal mediation analysis to separately identify these two effects, arguing that contemporary racial mix is relatively unimportant for understanding the effect of slavery on contemporary political attitudes.

Both approaches to mechanisms answer *why* questions of interest to social scientists. Both seem of value to us. For a theorist focused on building models, it is natural to answer *why* questions with reference to the features of the model that drive outcomes. For an empiricist focused on estimating causal effects, it is natural to answer *why* questions with estimates of intermediate causes. But taking a more integrated view of theory and empirics lets us see alternative ways to empirically assess mechanisms. Mechanisms have a variety of implications, about mediators, moderators, or other relationships. Assessing a theoretical mechanism's similarity to a target may involve confronting any of these kinds of implications with evidence.

4.3 Intentionality and Understanding

We have emphasized that models are built on principles that reflect theoretical traditions. Different theoretical traditions are interested in different kinds of explanations and thus result in models embodying different kinds of mechanisms. Joining a long tradition in the social sciences, we are interested in explanations that are *intentional*. An intentional explanation is one couched in terms of the opportunities, beliefs, and desires that make the behavior in question comprehensible (Dray, 1957; Davidson, 1963; Martin, 1969; Føllesdal, 1979; Dennett, 1989; Ferejohn and Satz, 1995; Landa, 2006). We say that we *understand* a phenomenon only when we have a successful intentional explanation of it.

Models help us achieve this kind of understanding by representing intentional mechanisms. Inquiry into the model reveals why the agents in the model act as they do, based on their beliefs, opportunities, and desires. If the agents in the model are similar to people in the world, then inquiry with the model provides understanding—the reasons people in the world act as they do will be similar to the reasons the agents in the model act as they do.

We have chosen the terminology of understanding deliberately. Dray (1957, p. 128) puts it well: "Only by putting yourself in the agent's position can you *understand* why he did what he did." Or, as Lucas (1987) argues, social scientists seek "to *understand* human behavior by visualizing the situations people find themselves in, the options they face and the pros and cons as they themselves see them" [p. 56, emphasis in original; a comma was deleted for clarity].

An intentional account is one kind of explanation. But it is not the only kind. Many nonintentional accounts are perfectly valid answers to *why* questions. Suppose someone asks, "Why did the people in one neighborhood vote at higher rates than another?" A good answer might be "because they were canvassed, and canvassing causes people to vote." That's a causal explanation, but not an intentional one. In our terminology, this answer explains the phenomenon, without providing understanding of it.

The model-building principles of rational choice theory demand that models be built with the elements of an intentional explanation—namely, agents and their opportunities, beliefs, and preferences or desires. This is not to say that an intentional model must be a canonical rational choice or game theoretic model. Far from it. For example, Kahneman and Tversky's (1979) prospect theory, Simon's (1956) bounded rationality, and Sen's (2004) reasoned choice are all also intentional theoretical traditions. But the rational choice approach does neatly illustrate how we can combine Giere's idea of theoretical principles with the demands of intentional understanding. In this sense, we agree with Guala and Steel (2011, p. 212) that the theoretical tradition reflected in rational choice (and other intentional) models "falls in the hermeneutic rather than the positivistic camp of social science methodology" and with Bates (1996) that "[t]he tools," of rational choice theory, "cannot be applied in the absence of *verstehen.*"

It is important to note that even models whose goal is understanding do not necessarily treat every agent in the model intentionally. For instance, consider a model whose goal is to understand how competition among candidates shapes campaign expenditures. Rather than treat the voters as intentional agents, a modeler might directly build in certain stylized facts about voters; for example, more campaign expenditure leads to more votes. Were the goal of the model to understand vote choice, this would be a problematic move. But if the goal is to understand the behavior of elites, it may be a productive simplification. Or it may not be. If there are important feedbacks between elite behavior and voter behavior, then treating voters as a black box may lead to misleading conclusions about the behavior of elites. So, while an intentional account does not require that every actor be modeled intentionally, it does require careful attention to the interaction of the various actors' intentions.

One final question concerns the status of intentional accounts of the behavior of collective agents.[2] It is, we think, straightforward why one might want an intentional account when the unit of analysis is an individual person. In such a setting, we can interpret model objects such as preferences and beliefs as representing mental states or internal justifications. But many social scientific models take the unit of analysis to be aggregate entities—such as political parties, states, or firms—that are not naturally thought of as having mental states. Why give an intentional account of the behavior of such entities?

Some scholars working in the rational choice tradition hold that it never makes sense to attribute intentionality to a collective agent. Riker and Ordeshook (1973, p. 78) argue that "[s]ociety, not being human, cannot have preferences in any proper sense." And Elster (1986, p. 3) makes a similar point, stating that a "family may, after some discussion, decide on a way of spending its income, but the decision is not based on 'its' goals and 'its' beliefs, since there are no such things." Shepsle (1992) puts it most pithily when he avers, "Congress is a they, not an it."

There is certainly some truth to this argument. But we think these defenders of methodological individualism take the argument too far. While collective agents may not literally have preferences or beliefs, the kinds of things represented by preferences and beliefs nonetheless sometimes play an important role in determining the behavior of such agents. In a decision about war and peace inside a government, various officials have preferences and beliefs. The foreign policy decisions of the state are made through a process involving both argumentation about preferences and beliefs and the exercise of power guided by preferences and beliefs. Ultimately, some group of people makes decisions that determine the behavior of the state. This behavior is comprehensible in terms of unitary intentions if that process led to a high level of agreement among the actors who have the power to act. In such a circumstance, treating the state as an intentional agent may be a productive simplification. As Frey (1985, p. 142) puts it, without sometimes treating collective agents as intentional, "we cannot even hope to fathom

---

2. See List and Pettit (2011) for one entry point into the philosophical literature on collective agents.

large-scale political systems." At the same time, he acknowledges that this makes sense only if "the relevant behavior of some few group members (leaders, spokesmen, representatives, etc.) permits prediction of the behavior of the rest," so that "[b]reaking up the group actors used into smaller components would only complicate the analysis without appreciably increasing its effectiveness."

To sum up, here is our view of how one uses a model to build social scientific understanding. The model is built on principles leaving blanks to be filled in corresponding to agents, their opportunities, beliefs, and desires. Within the model, agents do things for reasons. You then argue that those agents, and their beliefs, opportunities, and desires are similar to those of the real people we are seeking to understand. Hence, the reasons the people in the world behave as they do are similar to the reasons the agents in the model behave as they do.[3] And so, to the extent that the model provides an explanation for some phenomenon in the world, that explanation, by virtue of being intentional, also provides understanding.

4.4 Some Guidance on What Makes a Good Model

A model is supposed to provide understanding of a social phenomenon by developing implications of mechanisms that are embodied in the model and that are similar to mechanisms at work in the world. For a model to do this well, we want transparency about just which mechanisms the model embodies and we want those mechanisms to be plausibly similar to real-world targets.

These goals suggest two virtues that, to the extent possible, a good model strives to achieve. First, we would like to be able to "see through" a model so that we can identify which features of the model are crucial for which results. Second, we would like the model's features to be substantively interpretable, so that we can think about the plausibility of the similarity claim. Appreciating what makes a model transparent and substantively interpretable is particularly helpful for understanding why theorists make some of the modeling choices they do.

3. Lorentzen, Fravel, and Paine (2017) make a related argument, suggesting that, when evaluating the use of a theoretical model, one ought to ask whether individuals in an empirical circumstance actually perceived and thought about the main tradeoffs faced by the actors in the model.

Well-Understood Mechanisms

So far, we've talked about discovering a model's mechanisms as though it happens de novo with each theoretical inquiry. But many social-scientific models embody mechanisms that fit into well-understood categories. Examples include signaling, moral hazard, externalities, selection, commitment, coordination, complementarity or substitutability, and so on.

Building on well-understood mechanisms brings many benefits. It is particularly easy for a model to be transparent when its results are driven by mechanisms that have been extensively studied in other contexts. And when previous study has elucidated the substantive meaning of a mechanism, it is easier to assess similarity. Finally, having a collection of standard mechanisms facilitates seeing analogies across a variety of social phenomena, advancing the overall project of explanation in at least two ways.

First, we often run into mechanisms that we have seen before. Recognizing such patterns deepens our sense that we have explained what is going on—"feeling the key turn in the lock" as Peirce put it.[4] As Schelling (2006, p. 90) explains, "[r]ecognition of the wide applicability of a model, or of a family of models, helps in recognizing that one is dealing with a very general or basic phenomenon, not something specialized or idiosyncratic or unique."

Let us illustrate the idea. Someone puzzled by why national defense is nearly universally provided by a centralized authority can gain insight from a model of the private provision of public goods. Similarly, someone puzzled by the relative lack of success that large, diffuse groups have in lobbying can gain insight from Olson's (1965) model of concentrated versus diffuse interests. While each of these models is helpful on its own, deeper insight comes from noticing the common mechanism that unifies them. In each case, there are externalities—one agent's actions directly affect another agent's payoffs. And having noticed that well-understood mechanism, we start to see it elsewhere. For instance, Weingast, Shepsle, and Johnsen's (1981) model of the fiscal common pool explains the frequent overspending on earmarks and other pork by a legislature through externalities.[5]

4. Quoted in Hacking (1983).

5. Powell (2004) provides another example of unification of disparate phenomena via well-understood mechanisms. He shows how the same commitment-problem mechanism, in the presence of shifting power, underlies Fearon's (1998) model of civil wars, Acemoglu and Robinson's (2001) model of democratization, and de Figueiredo's (2002) model of inefficient bureaucracy.

Second, once we have a collection of well-understood and portable mechanisms, we can combine them with one another in various ways. This gives us an entry point for explaining new phenomena, using ideas we have already worked out. And we can reap an additional benefit. Seeing a mechanism working in the new context can suggest ways to modify or augment the analysis to represent important features of that new context and explore how they might interact with the mechanism. Thus, as Kreps (1990, p. 88) argues, the analogical approach to applying mechanisms allows us to "push intuitions into slightly more complex contexts" than we otherwise would be able to. For instance, consider models of electoral accountability (Ferejohn, 1986; Banks and Sundaram, 1993, 1998). These are built on mechanisms, such as moral hazard and signal jamming, that were already well understood from the study of managerial incentives (Holmström 1979, 1999). Building on these intuitions, and seeing how they change in the electoral setting, models of electoral accountability were able to provide insight into a variety of political phenomena, including the incumbency advantage, electoral pandering, term limits, and the effects of voter information, among many others (Ashworth 2012; surveys this literature).

Incrementalism

A second method for increasing transparency involves incrementalism. We can best evaluate whether some feature of a model is crucial for an implication if we have a benchmark for comparison—that is, we can compare what happens in that model with and without the feature in question. For this reason, theorists often try to work incrementally, building on canonical models that can serve as a benchmark.

An example illustrates the point. Calvert (1985) shows that in a one-dimensional model of platform competition, candidates' platforms do not converge when candidates are both policy motivated and uncertain of the median voter's ideal point. To understand the mechanisms driving platform divergence, we need to know which of these features is crucial.

Fortunately, Calvert is building on Downs's (1957) canonical model of platform competition. That model shows that platforms converge to the median voter's ideal point when voter preferences are single peaked, politicians are office motivated, and there is no uncertainty about voter preferences. Calvert maintains the assumption of single-peaked preferences, but proceeds incrementally from Downs's model with respect to the other two assumptions. First, he shows that in a model identical to Downs's model, except that politicians are policy oriented, platforms still converge to the median voter's ideal point. Then he shows that in a model that is identical to Downs's model except that politicians are uncertain of the median voter's ideal point, platforms converge to the median voter's expected ideal point. Thus, by proceeding incrementally, Calvert makes it transparent that what is crucial is actually the two features together—to get divergence, we need both uncertainty and policy-oriented politicians.

Seeing that incrementalism improves transparency helps make sense of a certain kind of conservatism in model building that we suspect troubles many outsiders. Theorists are more reluctant to abandon canonical models, even when those models have some assumptions that they don't like, than might appear optimal at first glance. But there is often a good reason for this reluctance. When we change too much at once, we often lose some of our ability to see which features are crucial. Incrementalism is in part the price of really grasping a model's mechanisms.

General and Substantive Assumptions

Seeing through a model to its mechanisms can be difficult, all the more so when implications are derived with heavy reliance on very particular assumptions about functional forms, distributions, and the like. Moreover, when those assumptions are technical (say, about two variables being summed or some function being differentiable) rather than substantive (say, about two variables being complements or substitutes in the production of some outcome), it is more difficult to know whether the similarity claim is plausible. So a third important goal for a formal model is to discover the fewest, most general, and most substantively interpretable assumptions under which some implication holds. We saw an instance of this in our preceding discussion about delegation. By moving away from a specific functional form, we were able to see with greater clarity the mechanisms underlying the model's implications.

This sort of concern explains some of the choices we made in the model of women's underrepresentation in Chapter 2. We did not, for example, assume that quality was uniformly distributed and then directly compute the quantities of interest. Leaving the distributions general enabled us to see that important implications of the model were not sensitive to the particular distribution.

There are a variety of techniques that advance the goal of making general and substantive assumptions. In what follows, we illustrate a few by talking through some examples.

In a famous argument about the political efficacy of concentrated versus diffuse interests, Olson (1965) points out that diffuse interests suffer from a greater externalities problem than do concentrated interests. In working toward some collective goal, each member of a diffuse interest, because there are more of them, internalizes the benefits to the group less and thus contributes less. As a consequence, Olson concludes, "the larger the group, the less it will further its common interests" (p. 36).

Olson provides a model to demonstrate the logic. Consider a version of that model. Suppose there are two groups, 1 and 2, with N_1 and N_2 members, respectively. Group 1 is the larger of the two groups (the diffuse interest), so $N_1 > N_2$.

The two groups are competing over the benefits from some policy. The total benefit to a group if they get their preferred policy is B, but those benefits must be shared among the members of the group, who each get an equal share. So if group i gets its policy, each member gets a benefit of $\frac{B}{N_i}$. If group i doesn't get its policy, its members get a benefit of 0.

Each group member decides how much to contribute to the group's lobbying efforts. Label individual j's contribution a_j. The total amount of lobbying expenditure by group i is A_i, which is just equal to the sum of the contributions of its members. Assume the cost of contributing a_j dollars to person j is just a_j. Denote the total amount of lobbying by the two groups combined by $A = A_1 + A_2$.

The probability group i wins is equal to its proportion of the lobbying. So group 1 gets its policy with probability $\frac{A_1}{A}$ and likewise for group 2. Since we are interested in whether the larger or smaller group is more likely to succeed, it will be useful to have notation for the probability group i wins. Write it as $\pi_i = \frac{A_i}{A}$. Olson's claim is that, since $N_1 > N_2$, it follows that in equilibrium $\pi_1 < \pi_2$.

Suppose each member of group 1 contributes a_1 and each member of group 2 contributes a_2. This implies $A_1 = N_1 a_1$ and $A_2 = N_2 a_2$. A member of group i's expected utility is the probability group i succeeds (π_i) times the individual's benefit if group i gets its policy ($\frac{B}{N_i}$) minus the cost of the individual's contribution (a_i):

$$\pi_i \frac{B}{N_i} - a_i.$$

We start finding an equilibrium by maximizing this expected utility for each person. This involves taking the first derivative with respect to one individual's contribution, holding fixed everyone else's contributions and setting it equal to zero. We aren't going to show you every step of the calculation, but once you do this, you get a condition that equates the marginal benefit and marginal cost for each individual. It implies that for each group $i = 1, 2$, the equilibrium probability of winning (π_i^*) must satisfy

$$\frac{1}{A}(1 - \pi_i^*)\frac{B}{N_i} = 1. \tag{4.2}$$

Notice that the right-hand side of Equation (4.2), representing the marginal cost to an individual of a contribution, is the same regardless of which group the individual is in. But the left-hand side, representing the marginal benefit to an individual of a contribution, depends on the group. Since the marginal costs are equal for the two groups, in equilibrium the marginal benefits must also be equal. This requires

$$\frac{1 - \pi_1^*}{N_1} = \frac{1 - \pi_2^*}{N_2}. \tag{4.3}$$

Now Olson's result is straightforward. Suppose the two groups succeed with equal probability, so that $\pi_1^* = \pi_2^*$. Since $N_1 > N_2$, the left-hand side of Equation (4.3) would be smaller than the right-hand side. So, in equilibrium, the two groups can't succeed with equal probability. To satisfy the equality in Equation (4.3), we need $1 - \pi_1^* > 1 - \pi_2^*$, which requires $\pi_1^* < \pi_2^*$. In equilibrium, the larger group succeeds with lower probability than the smaller group.

This model seems to confirm Olson's claim. The larger group has a bigger externalities problem than the smaller group. This is reflected in the fact that the marginal benefit of making a contribution is smaller for the members of the larger group. As a result, they each contribute less, the group as a whole collects fewer contributions, and so the diffuse interest is less politically effective.

Esteban and Ray (2001) agree with Olson that diffuse interests suffer a more severe externalities problem than do concentrated interests. And they agree that, as a consequence, each member of a diffuse interest will contribute less than each member of a concentrated interest. But they show this conclusion need not imply that the diffuse interest is less effective overall than the concentrated interest. It could be that the larger number of individually smaller contributions from a diffuse interest add up to more than the smaller number of individually larger contributions from a concentrated interest. Moreover, the fact that this was not the case in Olson's model was the result of a special functional form assumption that has a specific substantive meaning.

The issue Esteban and Ray raise has to do with Olson's assumption that the costs of contributions are linear—that is, that the cost of a contribution of a_j dollars is simply equal to a_j. One substantive meaning of this assumption is that the marginal utility of money is not diminishing. But we typically think that people do have diminishing marginal utility from money. All other things being equal, the first dollar a person contributes costs them less (in terms of utility) than the millionth dollar they contribute because, as they contribute more, they have less, so money is worth more to them. So linearity of the costs is probably best thought of as an auxiliary, rather than representational, feature of the model.

This is a concern because whether the marginal utility of money is decreasing is potentially consequential for the result that concentrated interests are more effective than diffuse interests. Olson points to a force associated with the externalities mechanism—because each individual in a diffuse interest internalizes less of the total benefit, they contribute less. If we allow diminishing marginal utility, there is a second force—because each individual in a diffuse interest is contributing less, the marginal cost of the next dollar is smaller to those individuals, making them inclined to contribute more. The first force implies that each individual in a diffuse interest will contribute less. The second force says, that doesn't necessarily imply that the total contributions from the diffuse interest will be smaller than the total contributions from the concentrated interest.

We can explore these ideas in a slight generalization of our model. Suppose everything is just as above, except that the cost of a contribution a_j is a_j^α, for $\alpha \geq 1$. When $\alpha = 1$, we have Olson's model. When $\alpha > 1$, the marginal cost of a contribution is increasing, so we have diminishing marginal utility in money.

Repeating the preceding analysis, suppose each member of group 1 contributes a_1 and each member of group 2 contributes a_2, so that $A_1 = N_1 a_1$ and $A_2 = N_2 a_2$. A member of group i's expected utility is the probability group i succeeds (π_i) times the individual's benefit if group i gets its policy $\left(\frac{B}{N_i}\right)$

minus the cost of the individual's contribution (a_i^{α}):

$$\pi_i \frac{B}{N_i} - a_i^{\alpha}.$$

Maximizing this expected utility for each person, holding fixed everyone else's effort, we get a condition equating marginal benefits and marginal costs, analogous to Equation (4.2). Each group i's equilibrium probability of winning, π_i^*, must satisfy

$$\frac{1}{A}(1 - \pi_i^*)\frac{B}{N_i} = \alpha \left(A\frac{\pi_i^*}{N_i} \right)^{\alpha-1}. \tag{4.4}$$

In Equation (4.4), it is somewhat harder, technically, to determine whether the larger or smaller group is more likely to win than it was with linear costs. Once we move away from the assumption of linearity, we don't get a nice explicit condition that isolates the probability a group wins on one side of an equation. As a result, we need to use a little more technique to deal with this more general setting. But we can still do it.

Once we do so, we find that, if α is sufficiently large, so that marginal utility is decreasing fast enough in money, Olson's result can be reversed. In particular, for any $\alpha \geq 2$, while it is still true that each member of a diffuse interest contributes less than each member of a concentrated interest, it is not true that diffuse interests are less effective than concentrated interests. When $\alpha \geq 2$, the diffuse interest is more likely to win than the concentrated interest.[6] And,

---

6. We want to know whether π_1^* or π_2^* is larger. Following Esteban and Ray's strategy, treat N_i as continuous and differentiate, holding A fixed at its equilibrium value. If π_i^* is decreasing (increasing) in N_i for a fixed A, then $\pi_1^* < (>)\pi_2^*$.

The implicit function theorem gives that the derivative of π_i^* with respect to N_i holding A fixed is

$$\frac{\dfrac{-(1-\pi_i^*)B}{AN_i^2} + (\alpha - 1)\alpha\dfrac{(A\pi_i^*)^{\alpha-1}}{N_i^{\alpha}}}{\dfrac{B}{AN_i} + \alpha(\alpha_1)\left(\dfrac{A}{N_i}\right)^{\alpha-1}(\pi_i^*)^{\alpha-2}}.$$

The denominator is positive, so π_i^* is decreasing in N_i if and only if

$$(\alpha - 1)\alpha\frac{(A\pi_i^*)^{\alpha-1}}{N_i^{\alpha}} < \frac{(1 - \pi_i^*)B}{AN_i^2}.$$

Substituting from Equation (4.4) into the left-hand side, we have that π_i^* is decreasing in N_i if and only if $\alpha < 2$.

indeed, Esteban and Ray show that this intuition extends beyond the extension we give, considering more general functions for the cost of contributions and an arbitrary number of groups.

A few lessons of this example are worth drawing out. First, Olson's model has two implications: (1) each member of a diffuse interest contributes less than each member of a concentrated interest and (2) diffuse interests are less likely to succeed than concentrated interests. He derives those results in a model that uses a special functional form assumption that embodies a substantive assumption—no diminishing marginal utility in money. Esteban and Ray's analysis shows that the first of these results holds quite generally in models embodying the externalities mechanism and is thus a pertinent implication if we want to assess whether externalities are at work. But they also show that the second implication depends on the extent to which the marginal utility of money is decreasing. So, for that implication to be pertinent, we have to believe that the assumption the marginal utility of money is not decreasing too much is also representational.

Second, once you see Esteban and Ray's point, you can start to think about additional arguments along these lines. We can now see that what really matters for the second force is whether the marginal cost of a contribution is higher or lower for members of the diffuse interest. Esteban and Ray point to a reason it might be lower—they are each contributing less and the marginal utility of money is decreasing. But there might also be reasons the marginal costs are higher for the members of diffuse interests in some applications. For instance, suppose that the diffuse interest is made up of workers and the concentrated interest of owners, so that the members of the diffuse interest have less wealth than the members of the concentrated interest. If we wrote a model with diminishing marginal utility of money that included each individual's wealth as a parameter, we might find that, even though they are making smaller contributions, the marginal cost of a contribution for a member of the diffuse interest is larger because they have less wealth to start with. In this kind of extension, we would recover Olson's original result, albeit for somewhat different reasons.

And this points to the third lesson. Having these kinds of substantive thoughts about what is going on in a model is facilitated by having enough technique to step back from making very specific functional form assumptions and calculating, and instead being able to see results that follow from more general properties and mechanisms. For our example concerning concentrated versus diffuse interests, we needed the implicit function theorem.

Below, we highlight another technique, called *monotone comparative statics* (Milgrom and Shannon, 1994; Ashworth and Bueno de Mesquita, 2006).

Our example of that technique is slightly different. Rather than focusing, as we did earlier, on a setting where we arguably get the conclusion wrong by making a specific functional form assumption, we focus on an example where the result we get with a specific functional form is right. But, as we saw from the example we just did, we can't really know that without having some technique that allows us to abstract from that specific functional form, which is what monotone comparative statics allows us to do. Moreover, once we see that the result follows from general, rather than specific, features of the model, we are freed up to do further theoretical exploration that wouldn't otherwise be possible.

Our example follows Powell (2002), who studies the following appeasement problem. Two states must divide some territory. There is a status quo division, but one state (call it D) is dissatisfied with that status quo. The other state (call it S) is satisfied with the status quo division.

S gets one chance to try to appease D by offering it some of the disputed territory. S believes that D will accept an offer of x with probability $p(x)$. The better the offer, the more likely D is to accept it, so p is an increasing function.[7] If D accepts the offer, then war is averted and S is left with $1 - x$ of its territory. If D rejects the offer, then there is a war. If S wins a war, it keeps all of its territory. If S loses a war, it ends up with none of the disputed territory. S wins a war with probability q. Given all of this, S will choose its appeasement offer, x, to solve the following maximization problem:

$$\max_{x} \overbrace{(1-x)p(x)}^{\text{Offer accepted}} + \overbrace{q\left(1 - p(x)\right)}^{\text{Offer rejected}}.$$

The question of interest is how the level of appeasement, x, changes with S's perception of its military strength, q. Does S offer more or less when it perceives itself to be strong? This is a classic comparative static question, asking how an endogenous outcome of the model (the level of appeasement) changes as we change a primitive (the probability that S wins a war with D), holding all else equal.

---

7. Notice that we are treating D as a nonintentional black box. That is just to keep the example simple. It is straightforward to flesh out this model in a way that treats D as intentional while preserving the fact that the probability an offer is accepted is increasing in x.

One way to find the comparative statics for this model is to choose a specific functional form for p and calculate the solution explicitly. For example, suppose $p(x) = x$. This means that S believes that if it offers $\frac{1}{2}$ of the disputed territory, then D accepts that offer with probability $\frac{1}{2}$ and likewise for all offers between 0 and 1. Under this assumption, S's maximization problem can be rewritten as follows:

$$\max_{x}(1 - x)x + q(1 - x).$$

We can solve this directly. If we differentiate and rearrange, the appeasement offer that maximizes S's expected utility is

$$x^* = \frac{1 - q}{2}.$$

This is decreasing in q—the stronger S is militarily, the smaller its appeasement offer to D.

While this conclusion is intuitive, the analysis made use of a strong assumption about the functional form of p. But the functional form was not chosen because of some compelling substantive political argument that the real-world probability of an offer being accepted is similar to a linear function. Rather, it was chosen because it simplified the algebra. This is troublesome for at least two reasons. First, if the conclusion, rather than just the derivation, relies on the functional form, then the conclusion is not pertinent unless we have a substantive argument that the functional form is in fact representational. Second, this approach makes it hard to generalize or add nuance to the results, since to solve a richer model we would still have to find functional forms that lead to explicit solutions, a process that gets harder and harder as the model becomes more involved.

With a little more technique, though, we can discover that this result is true under much weaker, and more substantively interpretable, assumptions. Standard results from monotone comparative statics show that the appeasement offer (x^*) is decreasing in S's military strength (q) as long as x and q are substitutes in S's expected utility function. Here, this simply requires something we already assumed, namely that p is increasing. Importantly, the result depends only on the substantively interpretable claim that better offers are more likely to be accepted. No technical auxiliary restrictions (e.g., linearity, concavity) are required. Thus, being able to characterize results in terms of minimal, general, substantive assumptions clarifies the mechanisms at work and allows a more substantive consideration of similarity. Moreover, it can facilitate deeper theoretical exploration. For instance, suppose we wanted to enrich our analysis by explicitly modeling how D's decision about whether to accept or reject an appeasement offer depends on domestic political bargaining. It is difficult to see how such a model would lead to the probability an offer is accepted being linear in the offer. But many models of domestic politics might imply the weaker condition that larger offers are more likely to be accepted, and that is all we actually need for the comparative static.

What to Include

Because theoretical models are simplifications that leave out so much of the messy reality that empiricists regularly confront, empiricists are often concerned about how theorists decide what gets included and what gets excluded from a model.

In thinking about this question, it is important to remember the purpose of a model. Models are not meant to be encompassing explanations of some phenomenon. Rather, they are meant to represent some mechanism that we believe might help explain the phenomenon. Thus, a feature of the world should be represented in a model only if doing so is important to representing the mechanism under study and its implications—that is, if excluding that feature changes the implications of the mechanism in important ways.

In this sense, the criterion for inclusion in a model is analogous to the criterion for whether to include a control variable in an empirical analysis. The empiricist interested in causal inference does not need to include every correlate of the outcome in her statistical analysis. She has to include those covariates that are correlated with both treatment and outcome. And the theorist doesn't need to include every feature of the world that matters for the phenomenon under study in her model. She has to include those features that matter for the way in which the mechanism relates to the phenomenon.

4.5 Conclusion

Models are radical simplifications. Their usefulness for social scientific explanation derives from two sources. First, they represent mechanisms. Inquiry into the model allows us to learn about how those mechanisms work and to derive implications of those mechanisms. Second, a model offers an explanation when it is similar to a real-world target. When similarity holds, we expect pertinent implications of the model to be reflected in the world.

The kind of explanation we get from such a model is inevitably limited. A model embodies at most a handful of mechanisms. As such, models are neither designed to provide nor capable of providing an encompassing account of how some phenomenon in the world works. Rather, they help us see the work that a particular mechanism is doing. Our simple model of the perception gap was not meant to be a complete account of electoral politics. But it did provide us with some insight into how that mechanism might affect women's underrepresentation. Simply put, it is not a model's job to explain everything; the hope is that it explains something.

Of course, this explanatory project requires that we have good reasons to believe the assertion of similarity between the model and the world. That belief must be grounded, at least in part, in qualitative and substantive knowledge of the target. But it also can be assessed empirically. An important contribution of our model of the perception gap is that it produced pertinent implications that we could compare to evidence. Since these implications are themselves all-else-equal claims, commensurability requires an empirical strategy that also holds all else equal. Research designs that do so credibly are the topic of the next chapter.

5

Research Design

Starting in applied microeconomics in the mid-1980s (e.g., LaLonde, 1986), a credibility revolution has spread throughout the empirical social sciences.[1] The core revolutionary move was to take seriously the assumptions required to interpret as causal the results of analyses of nonexperimental data. Scholars working within the credibility revolution have been dedicated to explicating those assumptions and to crafting research designs that render them more plausible.

The credibility revolution has awakened many scholars to just how difficult it is to estimate all-else-equal relationships. The *all* in all-else-equal covers a potentially enormous number of factors, many of which the researcher cannot observe.

If we could observe the outcomes for an individual unit in two different conditions (e.g., treatment statuses) at the same time, the credibility problem would evaporate. Comparing a unit to itself inherently holds all else equal. But that happy state is impossible. As we highlighted in Chapter 3's discussion of the fundamental problem of causal inference, at any given time, a scholar sees any given unit only in one condition.

What we can see are the average outcomes for different groups, one for each condition. The problem is how to compare these groups in a way that holds all else equal on average. This is where research design comes in.

In this chapter, we propose a tool for thinking about research design, which we call the *elements of research design* (ERD). This starts with an empirical strategy—that is, what the researcher will actually do to produce some estimate of a quantity of interest. It adds to that a set of assumptions under

1. See Angrist and Pischke (2010) for a discussion of the intellectual history in economics and Angrist and Pischke (2008) for the credibility revolution's emblematic treatise.

which the strategy works, and a collection of arguments—an argument for measurement validity, an argument for the plausibility of the assumptions, and an argument to bolster confidence that the findings are not due to chance or chicanery. The quality of these arguments determines how credible the research design is.

The ERD makes concrete the process of systematically articulating the claim of similarity between a research design and a target, represented in our framework as the right-hand side arrow across the top of Figure 2.1. Recall that this claim of similarity is based on two arguments: that the measures meaningfully represent the relevant features of the target and that the assumptions of the research design are plausible. The ERD involves an explicit statement of these arguments along with supporting evidence for them. Further, by specifying the precise quantity being estimated, it also facilitates clear thinking about commensurability.

We use the ERD to introduce some of the most popular research designs used in work inspired by the credibility revolution. Those research designs differ primarily in terms of substantive identification—the assumptions needed to estimate the quantity of interest and the kinds of arguments mustered for the plausibility of those assumptions. Our aim in discussing these research designs is not to replicate a textbook treatment of the statistical foundations of the techniques underlying them. Instead, this chapter focuses on clarifying the assumptions required for substantive identification, with a minimum of technicality.[2] We hope this discussion will guide the reader to a clearer understanding of the substantive arguments grounding claims of credibility and serve as a useful bridge for those planning to pursue a proper textbook treatment of the technicalities of research design (e.g., Angrist and Pischke, 2008; Dunning, 2012).

We conclude by using the ERD to analyze two bodies of research, one on politics and counter-narcotics policy and the other on the effects of treaty membership on government decision making. These analyses illustrate how the ERD clarifies what does, and what does not, count as progress toward credibility.

2. More technically, most of our discussion is focused on assumptions required for *point identification*, meaning that the value of the estimand could be known without uncertainty given infinite data. In Section 5.5, we briefly mention *partial identification*, meaning that an estimand can be known to be within a set of values. See Lewbel (2019) and Tamer (2010) for a discussion of these different notions of identification.

5.1 Elements of a Research Design

We draw a distinction between a statistical procedure and the broader concept of a research design. In our view, a credible research design must link two components. The first is an empirical strategy: the application of a statistical technique to data to estimate a quantity of interest (the *estimand*). The second is a series of arguments for that empirical strategy. Those arguments concern three things: measurement validity, substantive identification, and confidence building.

Measurement validity starts with an interpretive statement—it names the features of the target that the measures in the data are meant to represent. Substantive identification starts with a statement of assumptions—conditions under which the statistical procedure provides a good estimate of the estimand. The arguments tell us why we should believe those interpretations and assumptions. Importantly, the required arguments are substantive, not technical. Confidence building involves various further arguments that the findings are unlikely to be the result of chance or chicanery.

This terminology differs slightly from a commonplace usage. In a seminar, you often hear a researcher equate their research design and their statistical procedure. In our approach, a complete description of a research design must also convey the key interpretations and assumptions, as well as why those are plausible in their particular application. We follow convention by referring to families of research designs that share an empirical strategy by the name of that empirical strategy.

Table 5.1 is a template for the ERD, which can be used to understand any research design. Let's walk through its components.

An empirical strategy consists of three things. The *estimand* is the quantity we are attempting to estimate. Any characteristic of a population can be an estimand.[3] The *data* are information about that population. The *statistical procedure* is a set of mathematical operations on the data that yield as output both an estimate of the estimand and some measure of uncertainty of that estimate.

Let's step down in abstraction with an example. Social scientists are often interested in an average treatment effect among units in some population (as we discussed already in Chapter 3 and treat more formally later). Let's

---

3. For a discussion of the subtleties of this notion of population, see Imbens and Rubin (2015, Chapter 3).

TABLE 5.1. Elements of a Research Design

Empirical Strategy	
Estimand	The population-level relationship to be estimated
Data	Information drawn from the population under study
Statistical Procedure	A way to produce a quantitative summary of the data
Measurement Validity	
Interpretation	Statement of the features of the target that the variables in the data are claimed to represent
Arguments	Some combination of a substantive case and supporting evidence, lending credence to the interpretation
Substantive Identification	
Assumptions	Statement of conditions under which the statistical procedure yields a good estimate of the estimand
Arguments	Some combination of a substantive case and supporting evidence, lending credence to the assumptions
Confidence Building	A case and supporting evidence that the findings are unlikely to be due to chance or chicanery

imagine each unit has two potential outcomes—its outcome when treated and its outcome when untreated. The estimand is the average across the population of the difference in these two potential outcomes. The data include the recorded outcome under one or the other treatment status for each unit in the sample, which is some subset of the population. And the statistical procedure might be to calculate the difference in average outcomes between treated and untreated units, along with the associated standard error.

Sometimes innovations in data collection or statistical procedures open new questions to empirical inquiry. Many literatures have experienced great advances in the sorts of questions they can credibly answer due to advances in one or both of the data available or statistical procedures. Indeed, as machine learning and related techniques become increasingly important and well understood, we expect the speed of improvements on these fronts to accelerate.

Data and statistical procedures, however, are not our main focus. We instead concentrate on the other components of a research design: measurement validity, substantive identification, and confidence building. (Of course, improvements in data collection can sometimes lead to improvements in measurement validity or substantive identification.) Indeed, in keeping with our focus on the importance of all-else-equal relationships, we will mostly discuss substantive identification.

Measurement validity and substantive identification are ways of fleshing out the similarity claim represented by the right-hand arrow in Figure 2.1. Measurement validity concerns the similarity relationship between the variables in the data and the target, while substantive identification concerns the claim that the assumptions under which the statistical procedure yields good estimates of the estimand plausibly hold in the target. Our framework inextricably ties measurement validity and substantive identification to commensurability. It is often straightforward to describe a commensurable estimand. The key question is whether we have the right measures and can credibly estimate that estimand.

For results of a statistical procedure to be substantively interpretable in terms of relationships in the target, we need measurement validity. For instance, consider a study of the effect of legislator ideology on bill co-sponsorship. A political scientist might measure legislator ideology with a summary of roll-call voting, such as the NOMINATE score. It is then incumbent on the scholar to make a substantive argument that the NOMINATE score meaningfully represents legislator ideology, rather than, say, party pressure or constituent preferences.

We use the phrase *substantive identification* to cover two distinct, but related, ideas. The first is the statistical or econometric claim that the estimand, statistical procedure, and assumptions fit together: under the assumptions, the statistical procedure produces a good estimate of that estimand. Statistical and econometric theory address the precise assumptions under which various statistical procedures provide good estimates of particular estimands.[4] These technical issues are beyond the scope of this book, so we mostly leave them aside. We focus on procedures for which the relevant theory is well developed, and we will highlight the aspects of those results that are needed for our purposes as they arise.

The second aspect of substantive identification, and the one we primarily focus on, is the quality of arguments for the assumptions linking statistical procedures and estimands. We say that a research design is *substantively identified* if it includes arguments and evidence that would convince a reasonable interlocutor that the assumptions linking the statistical procedure and the estimand are plausible in the particular target under study. Focusing on

---

4. The features of a good estimate might include unbiasedness, consistency, efficiency, and so on (e.g., Wasserman, 2004, Chapter 6). Strictly speaking, "identification" is most closely related to consistency.

arguments for substantive identification is the central idea underlying the credibility revolution. That is, a research design can be credible only to the extent that the arguments for substantive identification are convincing.

A research design's assumptions typically cannot be tested directly. Rather, the argument for substantive identification is rooted in knowledge of the phenomenon and context under study. This knowledge often comes from descriptive or qualitative research. Sometimes, it is also possible to provide quantitative evidence that supports the plausibility of the assumptions—for instance, by showing that some implication of an assumption is true.

While measurement validity and substantive identification capture the similarity of the research design and the target, they do not exhaust what needs to be said about credibility. There is also the possibility that the findings under consideration may be the result of chance or chicanery. Addressing these concerns falls under activities that we refer to as confidence building.

The most direct way to address such concerns is by reporting measures of statistical uncertainty such as standard errors. For a research design to be credible, there needs to be an argument that the reported measures of uncertainty are appropriate, given the data and statistical procedure. For instance, the standard measures of uncertainty produced by statistical procedures are typically based on some kind of independence assumption across observations. If observations that are assumed independent are not, then we will underestimate our level of uncertainty. To build confidence in the credibility of a given approach, then, a researcher must use measures of uncertainty that appropriately account for dependence across observations in the data. Practically speaking, this might be accomplished through techniques such as clustering of standard errors.[5] The choice of and argument for the appropriate measure of uncertainty must be informed by substantive knowledge of the nature of the dependence across units.

There are forms of confidence building beyond showing evidence that the results were unlikely to be due to sampling variation. For instance, it builds confidence to show that results are not highly sensitive to particular choices about functional forms, covariates, bandwidths, and so on.

Finally, the whole apparatus by which we interpret statistical results builds in assumptions about how the researcher has behaved in generating those results. It is important both that you behave in a manner that is, broadly speaking, consistent with those assumptions and, in order to build confidence,

5. For more on this, see Bertrand, Duflo, and Mullainathan (2004) or Angrist and Pischke (2008, Chapter 8).

that you convince a reasonable interlocutor that you have not engaged in chicanery. This set of concerns is reflected in the growing literatures on multiple hypothesis testing, p-hacking, the garden of forking paths, publication bias, and related issues (Simmons, Nelson, and Simonsohn, 2011; Gelman and Loken, 2013, 2014; Simonsohn, Simmons, and Nelson, 2014).

Since the interlocutor can't always observe everything a researcher might have done, if you have engaged in good-faith behavior you have several ways of building confidence. For instance, you might adjust the standard for statistical confidence in a transparent way to reflect multiple hypothesis testing, report the results of many analyses to reassure a reader that any one result was not cherry-picked for its statistical significance, or pre-register the set of tests you intend to run. You can also allow other researchers to reach their own conclusions by making your data freely available.

Our discussion has thus far been relatively abstract. But even at this level of abstraction, you can see two benefits of the ERD. First, the credibility of an empirical claim, especially when working with widely accepted measures, is largely about the quality of the arguments for substantive identification. Second, a critical question for evaluating whether a new study increases the credibility of an empirical claim is whether the new study has changed either the assumptions or the argument for substantive identification. We return to each of these benefits, with an example, later in the chapter.

In what follows, we use the ERD to summarize various research designs. Given our focus on bringing together theory and empirics, the estimands of most interest to us correspond to all-else-equal relationships. Before introducing the particular research designs, we introduce *potential outcomes* more formally (Holland, 1986). The potential outcomes model helps us define one particular type of all-else-equal relationship, treatment effects. More importantly, it clarifies the assumptions under which aggregates of such relationships (e.g., average treatment effects) can be credibly estimated. As such, it is a useful tool for us, even though, as we argued in Chapter 3, the all-else-equal relationships we study when linking theory and empirics need not be causal.

5.2 Potential Outcomes and the Challenge of All Else Equal

In Chapter 3, we used the potential outcomes model as a way to clarify the idea of all else equal in empirical work at several points. Going forward, it will be helpful to have laid it out a bit more formally.

To keep things as simple as possible, let's focus on a context in which each unit is in one of two states: treated or untreated.[6] Each unit, i, has two potential outcomes—one when treated $(Y_i(1))$ and the other when untreated $(Y_i(0))$. The effect on unit i of moving from untreated to treated is the difference in its potential outcomes, $Y_i(1) - Y_i(0)$.

This definition of the unit-level potential outcomes already builds in an assumption. One unit's potential outcomes are not a function of the treatment status of any other unit. This rules out, for example, spillovers whereby the treatment assignment of one unit changes the outcomes for another unit. This "no spillovers" assumption is also referred to as the "stable unit treatment value assumption" (SUTVA). Because SUTVA is an assumption in all of the research designs that we discuss, we leave it implicit in what follows.

Consider some population of interest $(\mathcal{P})$ made up of $N_\mathcal{P}$ individual units. The average potential outcome if everyone in this population has treatment status T (which could be 0 or 1) is

$$\overline{Y}(T) = \frac{\sum_{i \in \mathcal{P}} Y_i(T)}{N_\mathcal{P}}.$$

The *average treatment effect* (ATE) in the population is just the difference in the average potential outcome when all units are treated and the average potential outcome when all units are untreated:

$$\text{ATE} = \overline{Y}(1) - \overline{Y}(0). \tag{5.1}$$

Each individual unit is actually either treated or untreated. Suppose the population is divided into two subgroups: those who happen to be treated, $\mathcal{T}$, and those who happen to be untreated, $\mathcal{U}$. These two subgroups have $N_\mathcal{T}$ and $N_\mathcal{U}$ members, respectively. So the share of the population in the treated group is

$$\delta = \frac{N_\mathcal{T}}{N_\mathcal{P}}$$

and the share in the untreated group is $1 - \delta$.

Because we've allowed for different units to have different treatment effects, it will sometimes also be important to discuss the average treatment effect within a subgroup. For any subgroup of the population, $\mathcal{G}$, the average

6. Our preferred terminology would be something like "exposed" and "not exposed." We follow convention by using "treated" and "untreated," with apologies to thinking people everywhere for medicalizing the discourse.

potential outcome in that group if everyone has treatment status T is

$$\overline{Y}_{\mathcal{G}}(T) = \frac{\sum_{i \in \mathcal{G}} Y_i(T)}{N_{\mathcal{G}}}.$$

The average treatment effects on the treated group and on the untreated group are particularly important. The *average treatment effect on the treated* (ATT) is

$$\text{ATT} = \overline{Y}_{\mathcal{T}}(1) - \overline{Y}_{\mathcal{T}}(0)$$

and the *average treatment effect on the untreated* (ATU) is

$$\text{ATU} = \overline{Y}_{\mathcal{U}}(1) - \overline{Y}_{\mathcal{U}}(0).$$

Recalling that the share of the population in the treated group is δ (so the share in the untreated group is $1 - \delta$), it is straightforward that

$$\text{ATE} = \delta \, \text{ATT} + (1 - \delta) \, \text{ATU}.$$

Further, notice that if the treatment effect happens to be the same for every unit, then $\text{ATE} = \text{ATT} = \text{ATU}$.

As we explained in our discussion of the fundamental problem of causal inference, we can't observe the group-level average outcomes that enter the definitions of the ATE, ATT, or ATU because we observe each unit either treated or untreated, not both. What we can observe is the average outcome with treatment for units that happen to be treated and the average outcome without treatment for units that happen to be untreated. This is called the *difference in means* (DIM):

$$\text{DIM} = \overline{Y}_{\mathcal{T}}(1) - \overline{Y}_{\mathcal{U}}(0). \tag{5.2}$$

At this point it is worth pausing and relating what we are talking about here to the kind of work scholars do in practice. Thus far, we've defined quantities—the DIM, the ATE, and so on—as characteristics of the population. A researcher typically observes a sample of data for some subset of the population, which introduces issues of sampling variation and statistical inference.[7] The researcher can then compute, say, a difference in means between treated and untreated units in that sample. We are going to ignore these issues of sampling, focusing instead on population-level relationships. We do so because if the DIM does not equal the ATE in the population,

7. Similar issues arise if we think of variation arising from the treatment assignment process. See Abadie et al. (2020) for a discussion.

then, while the difference in means in a sample may be a good estimate of the DIM in the population, there is no reason to think it is a good estimate of the ATE in the population, which is the quantity of interest. So let's return to the discussion of why the population DIM can fail to equal the population ATE.

It is helpful to start by comparing the DIM to the ATT and to the ATU:

$$\text{DIM} - \text{ATT} = \left(\overline{Y}_T(1) - \overline{Y}_U(0)\right) - \left(\overline{Y}_T(1) - \overline{Y}_T(0)\right)$$

$$= \overline{Y}_T(0) - \overline{Y}_U(0). \tag{5.3}$$

We refer to this difference as the *baseline untreated difference*. It is the difference in average potential outcomes between the treated and untreated groups, if they were all untreated.

$$\text{DIM} - \text{ATU} = \left(\overline{Y}_T(1) - \overline{Y}_U(0)\right) - \left(\overline{Y}_U(1) - \overline{Y}_U(0)\right)$$

$$= \overline{Y}_T(1) - \overline{Y}_U(1). \tag{5.4}$$

We refer to this difference as the *baseline treated difference*. It is the difference in average potential outcomes between the treated and untreated groups, if they were all treated.

Now, we can relate the DIM and the ATE by decomposing the DIM into three substantively meaningful terms:

$$\text{DIM} = \text{DIM} + \text{ATE} - \delta\,\text{ATT} - (1-\delta)\,\text{ATU}$$

$$= \text{ATE} + \delta(\text{DIM} - \text{ATT}) + (1-\delta)(\text{DIM} - \text{ATU})$$

$$= \text{ATE} + \delta\underbrace{\left(\overline{Y}_T(0) - \overline{Y}_U(0)\right)}_{\text{Baseline untreated difference}}$$

$$+ (1-\delta)\underbrace{\left(\overline{Y}_T(1) - \overline{Y}_U(1)\right)}_{\text{Baseline treated difference}}. \tag{5.5}$$

The first equality here follows from the fact that $\text{ATE} = \delta\,\text{ATT} + (1-\delta)\,\text{ATU}$, the second equality is rearrangement, and the third equality comes from substituting in the baseline untreated and treated differences from Equations (5.3) and (5.4).

This decomposition highlights how the DIM may fail to hold all else equal and therefore deviate from the ATE. The problem arises if there are baseline differences between units in the treated and untreated groups—that is, if average potential outcomes differ between the two groups. So to claim that we can interpret the DIM as the ATE, you need to assume that there are no baseline differences. That is, there must be no other factors, sometimes called *confounders*, that both systematically differ between the two groups and matter for outcomes. The standard sufficient condition for these assumptions to hold is that the potential outcomes are statistically independent of the treatment.

To get a sense of what can go wrong in interpreting the DIM as the ATE, consider a classic question from the field of political behavior: what is the average treatment effect of having seen a campaign advertisement on the decision to vote? Inspired by Equation (5.2), an initial approach would be to calculate the difference in means—comparing the turnout rate among voting age citizens who have and have not seen a campaign advertisement—and interpret it as the ATE.

This approach goes awry if there are baseline differences. And we have good reasons to worry that there are. Citizens who are more interested in politics are more likely to see campaign advertisements, since they are more likely to watch the news, televised debates, and other programs where political advertisements air. And citizens who are more interested in politics are more likely to vote than citizens who are not interested in politics, for reasons having nothing to do with whether they see a campaign advertisement. Thus, there are systematic baseline differences in voting between citizens who do and do not see campaign advertisements, just because the group that sees advertisements overrepresents politically interested citizens. Put differently, the difference in means fails to hold all else equal on average between those who do and do not see campaign advertisements.

Let's reframe this discussion in terms of the ERD. Suppose your estimand is the average treatment effect. If your statistical procedure is based on calculating the difference in means, then your research design can be credible only if you have a good substantive argument that there are no systematic baseline differences. The problem is that in many common settings, like in our example of campaign advertising, this assumption is implausible. This is what has motivated social scientists to develop more creative research designs to try to improve the credibility with which they learn about all-else-equal relationships.

5.3   The Major Research Designs

In this section, we use the potential outcomes framework to present each of the major research designs associated with the credibility revolution. In each case, we summarize the discussion using an ERD.

TABLE 5.2. Randomized Experiments

Empirical Strategy	
Estimand	Some weighted average of unit-level treatment effects (e.g., the ATE)
Data	Specific to application
Statistical Procedure	Difference in means, regression, matching, etc.
Measurement Validity	
Interpretation	Statement of the features of the target that the variables in the data are claimed to represent
Arguments	Some combination of a substantive case and supporting evidence, lending credence to the interpretation
Substantive Identification	
Assumptions	Conditional independence (aka, no omitted confounders or selection on observables)
Arguments	Treatment was randomized conditional on included covariates; evidence that randomization was faithfully implemented (e.g., balance tests)
Confidence Building	Argument that measure of uncertainty is appropriate (e.g., clustering, adjustments for multiple hypothesis testing); preregistration/preanalysis plan

5.3.1   Randomized Experiments

Experimental research designs randomize assignment to treatment. There is much to be said methodologically and practically about how to design and implement an experiment well (Gerber and Green, 2012). Those issues are beyond the scope of this book. For us, the key issue is to see why randomization is so valuable for substantive identification.

The DIM fails to equal the ATE when there are baseline differences. If assignment to treatment is determined randomly, then the treated and untreated groups are identical in expectation—there are no baseline differences. (There will still be sampling variation in any actual empirical study.) Experimental randomization thus makes the no omitted confounders assumption plausible. If the randomization was conditional on covariates, then those covariates must be conditioned on (e.g., through regression or matching) to make the no omitted confounders assumption plausible. For experimental research designs, then, randomization itself is the key argument for substantive identification, as emphasized in Table 5.2.

While experiments are great for credibility, their limitation is that many social science questions are not easily studied experimentally. This might be because it is infeasible to assign the treatment experimentally (e.g., major institutional reforms, coups), because random assignment of the treatment would be unethical (e.g., political violence), or because the subjects we wish to study will not participate (e.g., national leaders). In such situations, researchers must use other approaches to address confounding.

5.3.2 Just Controlling

Perhaps the simplest response to concerns over confounders, at least if they are observable, is to control for them statistically. Let's see how controlling works in the potential outcomes framework by focusing on a simple case where there is exactly one binary confounder.

As before, assume a binary treatment. But now, assume there are two types of units, A and B. Either type may receive the treatment. Within a type, all units have identical potential outcomes, meaning that within a type there are no baseline differences.

Suppose A types make up a share α_P of the total population (so B type's population share is $1 - \alpha_P$). The treated group ($\mathcal{T}$) and the untreated group ($\mathcal{U}$) are a mix of As and Bs. Let the share of As in the treated group be α_T and in the untreated group be $\alpha_\mathcal{U}$. (Again, the B type's share is the complement.) Finally, continue to let the total share of the population that is in the treated group be δ. Then, we have

$$\alpha_P = \delta \alpha_T + (1 - \delta)\alpha_\mathcal{U}.$$

Notice, this implies that $\alpha_T = \alpha_\mathcal{U}$ if and only if they both equal α_P. If this condition—which says that the share of each type in the treated and untreated groups is equal to their share in the population—holds, we say there is *no selection into treatment*.

The average treatment effect on the As is

$$\text{ATE}_A = \overline{Y}_A(1) - \overline{Y}_A(0).$$

And the average treatment effect on the Bs is

$$\text{ATE}_B = \overline{Y}_B(1) - \overline{Y}_B(0).$$

Since, by assumption, treatment effects are homogeneous within type, we could omit the averaging in these statements (i.e., $\overline{Y}_A(1) - \overline{Y}_A(0) =$

$Y_A(1) - Y_A(0)$ for each individual of type A). We keep it to maintain consistency of notation.

The ATE in the population is just the weighted average of these two type-specific average treatment effects, with the weights given by the population shares:

$$\text{ATE} = \alpha_P \text{ATE}_A + (1 - \alpha_P) \text{ATE}_B.$$

We can also write the ATE as the weighted average of the outcome with treatment minus the weighted average of the outcome without treatment (where the weights are the population weights):

$$\text{ATE} = \underbrace{\left[\alpha_P \overline{Y}_A(1) + (1 - \alpha_P)\overline{Y}_B(1)\right]}_{\text{Population average outcome with treatment}}$$

$$- \underbrace{\left[\alpha_P \overline{Y}_A(0) + (1 - \alpha_P)\overline{Y}_B(0)\right]}_{\text{Population average outcome without treatment}}. \tag{5.6}$$

Compare the ATE to the DIM. The average outcome for the treated group is

$$\overline{Y}_T(1) = \alpha_T \overline{Y}_A(1) + (1 - \alpha_T)\overline{Y}_B(1).$$

And the average outcome for the untreated group is

$$\overline{Y}_U(0) = \alpha_U \overline{Y}_A(0) + (1 - \alpha_U)\overline{Y}_B(0).$$

Thus, the difference in means between the treated and untreated groups is

$$\text{DIM} = \overline{Y}_T(1) - \overline{Y}_U(0). \tag{5.7}$$

Comparing Equations (5.6) and (5.7) shows that, if there is no selection into treatment—that is, $\alpha_T = \alpha_U = \alpha_P$—then the DIM equals the ATE. Why is this? When there is no selection into treatment there are the same proportions of each type in the treated and untreated groups as there are in the population overall. As a result, $\overline{Y}_T(1)$ equals the population average outcome with treatment and $\overline{Y}_U(0)$ equals the population average outcome without treatment.

By contrast, if there is selection into treatment, so that the proportions of As and Bs in the treated and untreated groups are not equal to their proportions in the population (i.e., one group is overrepresented among the treated and the other among the untreated), then the DIM does not equal the ATE.

To see this, let's write the decomposition of the DIM from Equation (5.5) in terms of our two types (we've skipped some algebra):

$$\text{DIM} = \text{ATE} + \delta \underbrace{\left(\alpha_\mathcal{T} - \alpha_\mathcal{U}\right)\left(\overline{Y}_A(0) - \overline{Y}_B(0)\right)}_{\text{Baseline untreated difference}}$$

$$+ (1 - \delta) \underbrace{\left(\alpha_\mathcal{T} - \alpha_\mathcal{U}\right)\left(\overline{Y}_A(1) - \overline{Y}_B(1)\right)}_{\text{Baseline treated difference}}.$$

Now the problem of confounding is clear. Suppose, for instance, that As have systematically bigger outcomes than Bs regardless of treatment status (i.e., $\overline{Y}_A(0) > \overline{Y}_B(0)$ and $\overline{Y}_A(1) > \overline{Y}_B(1)$). Unless the proportion of As in the treated and untreated groups is the same, so that $\alpha_\mathcal{T} - \alpha_\mathcal{U} = 0$, the DIM does not equal the ATE because there are baseline differences. If the proportion of As among the treated is greater than among the untreated, the DIM is larger than the ATE because it reflects the larger-on-average outcomes for As. And if the proportion of As among the treated is smaller than among the untreated, the DIM is smaller than the ATE. Of course, if the treatment effect is larger for As than for Bs, the opposite holds—if As are overrepresented (respectively underrepresented) in the treatment group, the DIM is larger (respectively smaller) than the ATE.

We can solve this problem by *controlling* for the confounder. In a simple case like ours, where the only confounder is group, controlling works in two steps. First, we find the DIM group-by-group. Then we average those group-specific DIMs according to the population shares. If group is the only source of baseline differences, this *conditional difference in means* (CDIM) corresponds to the ATE. Let's see how this works.

Start by writing down the difference in means for each group:

$$\text{DIM}_A = \overline{Y}_A(1) - \overline{Y}_A(0).$$

$$\text{DIM}_B = \overline{Y}_B(1) - \overline{Y}_B(0).$$

Now, notice that, because of our assumption that group is the only confounder, we have that $\text{DIM}_A = \text{ATE}_A$ and $\text{DIM}_B = \text{ATE}_B$. Thus, weighting by population share, we have

$$\text{CDIM} = \alpha_\mathcal{P} \, \text{DIM}_A + (1 - \alpha_\mathcal{P}) \, \text{DIM}_B$$

$$= \alpha_\mathcal{P} \, \text{ATE}_A + (1 - \alpha_\mathcal{P}) \, \text{ATE}_B$$

$$= \text{ATE}.$$

TABLE 5.3. An Example with Two Groups

	High interest	Low interest
Exposed to ad	300 vote 0 don't vote	100 vote 0 don't vote
Not exposed to ad	100 vote 0 don't vote	0 vote 300 don't vote

To reiterate, if there are indeed no other confounders, then each subgroup's difference in means equals its average treatment effect. As such, we can recover the overall ATE by taking a weighted average of the group-level difference in means with weights equal to the population shares. When we do so, we say we are *controlling for the confounder*.

To make this discussion a bit more concrete, let's return to our discussion of voter turnout and campaign advertising, where we were concerned that political interest was a confounder. Suppose the population is made up of 800 potential voters. Imagine that political interest is binary—people either have high interest or low interest in politics. And assume that the population, $\mathcal{P}$, is divided into two subpopulations: 400 high-interest (H) potential voters and 400 low-interest (L) potential voters.

High-interest voters always vote. But low-interest voters vote if and only if they see an ad. From this, we can already calculate this population's average treatment effect of exposure to an ad. The high-interest voters vote regardless of whether they see an ad, so each of them has a treatment effect of zero. The low-interest voters vote if and only if exposed to an ad, so each of them has a treatment effect of 1. Thus, the average treatment effect is

$$\text{ATE} = \frac{1}{2}\,\text{ATE}_H + \frac{1}{2}\,\text{ATE}_L = \frac{1}{2}.$$

For political interest to be a confounder, it needs to matter for both outcomes and treatment exposure. So assume there is selection into treatment: high-interest voters are more likely to see an ad than are low-interest voters. In particular, assume that $\frac{3}{4}$ of high-interest voters are exposed to an ad, while only $\frac{1}{4}$ of low-interest voters are. Table 5.3 shows the observed number of people who turn out for each combination of ad exposure and level of interest.

Given the selection into treatment, we know the DIM does not equal the ATE. But let's calculate it directly. All 400 voters exposed to the advertisement vote. Of the 400 voters not exposed to the advertisement, 100 vote. Thus, the difference in mean turnout between those exposed and not exposed to an advertisement is

$$\text{DIM} = \frac{400}{400} - \frac{100}{400} = \frac{3}{4} \neq \frac{1}{2} = \text{ATE}.$$

To see that controlling for political interest can recover the ATE, start by computing the group-specific differences in means. All 300 high-interest voters exposed to an advertisement vote. And all 100 high-interest voters not exposed to an advertisement also vote. Hence, the difference in mean turnout among high-interest voters is

$$\text{DIM}_H = \frac{300}{300} - \frac{100}{100} = 0 = \text{ATE}_H.$$

All 100 low-interest voters exposed to an ad vote. And none of the 300 low-interest voters not exposed to an ad vote. Hence, the difference in mean turnout among low-interest voters is

$$\text{DIM}_L = \frac{100}{100} - \frac{0}{300} = 1 = \text{ATE}_L.$$

Because there are no other confounders, the group-specific differences in means recover the group-specific average treatment effects.

The high- and low-interest groups have equal size, so the difference in means controlling for political interest is constructed by averaging these with equal weights:

$$\text{CDIM} = \frac{1}{2}\,\text{DIM}_H + \frac{1}{2}\,\text{DIM}_L = \frac{1}{2},$$

which is equal to the ATE we calculated earlier.

In this example, the DIM does not correspond to the ATE because it is confounded by political interest. If there are no remaining confounders, then the CDIM does correspond to the ATE. Thus, under certain conditions, controlling for confounders is a credible research design.

If there are other omitted confounders, you would need to control for them as well for a just-controlling research design to be credible. Typically, you would do so not by directly computing conditional means as we have here, but rather through a statistical procedure such as regression or matching.

There are three terms in common usage for describing a situation in which you have in fact controlled for everything you need to for the CDIM to equal the ATE: *conditional independence, no omitted confounders,* and *selection on observables.* We use these terms interchangeably.

In our experience, the overwhelming majority of just-controlling papers are subject to compelling critiques based on omitted confounders. A common reason is that some confounders may be unobserved in the data. This can be either because they are unobservable in principle or simply because the relevant variable hasn't been measured in the data currently available to you. If a confounder is unobserved, it obviously cannot be controlled for.

The exceptions tend to be papers that do two things. First, they substantively understand the process of treatment assignment—that is, where the variation in their key independent variable is coming from. Second, based on that understanding, they identify some component of that process that is plausibly random. Together, these allow the researcher to specify a set of control variables such that it is plausible that there are no omitted confounders. When a researcher has done this, we say they've identified a *natural experiment*. That is, a case can be made that treatment statuses are assigned as good as randomly, conditional on the control variables. Of course, sometimes the natural experiment does not entirely determine treatment assignment. When this is the case, the just-controlling design must be implemented in conjunction with an instrumental variables approach, which we discuss in more detail in Section 5.3.5.

Even in a situation in which a suspected confounder cannot be controlled for, all hope is not necessarily lost. Suppose a researcher wants to know, say, the direction of an all-else-equal relationship but is less concerned with its exact magnitude. Sensitivity and bounding analyses can help by revealing how likely it is that accounting for an omitted confounder could overturn the result. We discuss these techniques in Section 5.5.

In summary, at a conceptual level, the fundamental problem of causal inference is that we cannot observe the same unit in two different treatment statuses. Thus, we focus on estimands that are aggregate all-else-equal relationships, like the ATE. Practically, a researcher almost never has data for all of the variables that would need to be controlled for to make the CDIM correspond to the ATE. As a result, just-controlling research designs often are not credible if the stated estimand is the ATE. (They would be credible if the stated estimand were the CDIM, but that typically isn't a quantity that is commensurable with theoretical implications.) The main work of the credibility revolution has been to suggest alternative research designs that provide credible ways to estimate all-else-equal relationships without requiring data on every possible confounder.

TABLE 5.4. Just Controlling

Empirical Strategy	
Estimand	Some weighted average of unit-level treatment effects (e.g., the ATE)
Data	Specific to application
Statistical Procedure	Regression, matching, etc.
Measurement Validity	
Interpretation	Statement of the features of the target that the variables in the data are claimed to represent
Arguments	Some combination of a substantive case and supporting evidence, lending credence to the interpretation
Substantive Identification	
Assumptions	Conditional independence (aka, no omitted confounders or selection on observables)
Arguments	A substantive argument that there are no omitted confounders
Confidence Building	Evidence that the result is robust to reasonable variations in model specification (e.g., statistical procedure, covariates, functional form), placebo tests, and argument that measure of uncertainty is appropriate (e.g., clustering, randomization inference)

Table 5.4 highlights two points worth reemphasizing. First, just controlling can be implemented with multiple statistical procedures. Each of those procedures is associated, through statistical theory, with a slightly different estimand (e.g., the weights change). Second, and more importantly, the assumption of no omitted confounders is the same for any just-controlling research design, regardless of the particular statistical procedure employed (e.g., regression vs. matching).

5.3.3 Difference-in-Differences

Sometimes we have the advantage of repeatedly observing the same units over time. If units' treatment statuses change over time, we can calculate the difference in the units' outcomes from periods with and without the treatment. This might appear to solve the fundamental problem of causal inference—we are seeing the same unit both treated and untreated. But there's a catch. Things other than the treatment might change over time as well.

To capture this idea, continue to focus on binary treatments, but now imagine there are two time periods, $p = 1, 2$. And let's think about there being potential outcomes for each unit in each time period. Write the potential outcome for unit i under treatment status T in time period p as

$$Y_{ip}(T).$$

The treatment effect for unit i in period p is

$$TE_{ip} = Y_{ip}(1) - Y_{ip}(0).$$

Again, this treatment effect is unobservable because we can't observe the same unit both treated and untreated at the same time. But suppose unit i switches from untreated in period 1 to treated in period 2. Then we observe i's overtime difference ($DIFF_i$):

$$DIFF_i = Y_{i2}(1) - Y_{i1}(0). \tag{5.8}$$

$DIFF_i$ can be decomposed into the period 2 treatment effect and any overtime trend in i's potential outcome without treatment:

$$DIFF_i = \underbrace{(Y_{i2}(1) - Y_{i2}(0))}_{TE_{i2}} + \underbrace{(Y_{i2}(0) - Y_{i1}(0))}_{i\text{'s untreated trend}}. \tag{5.9}$$

If the potential outcomes are the same in both periods, then the treatment effect is the same in each period and the untreated trend is zero. In this case, $DIFF_i$ in fact captures the treatment effect for unit i (in any period). If potential outcomes are not the same in both periods, but there is no untreated trend, then $DIFF_i$ still captures the treatment effect for unit i in period 2.

Of course, either assumption (constant potential outcomes or no untreated trend) could be too strong. If we observe more than one unit, we can learn about the treatment effect for i under a different assumption. Suppose there is another unit, j, that remains untreated in both periods. For that unit we observe

$$DIFF_j = Y_{j2}(0) - Y_{j1}(0). \tag{5.10}$$

If we assume that units i and j have the same untreated trend, whether or not that trend is zero, then we have

$$DIFF_j = Y_{j2}(0) - Y_{j1}(0) = \underbrace{Y_{i2}(0) - Y_{i1}(0)}_{i\text{'s untreated trend}}.$$

Hence, if we consider the difference in the differences $(\text{DIFF}_i - \text{DIFF}_j)$, we recover the treatment effect for unit i in period 2. In other words, although unit j never changes treatment status, it allows us to calculate the untreated trend, which we can then use to recover the treatment effect for unit i in period 2. This is the simplest example of using a difference-in-differences approach.

As we move to observing more units, we can continue to find these period-specific, unit-level treatment effects as long as we are willing to assume that, for each unit that changes treatment status, there is some unit that does not change treatment status and that has exactly the same trend. That is an extremely onerous requirement. If we are satisfied with aggregate (e.g., average) treatment effects, we can considerably weaken the assumptions needed.

To see how this works, imagine our population is divided into two groups: the group that changes from untreated to treated $(\mathcal{UT})$ and the group that remains untreated $(\mathcal{UU})$. Define the average outcome in group $\mathcal{G}$ in period p under treatment status T as

$$\overline{Y}_{\mathcal{G}p}(T) = \frac{\sum_{i \in \mathcal{G}} Y_{ip}(T)}{N_{\mathcal{G}}}.$$

For group $\mathcal{UU}$, the average change in outcome between periods 1 and 2 is

$$\text{DIFF}_{\mathcal{UU}} = \underbrace{\overline{Y}_{\mathcal{UU}_2}(0) - \overline{Y}_{\mathcal{UU}_1}(0)}_{\text{Average untreated trend for } \mathcal{UU}}.$$

And analogously for group $\mathcal{UT}$ we have

$$\text{DIFF}_{\mathcal{UT}} = \overline{Y}_{\mathcal{UT}_2}(1) - \overline{Y}_{\mathcal{UT}_1}(0).$$

The difference-in-differences is

$$\text{DID} = \text{DIFF}_{\mathcal{UT}} - \text{DIFF}_{\mathcal{UU}}.$$

We can rewrite $\text{DIFF}_{\mathcal{UT}}$ as follows:

$$\text{DIFF}_{UT} = \overline{Y}_{\mathcal{UT}_2}(1) - \overline{Y}_{\mathcal{UT}_1}(0)$$
$$= \underbrace{\left(\overline{Y}_{\mathcal{UT}_2}(1) - \overline{Y}_{\mathcal{UT}_2}(0)\right)}_{\text{ATT}} + \underbrace{\left(\overline{Y}_{\mathcal{UT}_2}(0) - \overline{Y}_{\mathcal{UT}_1}(0)\right)}_{\text{Average untreated trend for } \mathcal{UT}}.$$

Using this, we can rewrite the difference-in-differences as the sum of the ATT and the difference in the average trends:

$$
\text{DID} = \underbrace{\left(\overline{Y}_{UT_2}(1) - \overline{Y}_{UT_2}(0) \right)}_{\text{ATT}} +
$$

$$
\underbrace{\left(\overline{Y}_{UT_2}(0) - \overline{Y}_{UT_1}(0) \right)}_{\text{Average untreated trend for } UT} - \underbrace{\left(\overline{Y}_{UU_2}(0) - \overline{Y}_{UU_1}(0) \right)}_{\text{Average untreated trend for } UU}. \qquad (5.11)
$$

$$
\underbrace{\phantom{\text{Difference in average trends}}}_{\text{Difference in average trends}}
$$

Now it is straightforward to see that the DID equals the ATT if the difference in average untreated trends is zero. This assumption is called *parallel trends*. Parallel trends is a weaker assumption than all units having the same trend. If we want to recover the ATE with the DID we need an additional assumption to ensure that the ATT equals the ATE; for example, constant treatment effects.

To get a slightly different sense of what is going on here, notice that assuming parallel trends is equivalent to assuming that any baseline differences are unchanged over time:

$$
\underbrace{\left(\overline{Y}_{UT_2}(0) - \overline{Y}_{UT_1}(0) \right)}_{\text{Average untreated trend for } UT} - \underbrace{\left(\overline{Y}_{UU_2}(0) - \overline{Y}_{UU_1}(0) \right)}_{\text{Average untreated trend for } UU}
$$

$$
= \underbrace{\left(\overline{Y}_{UT_2}(0) - \overline{Y}_{UU_2}(0) \right)}_{\text{Period 2 baseline untreated diff}} - \underbrace{\left(\overline{Y}_{UT_1}(0) - \overline{Y}_{UU_1}(0) \right)}_{\text{Period 1 baseline untreated diff}}.
$$

This shows that difference-in-differences is using the first period difference in average outcomes to eliminate the component of the second period difference in average outcomes that is due to baseline differences. This is important. As we saw in the previous section, with cross-sectional data, to deal with baseline differences, you have to control for a set of covariates and argue that there were no omitted confounders. With difference-in-differences, we are able to eliminate any baseline differences that don't vary over time without specifying any particular covariates that control for them. This means that we accounted for both any time-invariant confounders that we could have thought of and controlled for, as well as any time-invariant confounders that were unobservable or didn't occur to us.

TABLE 5.5. Turnout Example with Two Elections

	First Election	Second Election
Voters exposed to ad in second election	300 vote	400 vote
Voters never exposed to ad	100 vote	100 vote

Now that we've seen somewhat formally how difference-in-differences works in the simple two-group, two-period setting, let's return to the previous section's numerical example about campaign advertising exposure, political interest, and voter turnout. Continue to assume there are two equally sized groups—high-interest and low-interest—and that high-interest voters vote no matter what, while low-interest voters vote if and only if they see an ad. But unlike before, assume the researcher cannot observe political interest and so cannot control for it.

Suppose the first election is relatively uncompetitive. As a result, neither low- nor high-interest voters are exposed to any advertisements. But the second election is more competitive. As such, three quarters of high-interest voters and one quarter of low-interest voters see ads. Table 5.5 summarizes the example.

Since potential outcomes don't change between periods, the ATE is the same in each period. As before this ATE is one half—the treatment effect on the high-interest voters is zero and the treatment effect on the low-interest voters is one. Since we know who is exposed to treatment, we can also calculate the ATT. The treated group are the voters who are exposed to ads in the second election. This group is made up of three-quarters high-interest voters and one-quarter low-interest voters. So the ATT is $\frac{1}{4}$.

Parallel trends holds in this example. Among the untreated, turnout stays flat across the two elections. If the treated group was not exposed to ads in the second election, turnout for that group would also have stayed flat—the 300 high-interest voters would have voted in both elections and the 100 low-interest voters would not have voted in either election. Given this, we know that difference-in-differences analysis will recover the ATT. But let's see that directly.

Begin by calculating the within-group differences. The group that gets exposed to advertisements is analogous to what was earlier referred to as group $\mathcal{UT}$. In this example

TABLE 5.6. Turnout Example with Two Elections and Three Types of Voters

	First Election	Second Election
Voters exposed to ad in second election	300 vote (just high interest)	550 vote (300 high + 150 activated + 100 low)
Voters never exposed to ad	100 vote (just high interest)	150 vote (100 high + 50 activated)

$$\text{DIFF}_{UT} = \frac{400}{400} - \frac{300}{400} = \frac{1}{4}.$$

The group that is never exposed to a campaign ad is analogous to group UU. In this example,

$$\text{DIFF}_{UU} = \frac{100}{400} - \frac{100}{400} = 0.$$

The difference-in-differences is

$$\text{DID} = \text{DIFF}_{UT} - \text{DIFF}_{UU}$$

$$= \frac{1}{4} - 0$$

$$= \frac{1}{4} = \text{ATT}.$$

In this example, political interest is a source of baseline differences in voter turnout. Difference-in-differences recovers the ATT because it has effectively accounted for such baseline differences. This is true even though the researcher didn't observe political interest and so couldn't control for it directly.

We can enrich the example slightly to see why parallel trends is such an important assumption. In particular, augment the example so that there are now three groups. As before, there are 400 high-interest voters and 400 low-interest voters. But now there are also 200 activated voters, who were not interested in politics in the first election but become mobilized by some issue in the second election. In the first election, the activated voters weren't going to vote, even if they had been exposed to an ad. In the second election, these activated voters became like high-interest voters, voting no matter what. Three quarters of the activated voters are exposed to an ad in the second election. Table 5.6 summarizes this example.

Let's start by thinking about the ATE and the ATT. The high-interest voters still have a treatment effect of zero. The activated voters also have a treatment effect of zero: in the first election they would abstain no matter what and in the second election they would vote no matter what. The low-interest voters still have a treatment effect of one. The low-interest voters are now two-fifths of the population, so the ATE is two-fifths. The treated group is made up of 300 high-interest voters, 150 activated voters, and 100 low-interest voters. Thus, the ATT is $\frac{100}{550}$.

Importantly, parallel trends is not satisfied in this expanded example. In the untreated group, turnout between the first and second election goes from $\frac{100}{450}$ to $\frac{150}{450}$, an increase of $\frac{1}{9}$. If the potential voters in the treated group had not been exposed to an ad, turnout would have gone from $\frac{300}{550}$ to $\frac{450}{550}$—everyone in this group other than the 100 low-interest voters would have voted in the second election—an increase of $\frac{3}{11}$. Thus, even without the change in treatment status, the treated and untreated groups were on different trends. As such, we know the difference-in-differences will not recover the ATT. But let's compute it to see.

Again calculate the group-specific differences:

$$\text{DIFF}_{UT} = \frac{550}{550} - \frac{300}{550} = \frac{5}{11}$$

and

$$\text{DIFF}_{UU} = \frac{150}{450} - \frac{100}{450} = \frac{1}{9}.$$

The difference-in-differences is

$$\text{DID} = \text{DIFF}_{UT} - \text{DIFF}_{UU}$$

$$= \frac{5}{11} - \frac{1}{9}$$

$$= \frac{34}{99} \neq \text{ATT}.$$

(Recall the ATT is $\frac{100}{550}$, which is equal to $\frac{18}{99}$.) The parallel trends violation leads the difference-in-differences to overstate the ATT. The activated voters were going to change their voting behavior in the second election with or without ads. But because the activated voters are overrepresented in the treated group, the difference-in-differences attributes some of that change to the effect of the advertisement.

The assumptions underlying difference-in-differences designs are weaker than those underlying just controlling. We argued that credible just-controlling designs typically depend on a substantive understanding of the treatment assignment process that allows the researcher to find a natural experiment within it. Because difference-in-differences designs remove the influence of all time-invariant confounders, they reduce the burden on the researcher. Now the researcher must be able to find a natural experiment that affects changes to treatment status. This is a weaker requirement because explaining levels is sufficient for explaining changes, but the reverse is not true.

While this discussion captures the intuition behind difference-in-differences, things can get substantially more complicated as we move beyond the two-group, two-period setting. With multiple periods and multiple groups, if all units that ever change treatment status do so at the same time, things are exactly analogous to the two-group, two-period example we already considered. We can just let a unit's average outcome in the periods before treatment and a unit's average outcome in the periods after treatment take the place of the period 1 and period 2 outcomes in the two-group, two-period example. We refer to such a setting as a *simple difference-in-differences*.

Matters are more subtle when there is staggered timing of treatment; that is, when different units change treatment status at different times. But here is a way to start thinking about how it works. We can treat each period at which some group of units changes treatment status and others don't as a separate simple difference-in-differences. When we do so, the units that had previously changed treatment status will be part of the baseline comparison group, since, while they are now treated, they do not change treatment status in the relevant period. Then, the overall difference-in-differences with staggered timing of treatment is a weighted average of each of these separate simple difference-in-differences (Goodman-Bacon, 2018).

The nature of the weights that different statistical procedures give to the simple difference-in-differences that make up this weighted average is an area of active research (Goodman-Bacon, 2018; Callaway and Sant'Anna, 2020; Imai and Kim, 2019; Sun and Abraham, 2020). We suspect that knowledge of these issues and views about best practices will advance rapidly following the publication of this book and we encourage readers to follow such developments.

Two conceptual points are highlighted by this emerging literature. Both concern heterogeneity in treatment effects, one between units and the other within units over time.

First, in an important sense, there is more information in the simple difference-in-differences for units that change treatment status towards the middle of the time period covered by the data than for units that change treatment status toward the beginning or the end. This is because, for units that change treatment status in the middle, we get to observe them for multiple periods both treated and untreated. As such, a statistical procedure that forms the weighted average in a way that puts more weight on comparisons about which there is more information overweights units whose treatment status changes in the middle. So, if treatment effects differ for units that enter treatment at different times, there is no guarantee that the weighted average returned by the statistical procedure will be the ATT.

Second, if treatment effects change over time within a unit, this creates issues for the parallel trends assumption. Suppose, for instance, that a treatment's effect takes time to be realized, such that the effect in the period immediately after a unit becomes treated is less than in the period following and so on. As we've just said, in the simple difference-in-differences that become the components of the weighted average, units that have previously changed treatment status serve as part of the comparison group for units that later change treatment status. But if the effect of the treatment changes the longer a unit has been exposed to it, then it is not true that the newly treated and previously treated units would have been on the same trend, but for the newly treated units' change in treatment status. That is, over-time trends in treatment effects can lead to violations of parallel trends that introduce bias into a difference-in-differences when there is staggered entry into treatment.

As we've said, an active literature is exploring ways to diagnose and address these complex issues. Table 5.7 uses the ERD to explicate the basic structure of a difference-in-differences research design.

5.3.4 Regression Discontinuity

In some situations, treatment assignment is determined entirely by whether or not some observable variable (called the *running variable*) exceeds a threshold. In political science, elections provide a common setting since the 50% threshold determines the winner and loser. But elections are far from the only setting in which outcomes change according to thresholds. For instance, Italian municipalities use different rules for electing mayors depending on whether their population is above 15,000 (Bordignon, Nannicini,

TABLE 5.7. Difference-in-Differences

Empirical Strategy	
Estimand	Some weighted average of treatment effects for units that switch treatment status
Data	Specific to application, but must include repeated measures of same units over time, e.g., panel or repeated cross section
Statistical Procedure	Fixed effects regression, first differencing, etc.
Measurement Validity	
Interpretation	Statement of the features of the target that the variables in the data are claimed to represent
Arguments	Some combination of a substantive case and supporting evidence, lending credence to the interpretation
Substantive Identification	
Assumptions	No omitted time-varying confounders (a.k.a., parallel trends)
Arguments	A substantive argument about treatment status change that makes the case that there are no omitted time-varying confounders, evidence in support of this argument (e.g., test of parallel trends in the pre-trends, event study graph, robustness to inclusion of unit-specific time trends)
Confidence Building	Evidence that the result is robust to reasonable variations in model specification (e.g., statistical procedure, covariates, functional form), placebo tests, and argument that measure of uncertainty is appropriate (e.g., clustered standard errors, randomization inference)

and Tabellini, 2016). Does this allow for credible estimation of the effect of switching from one electoral rule to another?

At first blush, this structure seems to present a serious problem. Since the running variable entirely determines treatment status, you can never compare outcomes for treated and untreated units that have the same value of the running variable. Thus, if the running variable is conditionally correlated with the outcome, it is a confounder.

Despite these appearances, such a situation actually presents an opportunity to credibly estimate an all-else-equal relationship, albeit under a different set of assumptions. The key assumption is that the average potential outcomes are continuous functions of the running variable in a neighborhood of the threshold. If this continuity assumption holds, then units just above and just below the threshold have almost the same potential outcomes. But units just below are untreated and units just above are treated (or vice versa). Thus, the comparison of the outcomes for these two sets of units is very close to an actual treatment effect. Indeed, in the limit, it is the actual average treatment effect for a unit with a value of the running variable at the threshold. Research designs based on this approach are referred to as *regression discontinuity* (RD) designs.

Suppose that an individual unit's potential outcome function depends on both treatment and another variable, x. We can then write the potential outcome under treatment status T for unit i with $x = x_i$ as

$$Y_i(T) = F_i(T, x_i),$$

for some function F_i. Now, write the average potential outcome function at treatment status T and some value of the variable x as

$$Y(T, x).$$

This is the average of $F_i(T, x_i)$ for all individuals with $x_i = x$. Continuity around the threshold x^* means that the function $Y(T, \cdot)$ is continuous in its second argument at $x = x^*$ for $T \in \{0, 1\}$.

With this definition in hand, let's see how regression discontinuity designs work. Choose some small number $\epsilon > 0$, which defines three groups. One group, $\mathcal{B}(\epsilon)$, is just below the threshold, $x_i \in [x^* - \epsilon, x^*)$. Another group, $\mathcal{A}(\epsilon)$, is at or just above the threshold, $x_i \in [x^*, x^* + \epsilon]$. A third group, consisting of everyone else, is far from the threshold. Then, let

$$\overline{Y}_{B(\epsilon)}(T)$$

be the average of $F_i(T, x_i)$ for all individuals with $x_i \in [x^* - \epsilon, x^*)$ and

$$\overline{Y}_{A(\epsilon)}(T)$$

be the average of $F_i(T, x_i)$ for all individuals with $x_i \in [x^*, x^* + \epsilon]$.

The ϵ we choose corresponds to our notion of "very close." The comparison of the outcomes for the two sets of units very close to the cutoff yields the following difference in means:

$$\text{DIM}_\epsilon = \overline{Y}_{A(\epsilon)}(1) - \overline{Y}_{B(\epsilon)}(0).$$

Then, in the limit, as ϵ goes to zero, we have

$$\lim_{\epsilon \to 0} \text{DIM}_\epsilon = Y(1, x^*) - Y(0, x^*),$$

which is the average treatment effect for units with $x_i = x^*$. This means the average treatment effect is being identified only for units at the threshold and is thus very local.

In real data, we are always working with some interval around the threshold without the possibility of actually letting that interval shrink to the limit. Thus, implementing an RD in practice involves using the data to estimate the average potential outcomes at the threshold. One simple way of doing this on some interval is to estimate the difference in average outcome for the values of the running variable below the threshold (but in the interval) and the average outcome for the values of the running variable above the threshold (but in the interval). But, in general, this comparison of means is biased. How closely these averages approximate the averages we would get in the limit as the interval shrinks to zero depends on the size of the interval used, the amount of the data in the interval, and the shape of the average potential outcomes functions on the interval. Often you can improve this estimation with statistical modeling (e.g., by estimating the limit with some flexible function of the running variable).

The key identifying assumption for the regression discontinuity design is continuity of the average potential outcomes at the threshold. This continuity assumption may not be intuitive. So to get a sense of what it means, let's think about an example.

Suppose a campaign follows a strategy in which it sends mailers aimed at voter turnout, but only to people living in zip codes with a mean income of at least $75,000. Then, only residents of those zip codes are exposed to such mailers. This sets up a situation in which zip code mean income is the running variable and $75,000 is the threshold.

Figure 5.1 shows average potential outcomes as a function of the mean income in a person's zip code. The black line is the average potential outcome as a function of mean income when the zip code does not receive a mailer. The gray line is the average potential outcome as a function of mean income when the zip code does receive a mailer. Given the campaign strategy, residents of zip codes with mean income below $75,000 do not receive a mailer (indicated by the gray line being dashed and the black line being solid in that region) and zip codes with mean income at or above $75,000 do receive a mailer (indicated by the gray line being solid and the black line being dashed in that region). Because these average potential outcome functions are continuous at the threshold, the gap between the two lines at $75,000 is the average

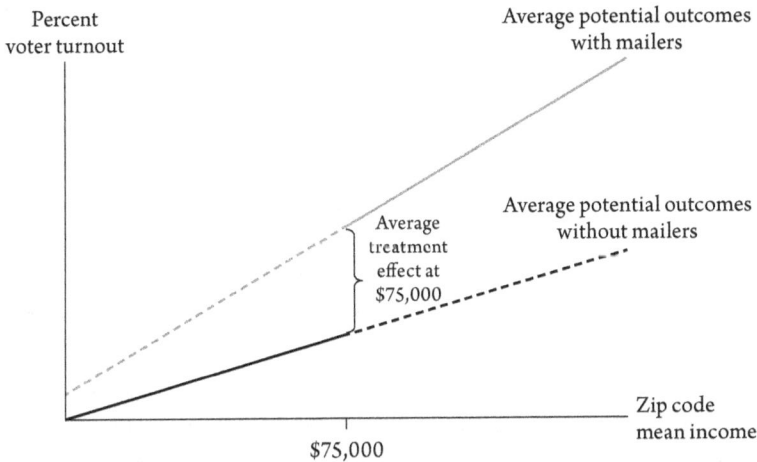

FIGURE 5.1. An example of the RD.

treatment effect of receiving a mailer for a resident of a zip code with mean income of exactly $75,000.

Let's use Figure 5.1 to think about the RD estimand and how it relates to the data one could actually observe. In the figure, we show the average treatment effect at the threshold of $75,000. This is the RD estimand. Recall, however, that residents in all zip codes with incomes at or above $75,000 receive mailers. Hence, we don't actually observe anyone at the threshold without treatment. So we can't directly compare treated and untreated voters at the threshold. Instead, the RD estimates the difference at the threshold using voter turnout in zip codes with average incomes above and below, but very close, to $75,000. Because the average potential outcomes functions are continuous in average zip code income (the running variable) at the threshold, the difference between these two averages approximates the average treatment effect at the threshold.

The continuity assumption feels different from the assumptions about no omitted confounders (of one sort or another) which were the foundation of just-controlling and difference-in-differences designs. But underlying the continuity assumption is a similar concern for omitted variables that may interfere with our ability to identify the treatment effect of interest. The concern is that if some variable other than treatment status changes discontinuously at the threshold, then it may lead to a change in the difference between the two average potential outcomes at the threshold that has nothing to do with the treatment. In this event, the RD would not in fact recover the average treatment effect at the threshold. The assumption of continuity rules out this possibility.

To make this a little more concrete, recall that in our earlier discussions of our example we were concerned about political interest as a confounder. Suppose that individual political interest is higher, on average, in zip codes with higher mean income. This could be because political interest is correlated with income at the individual level and individual incomes are, by definition, higher on average in zip codes with higher mean income. Under these circumstances, political interest would indeed be a confounder if it were omitted in a just-controlling regression of voter turnout on exposure to mailers. Individual income might be a confounder as well if it were correlated with turnout for reasons unrelated to political interest. But, if continuity at the threshold is true, then this is not a problem for the RD design. The RD compares zip codes just above and just below the mean income cutoff. The assumption of continuity implies that these zip codes have similar levels of political interest and individual income.

Why might continuity fail to be true? Suppose the state government implemented a civic education program that happened to also target zip codes with income below $75,000. This program might lead to an increase in political interest—and thus, voter turnout—in zip codes with incomes below $75,000. That might create a discontinuity at the threshold in the average potential outcomes functions both with and without treatment. The RD would be comparing zip codes with a mailer but without the civic education program to zip codes without a mailer but with the civic education program. Given that the civic education program increases political interest, which increases voter turnout, this comparison underestimates the average treatment effect of the mailer, as illustrated in Figure 5.2.

Finally, Figure 5.1 makes clear that the RD estimand is local. The identification comes from the jump at $75,000. We've drawn the figure so that the gap between average potential outcomes is different at every value of the running variable (the two average potential outcomes functions are diverging lines). Thus, there is in fact a different average treatment effect at each value of the running variable. For any given value of the threshold, the RD would correctly recover the appropriate *local* average treatment effect. In practice, you don't observe the complete average potential outcomes functions. So you can't know exactly how different the local effects are at different values of the running variable.

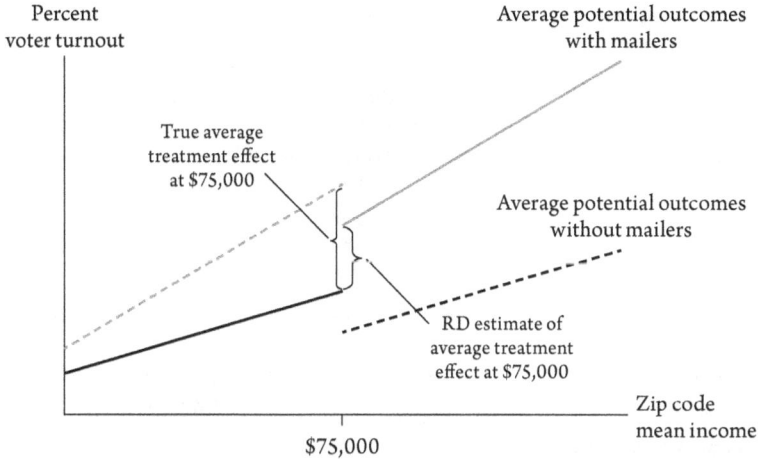

FIGURE 5.2. Failure of continuity at the threshold.

Table 5.8 uses the ERD to explicate the structure of a regression discontinuity research design.

5.3.5 Instrumental Variables and Noncompliance

Discussions of the credibility revolution often include instrumental variables
(IV) analysis as one of the major research designs. We are going to offer a
somewhat different take. Our view is that IV is best understood as a way to
address issues arising from noncompliance in the context of an otherwise
credible research design based on one of the approaches already described.[8]

To see what we mean, let's start by thinking about an experiment. Suppose
the staff of a campaign decided to use a randomized trial to evaluate the effectiveness of a particular ad. They ran the ad in the Facebook feeds of a randomly
selected group of potential voters.[9] Since this was an experiment, we don't
need to worry about confounders, so it seems that we can credibly estimate
the average treatment effect with the difference in means.

---

8. We are indebted to Anthony Fowler for pushing us to think more clearly about instrumental variables analysis.

9. Note to readers of the future: Facebook was an early twenty-first century platform for
sharing political misinformation.

TABLE 5.8. Regression Discontinuity

Empirical Strategy	
Estimand	Local average treatment effect at the threshold.
Data	Specific to application but must be from a setting in which treatment is assigned according to whether a running variable is above or below a threshold.
Statistical Procedure	Some type of regression applied to data from an interval around the threshold.
Measurement Validity	
Interpretation	Statement of the features of the target that the variables in the data are claimed to represent.
Arguments	Some combination of a substantive case and supporting evidence, lending credence to the interpretation.
Substantive Identification	
Assumptions	Treatment assignment changes discontinuously at the threshold.
	Continuity of the average potential outcomes functions at the threshold.
Arguments	A substantive argument that treatment and no pretreatment covariate changes discontinuously at the threshold. Evidence that treatment assignment is not manipulated near the threshold (e.g., McCrary test) and that there are no discontinuities in other variables at the cutoff.
Confidence Building	Evidence that result is not sensitive to reasonable variations in model specification, functional form, and bandwidth. Placebo tests at other values of the running variable. Argument that measure of uncertainty is appropriate.

The baseline turnout rate is 50%. Suppose the true average treatment effect of the ad is to increase the probability of turnout by five percentage points. (Of course, the researchers don't know this.)

Unfortunately for the campaign, not everyone in the treatment group logs on to Facebook on the day the ad runs, so they don't all see it.[10] Let's assume three-quarters of the treated group are what are called *compliers*. They log on and see the ad. In this case, turnout in the treated group is

$$.75 \cdot 55\% + .25 \cdot 50\% = 53.75\%.$$

None of the untreated group see the ad. Their turnout rate is 50%.

---

10. Note to readers of the future: Logging on is what we did before the neuro-chips came.

If the researchers calculate the difference in means between the treated and untreated groups, they find

$$DIM = 53.75\% - 50\% = 3.75\%,$$

which is smaller than the ATE.

What has gone wrong? The calculation that we just did is referred to as an *intention to treat* (ITT) analysis. We compared the average outcome for the people the researchers intended to treat to the average outcome for the people the researchers intended not to treat. But, because not everyone logged on to Facebook on the relevant day, not everyone the researchers intended to treat actually saw the ad. Only three-quarters of them did. When there is noncompliance like this, the ITT does not correspond to the ATE because some of the people who are being considered as members of the treated group are actually not treated.

Sometimes the ITT is in fact the quantity of interest. A campaign might anticipate that when they run ads for real, not all voters will see those ads. So the ITT might be relevant for, say, a cost–benefit analysis. But other times we genuinely want to know the ATE.

The question in such circumstances is whether there is any way to learn the average treatment effect despite noncompliance. In our example, if we know the rate of compliance in the group assigned to treatment (here, .75), the answer is yes. To see this, notice that we can rewrite the ITT as follows:

$$ITT = .75\,(55\% - 50\%).$$

That is, the ITT in our example is simply the average treatment effect (the term in parentheses) weighted by the rate of compliance in the group assigned to treatment. (Things would be slightly more complicated had there also been noncompliance in the untreated group, for example if they could have seen the ad through some other channel.) In our example, if the researcher gets to observe who actually complied with treatment, then it is straightforward to back out an average treatment effect from the ITT. The researcher finds an ITT of 3.75% and learns that the compliance rate is .75. Then the researcher can calculate the local average treatment effect (LATE) for the compliers from the ITT and the compliance rate by dividing:

$$\frac{ITT}{\text{Compliance rate}} = \frac{3.75\%}{.75} = 5\% = LATE.$$

Recovering the treatment effect in this way is a particularly simple version of instrumental variables analysis.[11] In this example, we assumed homogeneous treatment effects, so the LATE is in fact the ATE. But that need not always be the case.

As we've said, IV can be applied in conjunction with any of the research designs we've talked about to address noncompliance issues. But, to do so, you need an instrumental variable that satisfies assumptions above and beyond those needed for the underlying research design.

To understand the additional assumptions, it will help to reframe our preceding discussion of how IV analysis works in slightly different terminology. IV is best thought of in two steps (although not actually implemented that way). Conceptually, the first step isolates the part of the variation in treatment assignment that is due to variation in the instrument. That is, it estimates the effect of the instrument on treatment status. This is called the *first stage*. The second step estimates the effect of the instrument on the outcome. This is called the *reduced form*. Dividing the reduced form by the first stage recovers the LATE.

In our example, the instrument is the actual group assignment by the experimenter. The first stage, which estimates the effect of being assigned to the group whose Facebook feed gets the ad on the probability of seeing the ad, thus recovers the 75% compliance rate. The reduced form, which estimates the effect being assigned to the group whose Facebook feed gets the ad on turnout, recovers the 3.75% ITT. As we've seen, dividing yields the LATE.

Now let's consider what assumptions are needed for this to work.

First, we need a credible research design for estimating the effect of the instrument on the treatment in the first stage and the effect of the instrument on the outcome in the reduced form. Taken together, substantive identification of the first stage and reduced form is referred to as *exogeneity of the instrument*.

Second, the instrument must have an effect on treatment assignment. As we've seen, the way IV works is by dividing the reduced form by the first stage. If the first stage is zero, this won't work. Moreover, if the first stage is close to zero (i.e., the instrument has very little effect on treatment assignment), then, because of the division, the instrumental variables analysis is also highly sensitive to tiny fluctuations in the reduced form estimate (whether due to sampling error or violations of exogeneity of the instrument). In

---

11. This is sometimes called the *Wald estimator*.

this case, we say that the instrument is *weak*. A large literature discusses the problems associated with weak instruments (e.g., Angrist and Pischke, 2008, Chapter 4).

Third, the instrument must affect the outcome only by affecting treatment assignment. Suppose this were not true. Then the reduced form would reflect the effect of the instrument on the outcome through both the treatment and other channels. Therefore, even after dividing by the effect of the instrument on treatment status, we would not recover the LATE. The assumption that the instrument has no effect on the outcome other than through its effect on the treatment is called the *exclusion restriction*.

Fourth, the instrument must affect treatment status in the same direction for every unit, an assumption called *monotonicity*. In our example, monotonicity obviously holds since the only way to see the ad was to be in the group that had it put into their Facebook feed. If monotonicity doesn't hold, then the first stage relationship reflects a weighted average of the treatment effect for people whose treatment status responds positively to the instrument (the compliers) and the negative of the treatment effect for people whose treatment status responds negatively to the instrument (called defiers). Moreover, as a result, the reduced form reflects some positive and some negative effects of the instrument on the outcome. How big a problem this is depends on how large the fraction of defiers is relative to compliers.

Figure 5.3 provides a visualization of some of the key IV assumptions using directed acyclic graphs (DAGs). In these graphs, an arrow pointing from one variable to another means that the former has a causal effect on the latter. In the figure, Z is a candidate instrument, X is the treatment, Y is the outcome, and U_1 and U_2 are unobserved confounders. The DAG on the top row shows a situation where the exclusion restriction does not hold—the instrument affects the outcome both through its effect on the treatment and through another path. The DAGs in the bottom row show situations where exogeneity does not hold—on the left there is an unobserved confounder in the first stage and on the right there is an unobserved confounder in the reduced form.

While these assumptions seem straightforward, it is also easy to imagine ways in which prima facie plausible instruments might not satisfy them. For instance, suppose, in our turnout example, that the researchers did not run an experiment, but that a campaign released a new television and online ad on election day. Researchers learned that, by coincidence, there was a power outage in some neighborhoods but not others on that day. Because the power outage happened arbitrarily, and people in places with a power outage would

Exclusion restriction violated

Exogeneity violated for first stage   Exogeneity violated for reduced form

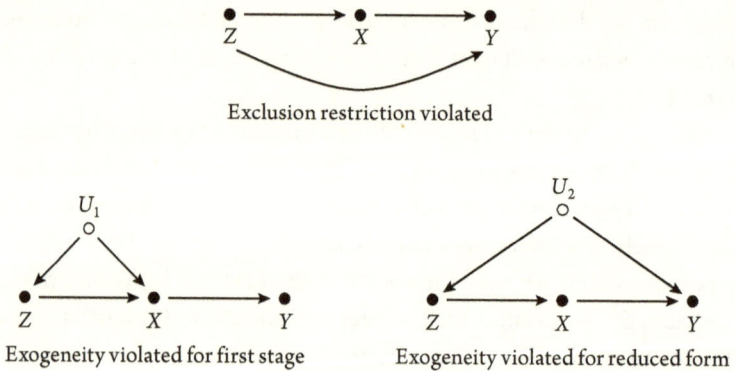

FIGURE 5.3. DAGs illustrating the exclusion restriction and exogeneity assumptions for IV.

be less likely to watch TV, this seems like a natural experiment for assessing the impact of the ad on turnout. But not everyone whose power went out failed to see the ad (maybe some of them were visiting friends in another neighborhood). And not everyone whose power stayed on saw the ad (maybe some of them weren't watching TV). So there is noncompliance. As such, it might seem sensible to use the locations of the power outage as an instrument for seeing the ad. But this instrument could plausibly violate each of the exclusion restriction, exogeneity, and monotonicity assumptions. Let's see why.

People dealing with a power outage on election day might have less free time and thus be less likely to vote for reasons having nothing to do with the ad. This violates the exclusion restriction. The power outage might last longer in poor neighborhoods because of slow response times. If socioeconomic status is a confounder in the reduced form relationship, this violates exogeneity—we can't credibly estimate the effect of the power outage on turnout. Finally, some people might respond to the power outage by spending more time online using their phones, while others might respond to the power outage by using fewer electronics of all sorts. This could violate monotonicity.

It is also important to note that the estimand that IV credibly estimates is an average treatment effect for the subpopulation of units whose treatment status is affected by the particular instrument (the compliers). This is why the estimand of an IV analysis is called the local average treatment effect (Angrist and Pischke, 2008). Because different instruments may influence different subpopulations, each instrument could potentially identify a different LATE.

TABLE 5.9. Instrumental Variables

Empirical Strategy	
Estimand	Instrument-specific, weighted local average treatment effect.
Data	Specific to application.
Statistical Procedure	Two-stage least squares, generalized method of moments, etc. applied to the appropriate underlying research design.
Measurement Validity	
Interpretation	Statement of the features of the target that the variables in the data are claimed to represent.
Arguments	Some combination of a substantive case and supporting evidence, lending credence to the interpretation.
Substantive Identification	
Assumptions	Exogeneity of the instrument
	Sufficiently strong instrument
	Exclusion restriction
	Monotonicity
Arguments	A substantive argument and (where possible) evidence for each of the assumptions (e.g., F-test for strong instrument in the first stage). Argument for exogeneity requires substantive identification of the reduced form and first stage. Discussion of differences between results with and without IV.
Confidence Building	Evidence that the result is robust to reasonable variations in model specification (e.g., statistical procedure, covariates, functional form), placebo tests, and argument that measure of uncertainty is appropriate (e.g., clustering, adjustment relative to strength of the instrument).

Any given LATE may or may not be equal to the overall population ATE, or to the LATE associated with a different instrument, and it is important to think about whether it is the right quantity for your question.

Table 5.9 uses the ERD to explicate the structure of an IV analysis. Importantly, as we've emphasized, IV is an approach that can be applied within the context of any of the four research designs we've already discussed. Hence, the table refers generically to the "underlying research design."

WHERE DO INSTRUMENTS COME FROM?

We've seen that IV is a potentially important way to deal with compliance problems that arise in other research designs. But only when the researcher can find a plausible instrument. Where do such instruments come from?

For two of the research designs we've discussed, experiments and regression discontinuity, there is a built-in candidate instrument: experimental treatment assignment and the running variable, respectively. The assumptions that underlie these research designs—random assignment and continuity at the threshold, respectively—are equivalent to exogeneity of the candidate instrument. But the researcher still needs to think about the validity of the other IV assumptions.

In experiments where there are issues of noncompliance, a natural first attempt at a solution is to use the experimental assignment as an instrument. For instance, Gerber and Green (2000) conduct a field experiment to study the effect of personal contact on voter turnout. Households are randomly assigned to be contacted (treated) or not (untreated). However, not all households assigned to treatment were successfully reached, creating a noncompliance problem. Gerber and Green address this problem by using experimental assignment as an instrument for being contacted and estimating the local average treatment effect with an IV analysis.

Something similar is possible in regression discontinuity research designs. A researcher might identify a threshold such that the probability of receiving the treatment changes discontinuously in the running variable at the cutoff. But that probability need not go from 0 to 1, as it did in our earlier discussion of RD. In this case, comparing those just above the threshold to those just below the threshold is not a comparison of exclusively treated units to exclusively untreated units. If continuity is satisfied, this reduced form is a valid RD, but does not estimate the average effect of the treatment at the threshold, it estimates an ITT—the reduced form relationship between the outcome and being above or below the threshold in the running variable.

As in our experimental example, this can be thought of as a problem of noncompliance. Some units do not change treatment status according to the rule associated with the threshold. Thus, as in experiments, we can think about using an IV design to fix the problem, an approach referred to as *fuzzy RD*. We do so by using an indicator for the running variable being above or below the threshold as an instrument for treatment status. For instance, Shoag, Tuttle, and Veuger (2019) use an RD to study the effect of home rule authority, which gives local government increased autonomy, on the fiscal behavior of cities. Cities above a population threshold are eligible to seek home rule authority, but not all of the eligible cities do so, creating a noncompliance problem. They address this problem with a fuzzy RD in which an indicator for whether the population is above or below the threshold is used as an instrument for home rule authority.

IV can also be used in the context of just-controlling or difference-in-differences research designs. But there is a catch. A candidate instrument that satisfies exogeneity is inherent in experimental and RD designs. In a just-controlling or difference-in-differences research design, the researcher has to think of an instrument that plays the same role as random assignment in an experiment. Exogeneity of the instrument rests on different assumptions in each of these settings. In the just-controlling context, exogeneity of the instrument requires that there are no omitted confounders in either the reduced form or first stage. In the difference-in-differences context, exogeneity of the instrument requires that there are no omitted time-varying confounders in either the reduced form or first stage (that is, it requires parallel trends). Since these research designs do not inherently suggest a candidate instrument, the application of IV to them requires the researcher to have a new idea for the instrument. This often takes the form of some sort of natural experiment.

If the instrument is in fact plausibly exogenous and perfectly predicts the treatment, then the researcher doesn't need to use IV. Instead, she has an argument for the validity of the just-controlling or difference-in-differences design on their own. This is because, if the instrument is exogenous and perfectly determines treatment, then the basic research design applied to the outcome and the treatment in fact satisfies the appropriate no-omitted-confounders assumption. But typically the plausibly exogenous instrument only imperfectly predicts treatment. In that case, the researcher is in a situation analogous to an experiment with noncompliance and has to use an IV design to recover a LATE. As always, exogeneity of the instrument is not enough. The instrument must also satisfy the other IV assumptions.

Broadly speaking, in political science, there are three common places people look for such instruments: natural, institutional, and economic processes. Natural processes include things like weather events, natural disasters, or geography. For instance, Strömberg (2004) uses ground conductivity as an instrument in a paper assessing the effect of radio penetration on the distribution of New Deal spending. Institutional processes include things like seniority norms, lotteries, rules for selection from waiting lists, and other ways in which institutional rules lead to decisions that are as-good-as random. For instance, because there is occasionally noncompliance with seniority norms for committee positions in the US Congress, Berry and Fowler (2018) use relative seniority on a committee, which is determined by elections in other districts, as an instrument for whether a member obtains a committee leadership position in their study of the effect of committee positions on federal distributive spending. Economic processes include things like price shocks or economic crises that result from events occurring in parts of the world distant from the location under study. For instance, Dube and Vargas (2013) use changes to the world price of coffee as an instrument for the local price of coffee in Colombia in a study of the effect of local economic conditions on conflict.

One other common approach to looking for instruments in just-controlling or difference-in-differences settings is to exploit historical events. Perhaps the most famous example is Acemoglu, Johnson, and Robinson's (2001) use of disease environment at the time of colonization as an instrument for contemporary property-rights institutions in a study of the effect of property rights protections on economic outcomes. Acemoglu, Johnson, and Robinson argue for their exclusion restriction on the grounds that disease environments have changed, so that the diseases that shaped colonial settlement patterns (and, thus, institutions) are unlikely to have any direct effect on contemporary economic outcomes. Glaeser et al. (2004) argue against the exclusion restriction on the grounds that settlement patterns had effects on things other than property rights institutions, such as investment in human capital, which might also affect contemporary economic outcomes.

This set of arguments has helped launch a large literature using historical lags as an instrument for all sorts of phenomena. As such, we think it is important to emphasize that the fact that something happened a long time ago is not, in and of itself, a convincing argument for the validity of an instrument. As we've just seen, the exclusion restriction clearly remains a concern—historical events may have many pathways to affecting contemporary outcomes. Moreover, the historical nature of an event is neither here nor there with respect to exogeneity. For instance, one would not want to use the date on which a state ended legal slavery as an instrument for contemporary minority voter disenfranchisement in a study of the effects of such disenfranchisement on contemporary party vote shares. Even though it happened a long time ago, states that ended slavery earlier are likely different from states that ended it later in all sorts of ways that matter for contemporary politics. For instance, one might worry that states that ended slavery later have different racial attitudes, which is a potential confounder in both the reduced form and the first stage. Hence, this historical instrument is not plausibly exogenous.

5.4 Putting the ERD to Work

The ERD is meant to be a useful tool for thinking through how the arguments in an empirical paper or literature work. The main point of the ERD is to focus attention on substantive identification as one of the cornerstones of credibility. In what follows we discuss two examples: one more successful and the other less successful in terms of building credibility. The first shows how credibility can be built through a combination of careful argument and large amounts of supporting evidence for substantive identification. The second exemplifies a common mistake. When a critique raised concerns about substantive identification, calling into question the credibility of an empirical finding, the literature responded methodologically, changing statistical procedures. But this technical move did not improve credibility because substantive identification under the new statistical procedure rests on the same implausible assumptions as it did in the earlier result. Taking steps toward better substantive identification adds nuance, but also offers support for the original theoretical hypothesis in the literature. In each case, the ERD helps make the sources of these successes and failures transparent. Compared to other research we discuss in this book, theory plays a relatively small role in these two examples, allowing us to focus squarely on research design.

5.4.1 The Mexican Drug War

Dell (2015) analyzes the extent to which Mexico's efforts to combat drug trafficking have contributed to the dramatic escalation in violence since 2007. A standard problem in the literature on the effects of government crackdowns on violent organizations is that, because government crackdowns do not occur at random, cross-sectional correlations between violence and crackdowns are unlikely to be all else equal. For instance, we'd observe a positive correlation between crackdowns and violence if governments were more likely to crack down in places where drug-related violence is already high. Even difference-in-differences estimates may be confounded if governments crack down preventatively in places where they expect violence to increase in the future.

We describe Dell's research design in Table 5.10. Her empirical strategy relies on an RD analysis that exploits variation in drug enforcement policy resulting from the outcomes of close mayoral elections. Specifically, the

TABLE 5.10. Dell's (2015) Research Design

Empirical Strategy	
Estimand	LATE of change in party control on drug-related violence for cities with close elections.
Data	Novel data set on drug-related violence, Mexican municipal election returns (2007–2010).
Statistical Procedure	Regression discontinuity using discontinuity at PAN win–loss threshold.
Measurement Validity	
Interpretation	PAN mayoral victories meaningfully represent drug enforcement crackdowns.
Arguments	PAN presidential candidate ran on drug enforcement platform; PAN mayors are more likely to cooperate in federal enforcement efforts.
Substantive Identification	
Assumptions	1. Mayoral elections decided by majority vote
	2. Continuity of expected potential drug-related violence at the PAN win–loss electoral threshold
Arguments	1. Winner of mayoral election is the candidate who won a majority of the vote.
	McCrary test showing no evidence of selective sorting around the PAN win-loss threshold.
	Qualitative description of Mexican electoral institutions (multipartisan state commission) that make electoral fraud unlikely.
	2. Twenty-five political, economic, demographic, road network, and geographic precharacteristics are balanced across the PAN win–loss threshold.
	No discontinuity in violence at the threshold in the preelection or lame-duck periods.
Confidence Building	Show robustness to alternative bandwidths, alternative polynomials in the running variable, and controls.

Partido Acción Nacional (PAN, National Action Party) candidate Felipe Calderon made combating organized crime, and drug trafficking in particular, a cornerstone of his administration (2006–2012). In addition to its victory at the federal level in 2006, PAN also won about one-third of mayoral elections, generally displacing incumbents of the *Partido Revolucionario Institucional* (PRI, Institutionalized Revolutionary Party), which had long dominated Mexican politics. Dell's key idea for measurement validity, therefore, is that drug enforcement was stronger in those municipalities with PAN

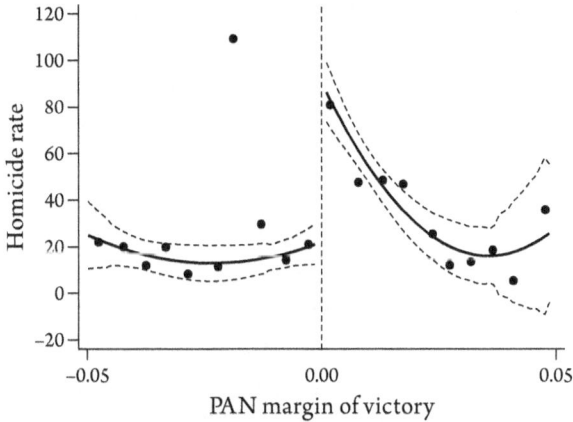

FIGURE 5.4. Election RD for drug-related homicide rate from Dell (2015).

mayors, who were, she argues, more likely to collaborate with the PAN federal government's crackdowns on organized crime. So, in Dell's design, PAN mayoral victories are meant to represent an increase in drug enforcement. Dell offers qualitative evidence for measurement validity by noting that the PAN ran on and implemented a policy of increased counter-narcotic crackdowns. Moreover, she offers some quantitative evidence that PAN mayoral victories are in fact associated with crackdowns.

Because municipalities that elect PAN mayors may systematically differ in other ways from municipalities that elect PRI mayors, Dell uses a regression discontinuity design, comparing municipalities where the PAN barely won with those where the PAN barely lost.

We reproduce the central results of Dell's analysis in Figure 5.4. The running variable is the PAN vote share minus the PRI vote share. The treated group includes places that elected a PAN mayor and the untreated group includes those that elected a PRI mayor. The idea is that the party of the mayor changes right when the running variable passes through 0. The outcome in the figure is the drug-related homicide rate in the year following the election. The figure shows that the drug-related homicide rate is roughly three times higher in municipalities where the PAN candidate barely won relative to those where the PAN barely lost.

To interpret the gap in Figure 5.4 as the effect of electing a PAN mayor on drug-related violence, one has to believe the RD assumptions. Thus, the key to establishing the credibility of this research design is Dell's arguments for those assumptions.

The first step is to argue that the treatment (assignment of a PAN versus PRI mayor) does indeed change discontinuously at the threshold. In this case, since electoral rules formally mandate that this be the case, the question is whether there is any evidence of electoral manipulation around the threshold. The first argument Dell makes in this regard is to point out some qualitative features of Mexican electoral institutions that make electoral fraud in local elections unlikely. Most importantly, there are state-level, multiparty commissions to which concerns about fraud in local elections can be addressed. The presence of this genuine recourse, her argument suggests, should either deter or rectify election fraud. In addition, Dell provides formal statistical evidence suggesting there probably was not electoral fraud. Specifically, she shows a test (due to McCrary, 2008) of whether there are more observations on one or the other side of the electoral threshold than would be expected by chance. Were this the case, we might worry that one of the parties was able to engage in some sort of systematic manipulation that allowed it to win close elections nonrandomly. There is no such evidence in this case.

The second step is to argue for the assumption of continuity of the average potential outcomes at the threshold. Here, again, Dell provides several types of evidence.

First, she shows that there is no discontinuity at the threshold for twenty-five political, economic, demographic, road network, and geographic variables. The argument is that if there was a discontinuity in average potential outcomes it would likely be the result of some other systematic difference between municipalities on either side of the threshold. If there were such systematic differences, they would probably manifest in some of these variables. Failure to find discontinuities in any of these variables, therefore, is evidence in support of the claim that there are not such systematic differences between municipalities on either side of the threshold.

Second, she shows that there is no discontinuity in drug-related violence between municipalities on either side of the threshold before the election or during the lame-duck period after the election but before the transition of power. The argument here starts with the assumption that potential outcomes functions are unlikely to change quickly over time. Therefore, if there is a discontinuity in the potential outcomes functions around the threshold, it should be evident before the inauguration of the new mayor. The fact that she finds no discontinuity therefore suggests that the continuity assumption is reasonable.

In addition to these arguments for substantive identification, Dell does a variety of things to build confidence that the results are not due to chance or chicanery. For example, she shows that the results are robust to alternative bandwidths around the threshold in the RD analysis, varying the degree of the polynomial in the running variable, and including different combinations of control variables.

Recall that the paper's motivating claim is that increased counter-narcotic crackdowns "caused large and sustained increases in the homicide rate" (p. 1740). Looking at the ERD, we conclude that Dell has produced a credible estimate of her estimand: the local average treatment effect of the change in party control on drug-related violence for cities with close elections. Even with a credible estimate of the estimand, we must also be convinced about measurement validity—that PAN mayor victories meaningfully represent crackdowns—to be convinced of the similarity of the research design to the target, both of which are discussed in the ERD.

Dell's argument for measurement validity is based on a combination of qualitative evidence that the PAN ran on a promise of crackdowns and quantitative evidence that more crackdowns actually took place in PAN municipalities. But this is not, on its own, fully satisfying. For instance, suppose political turnover itself is disruptive and leads to increased violence. Then the measure used, PAN victories, may capture a combination of crackdowns and political instability, rather than just crackdowns. Notice, this is not a question of the credibility of Dell's estimate of her estimand. Rather it is a question about the interpretation of the empirical evidence in terms of the phenomenon of interest in the world.

Dell goes on to provide various kinds of evidence to bolster her argument for measurement validity. We discuss that evidence and how it supports Dell's interpretative claims in Chapters 7 and 8.

5.4.2 The Effects of Treaty Membership

We've just seen an example where careful attention to substantive identification helped make a case for having credibly estimated an all-else-equal relationship. We now turn to an example where substantive identification took a back seat to statistical machinations, with less satisfying results. However, at the end, we will see that greater attention to substantive identification yields results that look supportive of the early hypotheses in the literature.

The effect of treaties on state behavior is a central question in international relations. Here we describe an exchange in this literature—focusing on the case of the IMF Articles of Agreement—that is often held up as an exemplar of a progressive research agenda, that is, a series of papers that built on one another to accumulate knowledge. By using the ERD to evaluate the key papers, we suggest that the literature's sense of knowledge accumulation is misplaced.

We should start by thinking about why this is a very difficult question to answer empirically. To do so, it is perhaps helpful to think about an analogous question from everyday life. Suppose you wanted to know whether the act of getting married causes people to become more likely to be monogamous. It clearly would not suffice to observe that married people are more likely to be monogamous than unmarried people. That might just be because people get married when they are more committed to their partner, creating baseline differences. So, if you wanted to make a credible comparison, you'd need to control for all relevant confounders—that is, features of individuals that affect their likelihood of getting married and their likelihood of being monogamous. This might include facts about their education, employment, genetics, age, location, religion, family background, dating history, commitment to their partner, desire for children, and who knows what else. That's a tall order. As we will see, the behavior of countries is similarly complicated.

In an important paper, Simmons (2000) asks whether signing an international legal agreement exerts a direct effect on a country's behavior. (In a separate analysis, the paper also looks at which countries take on the obligation, but that is not our focus.) She does so in the specific context of IMF Article VIII which, among other things, requires signatories to maintain an open current account. Importantly, becoming an Article VIII signatory is entirely voluntary.

Simmons is interested in the effect of treaty signing on state behavior. Evidence for such an effect requires showing that, all else equal, Article VIII signatories behave differently with respect to current accounts than non-signatories.

Table 5.11 uses the ERD to summarize Simmons's research design.

To try to provide evidence for this all-else-equal relationship, Simmons employs a just-controlling research design. She collects data on 133 countries observed from 1967 to 1997. Measurement validity is relatively

TABLE 5.11. ERD for Simmons (2000)

Empirical Strategy	
Estimand	"Logit average" difference in probability of current account restrictions between signers and nonsigners.
Data	133 countries observed from 1967 to 1997.
Statistical Procedure	Logit of Restrictions on Current Accounts against Article VIII Commitment controlling for a variety of country-level economic, fiscal, trade, etc. characteristics.
Measurement Validity	
Interpretation	Signing IMF Article VIII meaningfully represents commitment to an international legal agreement. Maintaining open current accounts meaningfully represents compliance with the agreement.
Arguments	These variables are direct measures of the features of interest.
Substantive Identification	
Assumptions	Selection on observables: there are no confounders other than those included in Table 5.12.
Arguments	In footnote 25 Simmons (2000) states that "the observable variables in the compliance model are very likely to control for nonrandom selection into Article VIII status," though does not provide supporting evidence or argument.
Confidence Building	Shows robustness of main result to different combinations of control variables.

straightforward in this case, as signing Article VIII is a direct measure of committing to an international treaty and current account restrictions are a direct measure of compliance with that treaty.

Simmons pools her country–year data and uses a logit model to regress a dummy variable for whether a country has current accounts restrictions in a given year on a dummy variable for whether the country was a signatory to Article VIII in that year, controlling for a variety of economic and political factors. The relevant results are found in Table 4, Model 3 of her paper, which we reproduce in Table 5.12.

The coefficient on Article VIII commitment is significant and negative, indicating that Article VIII signatories indeed are less likely to have current account restrictions, controlling for a variety of factors. As highlighted in Table 5.11, the key assumption for substantive identification in Simmons's just-controlling research design is no omitted confounders. Specifically, there must be no omitted pretreatment variables that (conditional on the included

TABLE 5.12. Replication of Simmons (2000) Table 4, Model 3 on the Relationship between Article VIII Commitment and Current Accounts

DV = Current Account Restrictions	
Constant	−.598
	(.355)
Article VIII Commitment	−1.111
	(.130)
Terms of Trade Volatility	.403
	(.094)
Balance of Payments/GDP	−.013
	(.007)
Reservers/GDP	.957
	(.353)
Change in GDP	.027
	(.011)
Use of Fund Credits	.880
	(.131)
Years since Last Restriction	−1.26
	(.109)
Observations	3100
Log-likelihood	−819.89
Pseudo-R^2	.62

The results are from a logit model that also includes three cubic splines in the number of years without current account restrictions. Robust standard errors in parentheses.

variables) affect both being an Article VIII signatory and having current account restrictions.

As we've already argued, a just-controlling design must be defended by a claim that the treatment assignment process is sufficiently well understood that no confounders are unaccounted for. Simmons provides a discussion of some factors that influence Article VIII membership. But she does not provide a substantive argument that there are not other, uncontrolled for factors that affect both Article VIII membership and current account restrictions. As such, she does not have a convincing argument that there are no omitted confounders. Moreover, there is actually direct empirical evidence suggesting the opposite.

If Simmons's controls really hold all else equal, then the current account restrictions of states that never sign should be the same on average as the

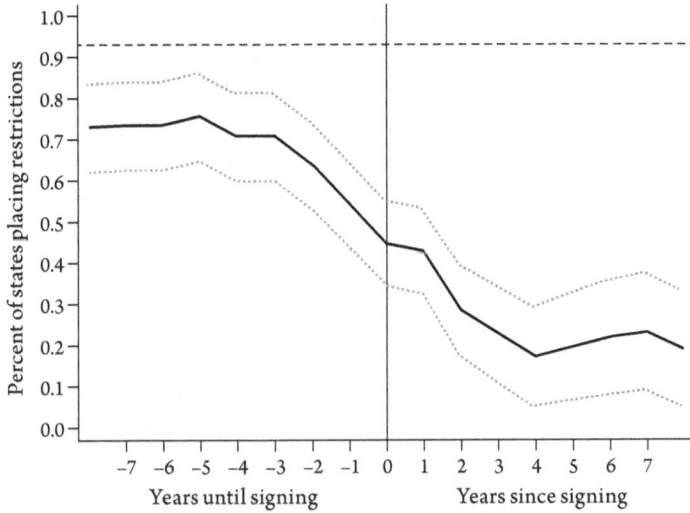

FIGURE 5.5. Replications of von Stein's (2005) Figure 1, on the relationship between Article VIII commitment and current accounts. The solid line represents restrictions among signatories before and after the commitment was actually made. The dashed horizontal line denotes average restrictions among states that never sign.

current account restrictions of states that do sign, prior to signing. If this is not the case, then some of the difference between signers and nonsigners reflects this baseline difference, rather than the effect of the treaty.

Von Stein (2005) argues that the no-omitted-confounders assumption is not plausible on the basis of just such evidence. She starts by pointing to a host of omitted potential confounders, both observable and unobservable. For instance, von Stein's notes that the IMF particularly encourages countries to sign when they have unrestricted current accounts. Moreover, she argues that the literature identifies other factors that might impact both Article VIII commitment and current accounts, including political will, trust, and negotiating posture.

She backs up this critique of the no-omitted-confounders assumption with evidence of baseline differences. Von Stein's Figure 1 (replicated here in Figure 5.5) shows two facts. First, countries that commit to Article VIII at some point had fewer restrictions on average even before they committed than do those that never commit. Second, countries that commit to Article VIII increase their compliance in the years before they sign the treaty. Both of these results point to the fact that countries that sign are different from those that do not in ways that are important for compliance. Hence, the key question is whether the controls in Table 5.12 account for these baseline differences.

Von Stein shows that they do not. She does so by running a regression similar to Simmons's, but including a dummy variable indicating the four years prior to becoming a signatory. This analysis shows that, among states that become signatories, behavior in the four years before signing is indistinguishable from behavior in the years after signing and different from the behavior of states that never sign. This is precisely the situation we indicated above would contradict the no-omitted-confounders assumption. Hence, von Stein provides pretty compelling evidence that all else is not held equal in Simmons's regression. That is, the fact that von Stein finds this evidence of baseline differences indicates that there are likely to be confounders not included in Simmons's regression.

Von Stein concludes that "the empirical record reveals ... that there is something fundamentally different about signatories, even long before they sign. This is more suggestive of a selection process whereby a certain 'type' of state will assume the treaty obligation" (p. 616).

In a response to von Stein, Simmons and Hopkins (2005) don't dispute the claim that there are baseline differences between signatories and nonsignatories of Article VIII. Rather, they retort,

> Our theory of how and why international law works implies that governments do not enter into legal commitments randomly. If they did, commitments would hardly be credible and markets would have no reason to take Article VIII commitments seriously. The theory suggests that treaties screen and constrain. Von Stein's estimator does not convincingly show that the screening effects overwhelm the constraining effects of legal commitments. (p. 627)

In essence, Simmons and Hopkins contend that there is both nonrandom selection into treatment (screening) and a treatment effect on subsequent behavior (constraining). Both Simmons and von Stein provide evidence of screening. However, showing evidence that treaties also constrain requires controlling for screening. That is, providing evidence for a constraining effect of treaties would require controlling for any observable or unobservable difference between countries that sign the treaties and those that don't sign. Von Stein argues that Simmons failed to fully control for screening because signatories are already different from nonsignatories before they sign, even after controlling for observable characteristics.

Simmons and Hopkins attempt to defend the credibility of Simmons's original estimates of the constraining effects of treaties. To do so, they adopt a different statistical procedure—propensity score matching. After matching on observable characteristics, they find that the difference in behavior between signatories and nonsignatories is roughly unchanged relative to Simmons's original findings.[12] They conclude that their matching analyses, "confirm yet again that these estimated treaty effects are quite robust: they show up consistently across a wide range of modeling approaches and specifications."

To what extent is this conclusion warranted? While a discussion of the similarities and differences between regression and matching is beyond the scope of this book, the key point is that, while matching is more robust with respect to functional form assumptions, it still requires the assumption of no omitted confounders for substantive identification (Sekhon, 2009). If the no-omitted-confounders assumption was not plausible in the original paper's regressions, it is not plausible in the latter paper's matching.

But you don't need a deep understanding of matching to see why such an analysis does not address von Stein's critique. Recall our monogamy example. Suppose that marriage both screens and constrains. That is, those who intend to be monogamous are more likely to get married, but marriage also causally affects monogamy. Even if you exactly matched married and unmarried people on all their observable features—that is, if you compared married and unmarried people who were otherwise identical on observable features like age, gender, years in the relationship, and so on—you would still be skeptical that doing so controlled for all the differences that might affect monogamy other than the simple fact of having signed a marriage license.[13] If there are such unobservable differences, then you won't be able to distinguish the screening effect from the constraining effect.

Table 5.13 summarizes Simmons and Hopkins's research design. Recall, von Stein's critique of Simmons's original research design was not about the statistical procedure or estimand, it was about substantive identification— the claim that no omitted confounders was plausible. While Simmons runs a logit and Simmons and Hopkins use propensity score matching to preprocess

12. Whether the matching exercise was successful is open to question. The authors acknowledge that, even after matching, the treated and untreated groups differ in their propensity scores (Simmons and Hopkins, 2005, footnote 14). We leave this issue aside to focus on the bigger point that the matching analysis could not have answered Von Stein's critique even if it attained balance on the propensity scores.

13. The fifth element is love.

TABLE 5.13. ERD for Simmons and Hopkins (2005)

Empirical Strategy	
Estimand	"Probit average" difference in probability of current account restrictions between signers and nonsigners.
Data	133 countries observed from 1967–1997.
Statistical Procedure	Propensity score matching to pre-process data before running probit model of Restrictions on Current Accounts against Article VIII Commitment
Measurement Validity	
Interpretation	Signing IMF Article VIII meaningfully represents commitment to an international legal agreement. Maintaining open current accounts meaningfully represent compliance with the agreement.
Arguments	These variables are direct measures of the features of interest.
Substantive Identification	
Assumptions	No omitted confounders: there are no confounders other than those used to compute the propensity score, which include those in Table 5.12 plus three new variables used to measure a country's "political will."
Arguments	Argue that signatories and nonsignatories are balanced on observable characteristics. Similar to Simmons (2000), Simmons and Hopkins (2005) claim that "important influences on commitment and compliance can be theorized, observed, and (imperfectly) measured."
Confidence Building	No explicit argument.

the data and then run a probit, both are implementing a just-controlling research design. As such, Simmons and Hopkins have the same key assumption for substantive identification (though with a somewhat larger list of control variables).

The progression from Simmons to von Stein to Simmons and Hopkins illustrates how important it is to recognize the difference between statistical method and substantive identification. There may be an appearance of progress across the papers in this literature. But, in truth, all that is changing is statistical method, while nothing was done to address the real problem that von Stein pointed to—implausible identifying assumptions. Thus, in the end, we are left with no more credible an estimate of the constraining effects of treaties than we began with.

How might a researcher attempt to make progress on this problem? Start by recalling the essence of von Stein's argument. She asserts that signatories and nonsignatories are fundamentally different types of states, whose behavior was different long before any treaty was signed. We already discussed one research design that accounts for time-invariant differences between units: difference-in-differences. If the parallel trends assumption holds, a difference-in-differences analysis separates the screening and constraining effects by basing the analysis on changes within a country before and after treaty signing.[14]

We used the replication data from Simmons and Hopkins to conduct a difference-in-differences analysis and compare the results with those obtained in the three prior studies. (This research design is summarized in Table 5.15.) For the sake of simplicity and transparency, we use a linear probability model.[15] Table 5.14 shows the results. To establish a baseline, Model (1) presents an analysis in the spirit of Simmons's Table 4.[16] In this just-controlling design, we see that countries that have signed Article VIII are 13 percentage points less likely to have current account restrictions.

Model (2) implements a version of von Stein's analysis. This model includes a dummy variable coded as 1 if the state will sign Article VIII within the next four years and 0 otherwise. It also includes a dummy variable for the year of signing Article VIII, and a dummy variable for all subsequent years as an Article VIII signatory. Hence, the omitted category is years not within four years of signing Article VIII, and the coefficients on the dummy variable should be interpreted relative to that baseline. The results show that countries are about 37 percentage points less likely to have current account restrictions in the year when they sign Article VIII, and 13 percentage points less likely to have restrictions after the first year. However, countries are already less likely to have current account restrictions in the four years before signing Article VIII. Indeed, we cannot reject the hypothesis that the coefficient on the four years before signing is equal to the coefficient on the years subsequent to signing ($p = .27$). These results are similar to von Stein's, as expected.

Model (3) adds country fixed effects to implement a difference-in-differences analysis.[17] Notably, the coefficients on the year-of-signing and the post-signing years are nearly unchanged relative to Model (2), suggesting that, even within a country, current account restrictions are less likely after signing

14. While Figure 5.5 looks like a within-country analysis, this appearance is misleading. In fact, von Stein merely plotted cross-sectional averages over time.

15. Simmons and von Stein use logit and probit models, respectively.

16. In contrast to Simmons we use a linear probability model and include year fixed effects.

17. See Angrist and Pischke (2008, Chapter 5) for a discussion of how unit-level fixed effects create a difference-in-differences design.

TABLE 5.14. Difference-in-Difference Analysis of Joining Article VIII of IMF and Current Account Restrictions

DV = Current Account Restrictions	Model			
	(1)	(2)	(3)	(4)
Article VIII dummy	−.130			
	(.0257)			
Year of signing Article VIII		−.367	−.316	−.283
		(.0599)	(.0691)	(.0652)
Article VIII after year of signing		−.134	−.153	
		(.0255)	(.0567)	
1–4 years before signing		−.0944	−.0507	
		(.0323)	(.0349)	
4 years before signing				−.0406
				(.0368)
3 years before signing				.0130
				(.0391)
2 years before signing				−.00993
				(.0416)
1 year before signing				−.0997
				(.0548)
1 year before signing				−.319
				(.0784)
2 years after signing				−.282
				(.0788)
3 years after signing				−.215
				(.0671)
4 years after signing				−.148
				(.0616)
More than 4 years after signing				−.0139
				(.0581)
Country fixed effects	No	No	Yes	Yes
Observations	2974	2974	2974	2974
R^2	.667	.672	.727	.734

All models include year fixed effects. Robust standard errors clustered by country in parentheses. All models control for the covariates in Simmons (2000), Table 4.

Article VIII. However, the coefficient for being within four years of signing Article VIII is smaller and we are able to reject at the 10% level the hypothesis that the four years prior to signing are the same as the years subsequent to signing ($p = .08$). The reason for the difference between Models (2) and (3) is that (2) compared the average restrictions for all countries within four years of signing Article VIII to the average for all countries not within four years of signing, whereas (3) compares the average restrictions within four years of

TABLE 5.15. Differences-in-Differences on Simmons's (2000) Data

Empirical Strategy	
Estimand	"Regression average" difference in probability of current account restrictions within countries before and after signing Article VIII.
Data	133 countries observed from 1967 to 1997.
Statistical Procedure	Differences-in-differences via fixed-effects regression of current account restrictions against Article VIII Commitment, controlling for a variety of time-varying country-level characteristics.
Measurement Validity	
Interpretation	Signing IMF Article VIII meaningfully represents commitment to an international legal agreement. Maintaining open current accounts meaningfully represents compliance with the agreement.
Arguments	These variables are direct measures of the features of interest.
Substantive Identification	
Assumptions	Parallel trends: after controlling for time-varying confounders in Table 5.12, signatories would have followed the same trend in restrictions as nonsignatories but for the signing of Article VIII.
Arguments	While this analysis is merely an illustration, a natural argument would rely on the event study graph showing that differences between signatories and nonsignatories emerge in the year prior to signing. We would need to argue that year-before difference is actually an effect of the treaty, as countries get into compliance in order to sign. Would be nice to see additional event-history analyses of trends in covariates to show that nothing else was changing differentially for signers around the time of signing.
Confidence Building	Standard errors are clustered by country to account for nonindependence. If this were a more fully fleshed out study, we might want to include additional robustness checks, such as randomization inference for the standard errors.

signing to the average restrictions not within four years of signing within the same country (adjusted for secular trends). Baseline differences between signatories and nonsignatories are reflected in the estimates from (2) but not (3). Based on the results from (3), the evidence for a constraining effect of treaties is stronger, although hardly conclusive.

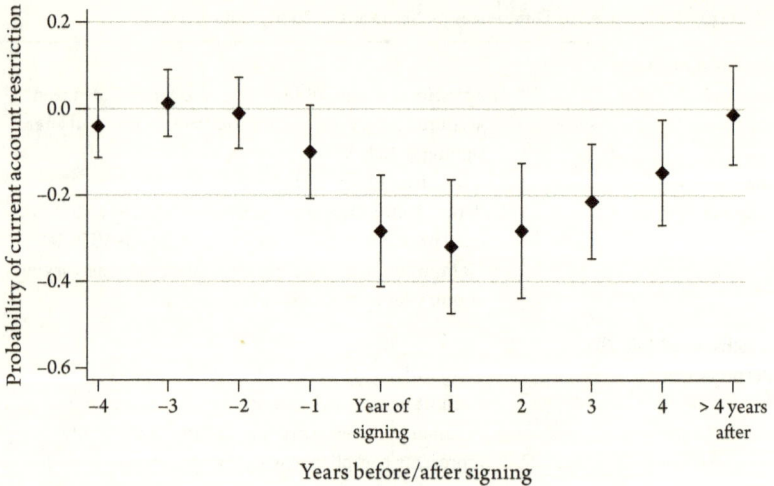

FIGURE 5.6. Current accounts restrictions before and after joining Article VIII of IMF. Coefficients and confidence intervals from model (4) of Table 5.14.

Model (4) shows a simple way to further understand trends in current account restrictions around the time of a country's signing Article VIII. Rather than having one indicator for being within four years of signing, as in von Stein's analysis, we use a dummy variable for each of the four years leading up to signing and another set of dummies for each of the four years after signing.[18] To make it easier to visualize the results from this analysis, Figure 5.6 plots the coefficient estimate and 95% confidence interval for each of these dummies.

The only pretreatment year that is significantly different (albeit at the 10% level) is the one year immediately prior to signing. Countries are roughly 10 percentage points less likely to have current account restrictions in the year immediately prior to signing Article VIII. However, coefficients for all other presigning years are small and insignificant. Model (4) also shows that restrictions are least likely during the year of signing and the year immediately after signing. In years two to four after signing, the difference gradually diminishes. And after five or more years post-signing, there is essentially no difference in the probability of a country having a current account restriction (relative to the omitted category, which is more than four years presigning).

18. This is an event-study analysis. Such analyses can be particularly useful when there are multiple periods with staggered adoption of a treatment (Goodman-Bacon, 2018; Callaway and Sant'Anna, 2020; Sun and Abraham, 2020).

What should we make of the pattern of results shown in Table 5.14? Countries do appear to reduce their current account restrictions even before signing Article VIII, as von Stein argued. However, when we look at within-country changes in Model (4), we see that the reduction in restrictions comes only in the year immediately prior to signing. Moreover, there is a significant reduction in restrictions in the year of signing and the first few years after signing. In other words, while states that sign Article VIII may be fundamentally different types from those that don't, as von Stein argued, nevertheless there is evidence that signatories change their behavior around the time of signing.

Should we think of the change in current account restrictions in the few years around the time of signing as a constraining effect of Article VIII? Or is it merely another aspect of the screening effect? Von Stein argues that the IMF urges members not to commit to Article VIII until restrictions have already been eliminated. The observed pattern of results appears consistent with states eliminating restrictions in order to sign Article VIII, and then fairly quickly reverting to their presigning behavior. This strikes us as more akin to a screening effect than a constraining effect. At the very least, this analysis suggests that any constraining effect is relatively shortlived.

A causal interpretation of the difference-in-differences model hinges on the parallel trends assumption, which, as we have emphasized, is not directly testable. How plausible is the assumption in this case? We can see from Model (4) that there is a difference between signatories and nonsignatories even before signing. Ordinarily, preexisting differences in trends are taken as strong evidence against the parallel trends assumption. But this difference emerges only in the year immediately before signing. If one were willing to believe that this change in behavior is part of the IMF-imposed requirement for signing Article VIII, then one might call it part of the effect of signing. Importantly, however, recall that the parallel trends assumption does not pertain to trends prior to signing; it pertains to counterfactual trends after signing. That is, the parallel trends assumption in this case states that countries that signed Article VIII, but for signing, would have followed the same trends in account restrictions in the years after signing as did those countries that didn't sign Article VIII.

Not being scholars of international relations, we leave it to others with more expertise to adjudicate the plausibility of the parallel trends assumptions and other issues of substantive interpretation.[19] Our goal in this exercise

---

19. And to write the obvious APSR paper.

was to illustrate how changing the assumptions for substantive identification contributes to credibility. In this case, we find strong evidence against one previously offered interpretation: namely, that the differences in restrictions between signatories and nonsignatories of Article VIII were entirely due to baseline differences between the types of states that do and don't sign. This explanation cannot account for the differences we observe within countries before and after signing. Being able to rule out one explanation that previously appeared plausible is one step forward, but leaves plenty of open questions. This sort of incrementalism is characteristic of how most literatures make progress and accumulate knowledge over time.

5.5   Sensitivity Analysis

In our discussion of the major research designs and the examples, we have emphasized that the credibility of a research design hinges on the plausibility of the assumptions required for substantive identification. Such assumptions are inherently untestable and there are situations in which a researcher does not have sufficient arguments to convince a reasonable interlocutor—or perhaps even herself—that the assumptions are sound. Is there any hope of progress in such situations? Thankfully, hope abides.

When the assumptions required for substantive identification are suspect, there are several approaches a researcher can take to probe whether the claim that an all-else-equal relationship exists is credible. In this section, we discuss one such approach, sensitivity analysis. The goal of a sensitivity analysis is to assess how sensitive a given estimate is to violations of the assumptions required for substantive identification (Rosenbaum, 2005; Imbens and Rubin, 2015).[20] While these methods are not widely used in social science, we believe they should be, especially in the context of just-controlling research designs.[21]

As we've said, it is not possible to test the assumption of no omitted confounders. But it is often possible to assess how much confounding would be required to overturn a given result. For example, one could ask how much confounding would be required to change the sign of a coefficient or to reduce its magnitude by some specific amount. Being able to answer such questions

20. A related approach, partial identification, asks what can be learned about the relationship of interest under weaker, more plausible assumptions (Manski, 2007; Tamer, 2010).

21. For a more technical and thorough introduction to these topics, see Gangl (2013).

can be particularly useful when linking theory and empirics if the question of interest is whether the evidence agrees with a theoretical all-else-equal claim, which would typically be a qualitative claim about the direction of a relationship rather than a specific claim about its magnitude. (Of course, knowing the magnitude is also of interest, since we want to know not just whether mechanisms are at work, but whether they are important.)

To understand the intuition behind sensitivity analysis, it will be helpful to note that if the conditional independence assumption is true, then, controlling for covariates, individuals in the treated and untreated groups are equally likely to have received the treatment. If these probabilities are not equal, it suggests nonrandom selection into treatment, which could confound our estimates of the treatment effect.

Let Γ be the ratio of the largest probability of receiving treatment in the treated group relative to the smallest probability of receiving treatment in the untreated group. Note, Γ is not directly observable, it is a conceptual quantity. In a simple random experiment, every subject has the same probability of being assigned to treatment, so $\Gamma = 1$. Similarly, if the conditional independence assumption holds, then $\Gamma = 1$ for subjects with the same value of the observed covariates. A Γ exceeding 1 indicates that units in the treated group were more likely to receive the treatment than units in the untreated group, which is evidence of nonrandom selection into treatment. Although Γ is not an observable quantity, sensitivity analysis allows us to estimate how different values of Γ (i.e., differing degrees of selection into treatment) would alter our estimated treatment effects. Of particular importance, sensitivity analysis allows us to estimate the value of Γ that would be required to generate an observed result spuriously, say when the actual ATE is 0.

The canonical method for carrying out such a sensitivity analysis was developed by Rosenbaum (2005). Various flavors have been subsequently offered (Imbens and Rubin, 2015, Chapter 22). A particularly useful variant comes from Imbens (2003), who casts sensitivity analysis within the framework of omitted-variables bias. Imbens's method allows a researcher to ascertain how great the bias due to omitted variables would have to be in order to invalidate a particular observed result. That is, how strong would the correlation have to be between a hypothetical confounder and the treatment or the outcome in order for the true treatment effect—the effect that would be observed if the confounder were included in the regression—to be insignificant? While the method cannot reveal whether such a confounder exists, it helps the researcher assess, based on substantive expertise, the likelihood of such a confounder existing. Often, a researcher gains traction on this question by evaluating the properties of the included covariates and asking whether there is likely to exist an omitted confounder that is equally influential.

Blattman (2009) provides one of the rare social science applications of a sensitivity analysis to bolster a just-controlling research design. Blattman is interested in the political legacy of violent civil conflict. Specifically, he studies Uganda's twenty-year civil war and asks whether individuals who were abducted and forced to serve in the Lord's Resistance Army (LRA) exhibit different patterns of political participation after the war than comparable individuals who did not participate in the violence. His main finding is that former abductees are more likely to vote and to participate in other aspects of politics than are non-abductees.

The key to substantive identification in Blattman's study is the assumption that abductees and non-abductees do not differ in other respects that might influence their political participation (i.e., there are no omitted confounders). To support this assumption, he makes the argument that abductions by the LRA were so unplanned and arbitrary as to produce "nearly exogenous variation." He supports this argument with evidence that abducted and non-abducted individuals are comparable on observable prewar traits gathered from a survey. Nevertheless, Blattman is attuned to the possibility of unobserved differences between abductees and non-abductees. For instance, he conjectures that if less able abductees were less likely to survive the war, then the postwar populations of abductees and non-abductees will differ even if the two groups were identical before the war. And if the attributes that help a person survive the war also make them more politically engaged, these attributes are a potential source of bias in his analysis.

As a response to such concerns, Blattman conducts a sensitivity analysis. Figure 5.7 presents one of Blattman's analyses, which is based on Imbens's (2003) method of testing sensitivity to exogeneity assumptions. The vertical axis represents the increase in the R^2 statistic that comes from adding a variable to a regression of voting (the outcome of interest) on all the other controls. The horizontal axis represents the increase in R^2 that comes from adding the same variable to a regression of abduction (the treatment of interest) on the other covariates. The points on the graph show the actual values of incremental R^2 for each covariate included in the analysis. The dashed line represents all the combinations of incremental R^2 for a hypothetical confounder that would be sufficient to reduce the coefficient on abduction by half.

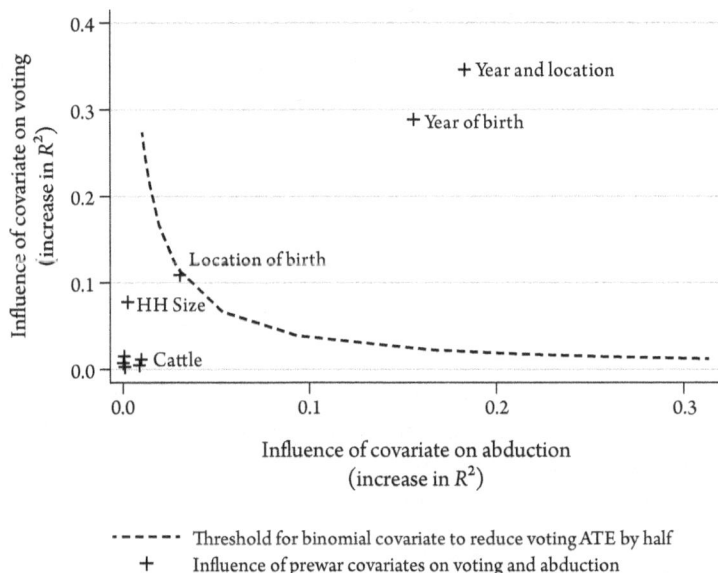

FIGURE 5.7. Impact of relaxing the assumption of unconfoundedness from Blattman (2009).

This sensitivity analysis allows an assessment of how much confounding, relative to observed covariates, would be enough to change the conclusions of the analysis. Among the observed covariates, only age and location of birth have sufficient correlation with both voting and abduction to significantly change the result, had they been omitted. These observable covariates provide a benchmark by which to assess potential omitted confounders. That is, an omitted confounder would have to be as influential as one of the two most powerful observable determinants of abduction in order to halve the observed treatment effect. The sensitivity analysis does not, and indeed cannot, test whether such confounders exist. Rather, it provides a basis for the analyst to make a substantive argument about how likely it is that a confounder, or combination of confounders, of such a magnitude exists. Blattman argues that such a confounder is unlikely in his setting.

Stepping back from this particular application, let's think about what a sensitivity analysis accomplishes within the research design framework we've offered in this chapter. Sensitivity analysis does not produce evidence in support of the assumptions for substantive identification; that is, the assumptions under which the statistical procedure produces a good estimate of the estimand. Instead, sensitivity analysis provides evidence to support an argument that, while the statistical procedure may not produce a good estimate of the estimand in general, in the particular case at hand the bias due to omitted confounders is likely small. So a sensitivity analysis shifts the argument from being about general properties of the procedure to being about the particular application of the procedure. As such, a sensitivity analysis does not bolster the credibility of the research design but rather suggests that a less than credible research design may nevertheless produce an estimate that is not far from the one that would be obtained by a more credible design.

Although details of implementation are beyond the scope of our discussion, sensitivity analysis can be applied to many research designs based on regression or matching (see Imbens and Rubin, 2015, Chapter 22). Sensitivity analysis sometimes shows that even a small amount of confounding could overturn a particular result, in which case we should probably be fairly skeptical. What is important is that sensitivity analysis provides researchers with a path forward even when the argument for substantive identification is not as strong as we might like.

5.6   Conclusion

The most important point to take away from this chapter is that the credibility of any research design hinges on the quality of the arguments for substantive identification and measurement validity. These arguments cannot be based on statistics alone. They depend crucially on making a substantive case, grounded in both evidence and subject area knowledge.

How convincing such arguments are is a matter of degree. Taking seriously the injunction to hold all else equal does not mean insisting on research designs that are bulletproof. Even well-designed studies are often susceptible to a variety of reasonable concerns about credibility. The point of the ERD is to help you do your duty as a scholar—state your assumptions clearly and present the arguments in support of those assumptions explicitly. If you do this, you make it possible for the literature to draw the appropriate conclusions from even imperfect analyses.

Interlude

In Part I we developed a framework for connecting theory and empirics based on three links—two similarity relations and commensurability. The framework makes clear that, when there is agreement or disagreement between a theoretical implication and an empirical finding, how much we learn about any one of the links depends on the strength of our reasons for believing the other two. As such, strengthening any of the links advances our ability to understand the mechanisms that explain important political phenomena.

The foundations offered by our framework support what we might think of as the textbook scientific method: write a theory (model), derive hypotheses (theoretical implications), and test them (assess using a credible estimate of a commensurable estimand). But there is much more to research linking theory and empirics than that.

Part II discusses in greater depth a variety of activities at the nexus of theory and empirics supported by the foundations laid in Part I. Each chapter considers one such activity: reinterpreting, elaborating, distinguishing, disentangling, and modeling the research design. Taken together, these activities exemplify the back-and-forth between theory and empirics through which social scientific knowledge accumulates.

PART II

Interactions

6

Reinterpreting

As a literature develops, a conventional wisdom often enshrines a particular theoretical interpretation of some empirical findings. This might be a sign of success—agreement between empirical findings and theoretical implications provides evidence for similarity between the theoretical model and the target and thus evidence the interpretation is correct. But we should always ask about other plausible interpretations. Offering such reinterpretations often productively moves a literature forward.

To be a reasonable interpretation of a set of empirical findings, a model must satisfy two conditions. First, it must be plausibly similar to the target. Second, its implications must agree with the empirical findings. Suppose there is already one such interpretation. A scholar reinterprets by proposing a different model, embodying different mechanisms, that is also a reasonable interpretation of those same empirical findings.[1] Looked at through the lens provided by our framework, this means the scholar could plug in the new theoretical model on the left-hand side of Figure 2.1 while maintaining commensurability, agreement between the theoretical implications and empirical findings, and the plausibility of similarity.

Some additional terminology can help clarify what's going on here. Call an implication shared by two theoretical models a *common implication* of those two models. A reinterpretation involves pointing out that some existing empirical findings actually agree with common implications of a model embodying the old mechanism and a model embodying the new mechanism. If the two models are both plausibly similar to the target, then that agreement does not favor one interpretation over the other.

1. The requirement that the new model embody different mechanisms is to exclude trivial cases in which the two models differ only in auxiliary features.

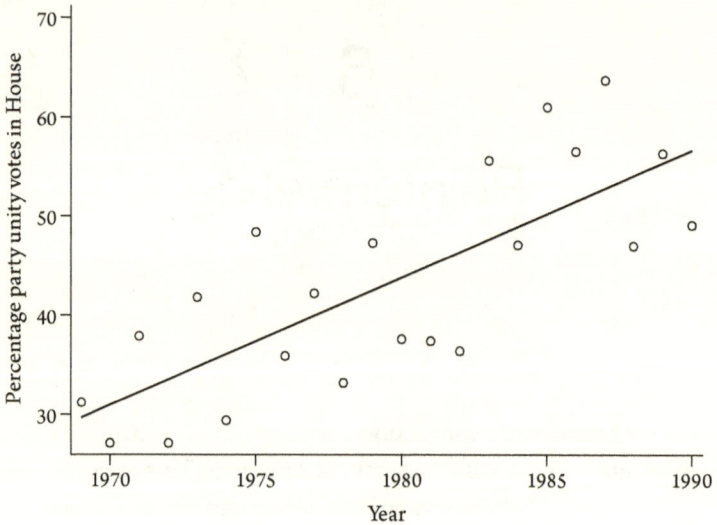

FIGURE 6.1. History of party unity voting, 1969–1990.

Importantly, a reinterpretation need not assert that the previously posited theoretical mechanism is absent, nor need it assert that the newly proposed one is present. It is instead an argument about the evidence on offer. Because that evidence is consistent with more than one mechanism, a reasonable interlocutor is not forced to accept one interpretation over the other.

In this chapter, we explore these ideas through three substantive literatures. The first concerns the influence of parties on the roll-call votes of members of the US Congress. The second concerns mobilization and recruitment for terrorist groups. And the third, which we alluded to briefly in Chapter 1, concerns the effect of natural disasters on the electoral fortunes of incumbent leaders.

6.1   Party Effects in Congress

During the 1980s, students of the US Congress observed a resurgence in party unity voting—the proportion of roll-call votes in which a majority of Democrats vote one way and a majority of Republicans vote the other. Figure 6.1 plots the history of party unity voting, revealing an upward trend, with a noticeable uptick in the eighties. Scholars including Rohde (1991) and Patterson and Caldeira (1988) interpreted this rise as evidence that political parties and their leaders were exerting increasing influence over the votes of

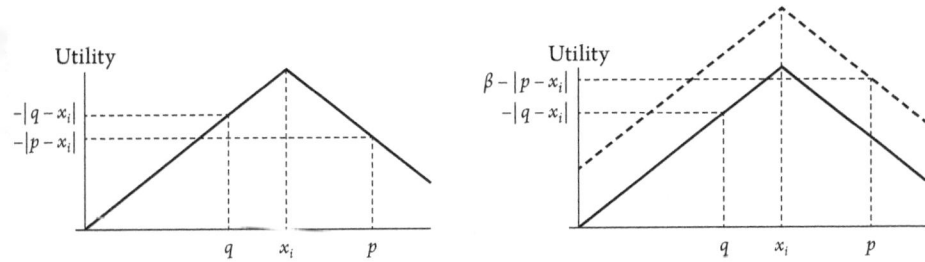

FIGURE 6.2. Increased party influence can change a legislator's vote.

rank-and-file members. A literature emerged explaining this apparent resurgence in terms of the power congressional parties wield over their members (for a review, see Rohde, 2013).

Krehbiel (1993) responded to this emerging literature with a textbook example of reinterpreting, asking "Where's the Party?" Krehbiel did not challenge the empirical claim that roll-call voting was becoming increasingly partisan. Instead, he made two points. First, an increase in party influence would matter only if legislators had some other motivation that also affected their votes. An example is close to hand. Democrats and Republicans typically have different ideologies on top of being members of different parties. Liberals tend to be Democrats, and conservatives tend to be Republicans. Second, changes to the distribution of this ideological motivation can also affect roll-call voting. Taken together, these two points make up Krehbiel's reinterpretation—the increase in party unity voting could arise from greater ideological sorting into parties.

We can represent these two mechanisms in a canonical model. To capture the party influence mechanism, assume that a legislator gets a benefit of $\beta \geq 0$ when voting as directed by the party leader. This benefit represents party-directed campaign funding, support from party leaders on other initiatives, and so on. If β is large, then legislators are highly responsive to party influence. To capture the ideological sorting mechanism, assume that bills are located in a one-dimensional policy space, and each legislator i has an ideal point x_i. Legislator i evaluates a bill with location x according to the utility function $-|x - x_i|$. An ideal point, x_i, represents the policy position this legislator would adopt without any influence from the party. This need not represent her personal policy preferences—the ideal point can also reflect electorally induced position taking.

To see Rohde's idea, consider the effect of an increase in a legislator's direct benefit from voting with the party, β. The left-hand panel of Figure 6.2

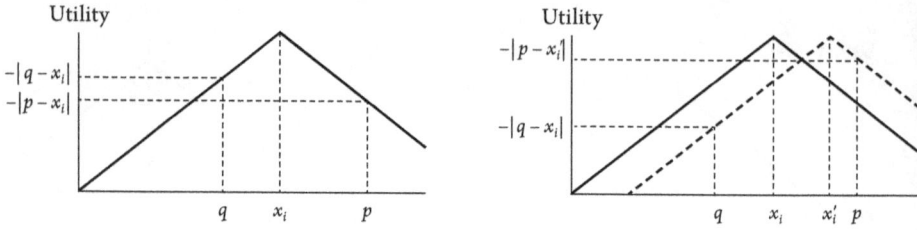

FIGURE 6.3. A shift in preferences can change a legislator's vote.

illustrates the legislator's utility function when $\beta = 0$, so there is no benefit to voting with the party. This panel shows a case in which a Republican legislator's ideal point is between the status quo policy q and a Republican party proposal p. Since the legislator's ideal point is closer to q than to p, and the legislator doesn't care at all about party pressure, the legislator votes against the proposal.

In terms of this model, Rohde's interpretation of the increased frequency of party unity voting is about a change in β, the size of the direct benefit from voting with the party leader. The right-hand panel of Figure 6.2 shows the same situation as before, but now the legislator gets benefit $\beta > 0$ if she votes for the proposal. As a result, her payoff to voting for p is given by the dashed curve, while her payoff to voting against p is still given by the solid curve. In the depicted case, the shift up by β is enough to reverse the legislator's vote.

Krehbiel's reinterpretation can also be represented in the model. Increased ideological sorting corresponds to shifting the legislator ideal points to be more in line with party proposals. Figure 6.3 starts with the same situation as in Figure 6.2. But this time the right-hand panel shows what happens if the Republican legislator's ideal point is shifted to the right (from x_i to x_i'). This shift is enough to reverse the legislator's vote, even though the direct benefit to supporting the party remains 0.

In other words, Krehbiel argues that increased party unity voting is a common implication of both increased partisan pressure and increased ideological sorting. As a result, Rohde's findings can be reasonably interpreted in terms of a model in which parties play no role, congresspeople vote based on ideology, and ideological sorting by party has increased over time.

Recall, to reinterpret an empirical finding is not necessarily to argue that the initial interpretation is wrong. Indeed, referring to Rohde's interpretation that increased party unity voting is evidence of increased party discipline,

Krehbiel writes, "such inferences are not necessarily wrong, but they are not necessarily right either" (p. 238). Krehbiel shows that Rohde's findings can be explained entirely in terms of a different theoretical mechanism. More evidence, of a different kind, is needed before we can conclude that the party influence mechanism is at work. Later in his article, Krehbiel attempts to provide evidence that the party influence mechanism is not at work in the committee assignment process, but Krehbiel's reinterpretation of Rohde's findings does not stand or fall with that exercise.

Finally, it is worth relating Krehbiel's particular reinterpretation of the party effects literature back to the framework in Chapter 2. Once we see that the party influence mechanism works alongside an ideological sorting mechanism, it becomes apparent that Rohde is implicitly holding ideologies constant in deriving his theoretical implication. Thus, commensurability of that implication and an empirical result requires a research design that also holds ideologies constant. But, as Krehbiel's argument makes clear, ideology is an omitted variable in Rohde's analysis, so commensurability fails here. The same goes for an assessment of the ideological sorting mechanism— a commensurable estimand would hold party influence fixed, asking how party-unity voting changes with changes in the distribution of ideology, all else equal. In Chapter 8 we discuss research designs that do better on commensurability for related questions.

For our purposes, it is not central that this argument can be understood in terms of omitted variables. As we will see in the rest of this chapter, theoretical reinterpretation is often possible and productive even absent an omitted-variables bias problem.

6.2   Who Becomes a Terrorist?

Scholars and policymakers share a common intuition that people often turn to political violence out of a lack of economic opportunity. Improvements in economic opportunity are thus expected to reduce mobilization for political violence. This economic opportunity-cost mechanism can be empirically assessed in a variety of ways. For instance, in Chapter 1 we discussed work examining the relationship between economic shocks and civil war, which we return to in Chapter 9. Parts of the terrorism literature take another approach, which is our focus here. The idea is to assess the opportunity-cost mechanism through a comparison of the characteristics of individuals who do and don't mobilize for armed conflict.

Krueger and Maleckova (2003) and Berrebi (2007) use this approach in studies of the individual characteristics of operatives from *Hezbollah* and *Hamas*, respectively. They show that these operatives have economic and educational statuses above the averages in their societies. For example, Berrebi reports that only 16% of Hamas operatives are poor, compared to 31% of all Palestinians. Krueger and Maleckova argue that, since those who mobilize for violence are neither poor nor poorly educated, economic opportunity must not be an important determinant of terrorist mobilization. Indeed, based on this evidence, Krueger (2007) argues, "there is not much question that poverty has little to do with terrorism."

Bueno de Mesquita (2005) offers a reinterpretation. Without disputing the empirical findings, he argues that the individual-level evidence does not entail the conclusion that economic opportunity is unimportant for understanding why individuals are willing to mobilize for political violence.

To do so, he adds organizational behavior to a model of mobilization. The idea is that two decisions must be made before someone becomes a terrorist operative—an individual decides to mobilize and a terrorist organization decides to recruit that individual. The key mechanism is screening—terrorist organizations select potential recruits based on ability, which is positively correlated both with efficacy as a terrorist operative and with economic success. (Hassan's [2001] qualitative evidence is consistent with that assumption.) The model implies that terrorist operatives will be neither poor nor ill educated, and is thus consistent with the empirical evidence. But it also implies that mobilization is responsive to economic opportunity costs.

To see the argument, let's start with a model designed to capture just the opportunity-cost mechanism that Krueger is implicitly testing and rejecting. Consider a set of individuals, each of whom has an ideological affinity with the terrorist group and so might consider mobilizing. Individual i has an underlying ability, θ_i. Each individual chooses between working in the regular economy or joining a terrorist organization. Individual i's payoff is $u_E(\theta_i)$ if she works in the economy, while her payoff is $u_T(\theta_i)$ if she joins the terrorist organization.

The parameter θ represents an individual's talents and level of education. As we illustrate in Figure 6.4, each of the functions u_E and u_T is increasing in ability; that is, individuals with higher ability expect to be more successful in the economic arena and more efficacious as terrorist operatives. The economic arena allows greater sorting according to ability, so payoffs increase faster in that sphere, as reflected in the curve labeled "Payoff from economy"

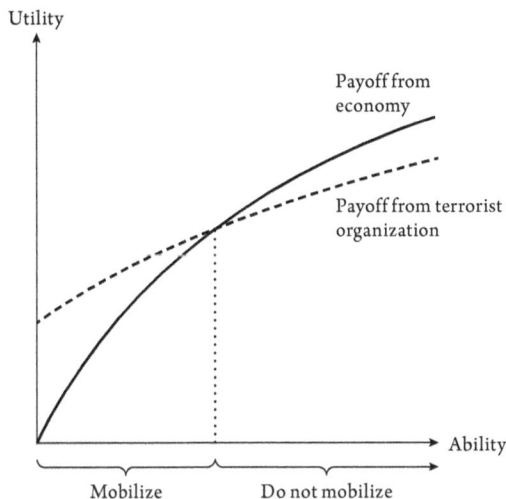

FIGURE 6.4. Terrorist mobilization decision.

being steeper than the curve labeled "Payoff from terrorist organization." An individual mobilizes for terrorism if the payoff to terrorism is greater than the payoff to economic activity. As Figure 6.4 shows, this means an individual is willing to mobilize only if her ability is below some threshold. As a result, poorer and less educated individuals, who face lower opportunity costs, are more likely to mobilize for terrorism. Krueger argues against such a model on the grounds that he does not find terrorist operatives to be poor or uneducated. Rather, he concludes, the right model has individuals choosing whether to mobilize for reasons unrelated to the economy.

But suppose we add the screening mechanism to the model in Figure 6.4—allowing terrorist organizations to choose whom to recruit from among those individuals who are willing to mobilize. There are costs and benefits to accepting a recruit. The more operatives recruited, the more attacks the organization can carry out. But accepting an operative also brings costs for the organization, for example, increased financial costs, risk of disloyalty, and so on.

Bueno de Mesquita captures these qualitative features of terrorist organizations in a variant on the model discussed earlier. Individuals' payoffs are the same. The terrorist organization cares about efficacy, which is increasing in the quality of its operatives. Since each operative also imposes some costs, the organization might not be willing to take all comers.

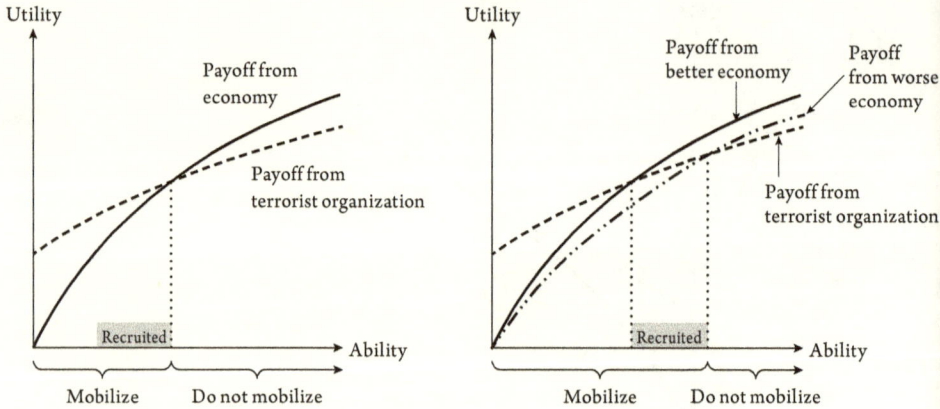

FIGURE 6.5. Terrorist mobilization decision.

The first cell of Figure 6.5 illustrates the equilibrium of this expanded model. Among those willing to mobilize, the organization accepts only individuals whose ability lies in the rectangle labeled "Recruited." These are the highest quality operatives available to the organization. So, in this model, terrorist operatives are not the lowest ability individuals. This agrees with the empirical finding that terrorist operatives are neither poor nor ill educated relative to the societies from which they are drawn.

In this model, the economy matters for terrorist mobilization and efficacy, even though terrorist operatives are not those with the least economic opportunity. A comparative static makes this clear. The second cell of Figure 6.5 shows what happens if the economy worsens (denoted by the dash-dot curve labeled "Payoff from worse economy"). The pool of potential recruits expands. As a result, the quality of terrorist operatives and the efficacy of the terrorist organization increase.

This theoretical argument is not sufficient to establish that the economic opportunity cost or screening mechanisms are at work. But it does offer a reinterpretation of the empirical evidence, showing that the data do not entail the conclusion that the motivation for mobilization must be unrelated to economic opportunity. That is, the data showing that terrorist operatives are neither poor nor ill educated is consistent both with a reasonable theoretical interpretation in which lack of economic opportunity does matter for mobilization and with a reasonable theoretical interpretation in which economic opportunity does not matter.

Unlike Krehbiel's reinterpretation that we discussed earlier, Bueno de Mesquita is not making an omitted-variables bias critique. Suppose we randomly assigned incomes in the population and then found that terrorist operatives were not poor relative to the population. This would still be a common implication of a model in which economic opportunity doesn't matter and of a model embodying the opportunity cost and screening mechanisms. After all, in the latter case, the terrorist organization would still select the highest quality operatives from among those who mobilized. The interpretive problem is not one of confounding.

This does not mean that different data could not be used to adjudicate between these two theoretical interpretations. To take the best case, suppose we had complete data on willingness to mobilize and ability. Bueno de Mesquita's argument implies that, among those willing to mobilize, recruitment should be positively related to ability. Krueger's argument would suggest no such relationship.

In practice, we are rarely in that kind of best case. To go further, we need to identify other empirical implications that differ between the two models, so that data might distinguish between them. In Chapter 8 we return to this and discuss empirical work that attempts to shed further light on this debate.

6.3 Elections and Natural Disasters

Students of voter behavior have long debated whether voters are up to the job given them in a democracy. The early literature on voter competence was concerned with whether voters were sufficiently informed to make good decisions (Campbell et al., 1960; Fair, 1978; Kinder and Sears, 1985; Popkin, 1991; Sniderman, Brody, and Tetlock, 1993; Lupia, 1994; Delli Carpini and Keeter, 1996). A more recent literature focuses on another aspect of voter competence—their rationality.

To assess whether voters behave rationally, that literature asks how election outcomes change in response to various shocks to voter welfare. One strand examines the electoral consequences of natural disasters and government responses to them (Abney and Hill, 1966; Achen and Bartels, 2004; Healy and Malhotra, 2010; Healy, Malhotra, and Mo, 2010; Bechtel and Hainmueller, 2011; Gasper and Reeves, 2011; Cole, Healy, and Werker, 2012; Huber, Hill, and Lenz, 2012; Chen, 2013). Another strand examines the electoral consequences of economic shocks (Ebeid and Rodden, 2006; Wolfers, 2002; Leigh, 2009; Kayser and Peress, 2012). Many such studies report that incumbent electoral fortunes suffer following negative events outside the control of policymakers (Achen and Bartels, 2004; Wolfers, 2002; Leigh, 2009; Healy, Malhotra, and Mo, 2010). These results are typically interpreted as evidence of voter irrationality. The basic argument is that, if voters are rational, then they should not blame incumbents for events outside of the incumbents' control.

Ashworth, Bueno de Mesquita, and Friedenberg (2018) offer a reinterpretation, challenging the claim that such empirical findings imply that voters are not behaving rationally. They present a model in which incumbent electoral fortunes can suffer following a natural disaster or economic downturn, even though voters are rational and politicians exert no control over the occurrence of such events.

To see how the argument works, consider a model of the effect of shocks on electoral fortunes. Each politician has quality θ that can be high ($\overline{\theta}$) or low ($\underline{\theta}$). The incumbent is high quality with probability p_I and the challenger is high quality with probability $p_C < p_I$. The assumption that the incumbent is higher quality, in expectation, than the challenger is meant to represent things like learning on the job and the fact that the incumbent has already been positively selected by winning an earlier election. Rational voters prefer higher quality politicians because they are expected to provide better governance outcomes in the future.

Before the election, the voter observes two things—a random shock ω and a governance outcome. The shock is either small ($\underline{\omega}$) or large ($\overline{\omega}$), and its value is completely random, not influenced in any way by the incumbent.

The governance outcome g depends on both the incumbent's quality and the shock. Its values satisfy the following relations:

$$g(\overline{\theta},\underline{\omega}) = g(\underline{\theta},\underline{\omega}) > g(\overline{\theta},\overline{\omega}) > g(\underline{\theta},\overline{\omega}). \qquad (6.1)$$

The equality says that the incumbent's quality is irrelevant for governance outcomes when the shock is small. The first inequality implies that a large value of the shock reduces the governance outcome, no matter the incumbent's quality. The second inequality says that, when the shock is large, high-quality incumbents produce better governance outcomes than do low-quality incumbents.

The shock represents a natural disaster, such as a hurricane or the emergence of a novel virus. A hurricane is an act of God, not something the incumbent can influence. This is represented by the assumption that the value of the shock is independent of the incumbent's quality. Moreover, hurricanes are destructive, so damage (similar to governance outcomes) is avoided when storms do not occur. But when storms do land, the damage depends on infrastructure investment, emergency preparedness and response, and so on. The incumbent's quality is meant to represent the capacity and willingness to engage in such preparations.

The inequalities in Condition 6.1 have implications for voter learning. The size of the shock affects how much information the voter has about the incumbent. The voter perfectly learns the incumbent's quality if there is a large shock, but the voter learns nothing if there is a small shock.

This kind of assumption about informativeness is plausibly representational. Suppose better incumbents do a good job preparing for storms than do worse incumbents. If the weather is calm, the voter does not see the difference in preparedness. If a hurricane comes, the voter does see the difference in preparedness, because good preparation leads to only minor damage. Of course, the assumption made here is too strong. It is surely not true that voters learn nothing about the incumbent in the absence of a disaster and learn everything about the incumbent in the presence of a disaster. Ashworth, Bueno de Mesquita, and Friedenberg show, in their paper, that all that is needed is that the voter learns more when there is a disaster than when there is not. We make the stronger assumption here just to ease exposition.

Because the voter wants to elect whichever candidate is most likely to be high quality, the first step in solving the model is to determine what the voter believes about the incumbent, based on what the voter observes. If there is a small shock, the voter learns nothing and continues to assess probability p_I that the incumbent is high quality. We record this in the top row of Table 6.1 on the left. If there is a large shock, the voter observes either $g(\overline{\theta}, \overline{\omega})$ or $g(\underline{\theta}, \overline{\omega})$, depending on the true quality of the incumbent. The better outcome reveals that the incumbent is high quality, while the worse outcome reveals that the incumbent is low quality. We record this in the bottom row of Table 6.1 on the left.

Next, we determine how the voter votes. Because $p_I > p_C$, when there is a small shock and the voter learns nothing new, she continues to believe the incumbent is more likely to be high quality than is the challenger. As a result, the voter reelects the incumbent whenever there is a small shock. If there is a large shock, the voter learns the incumbent's quality from her observation of damage and preparedness. If that quality turns out indeed to be high, the incumbent wins reelection. But if that quality turns out to be low, the incumbent loses. We record these electoral outcomes in Table 6.1, right side.

TABLE 6.1. The Voter's Posterior Probability Assessment That the Incumbent Is High Quality and the Incumbent's Electoral Fortunes, as a Function of the Incumbent's Actual Quality and the Size of the Shock.

(a) Posterior probability			(b) Electoral fortunes		
	High quality	Low quality		High quality	Low quality
Small shock	p_I	p_I	Small shock	Reelected	Reelected
Large shock	1	0	Large shock	Reelected	Defeated

Because there is a positive probability that the incumbent is low quality, there is a positive probability that the incumbent is defeated following a large shock. But the incumbent is reelected for sure if there is a small shock. Hence, by providing the voter with new information, the large shock reduces the ex ante probability the incumbent is reelected, even though the shock itself is not the incumbent's fault.[2]

This result is quite stark and, as stated, implausible as a representation of the world. It is clearly not the case that incumbents win reelection for certain when there is no disaster. But, as we've already mentioned, the strong informational assumption that gives rise to this stark result on reelection rates is not necessary for the key implication that the incumbent's probability of reelection is higher when there is no disaster. For instance, Ashworth, Bueno de Mesquita, and Friedenberg show that in nearby models in which governance outcomes depend on other, unobservable factors in addition to natural disasters or incumbent quality, it is still true that natural disasters affect electoral fortunes, but it is no longer true that incumbents win for certain absent a disaster.

In this model, there is a negative correlation between the exogenous shock and incumbent electoral fortunes. To relate this to the empirical literature, consider a large population of locations, each of which is represented by the model just sketched. Some of these locations have a hurricane and some do not. Since hurricanes happen by chance, the distribution of high- and low-quality incumbents is the same in each subpopulation. The model's implication is that incumbents win at a higher rate in locations that do not have hurricanes than in locations that do. Hence, the difference in electoral fortunes is a common implication of this rational-voter model and the irrational-voter

2. If the voter started with the belief that the incumbent was less likely to be high quality than the challenger, then the effect of the shock would be reversed.

story offered in the prior literature.[3] As such, this reinterpretation does not require an interlocutor to conclude that voters are rational; it merely shows that the evidence on offer does not entail the conclusion that voters are irrational.

6.4 Gleanings

We've just looked at three debates in three different literatures. We deliberately chose examples in which the associated theoretical models were relatively accessible and simple to present. But a growing body of theoretical research has taken up the challenge of reinterpretation on topics ranging from media bias (Wolton, 2019) to electoral violence (Harish and Little, 2017) to lobbying (Schnakenberg, 2017).

None of the papers we discussed is anything like the last word on these substantive topics. It is always a good bet that scholars will come up with new evidence and new reinterpretations. That doesn't make it a mistake to offer an interpretation or think about the implications of a particular mechanism. Doing so, even knowing the risk of a future reinterpretation, is an important step in the accumulation of knowledge.

The particular works we discussed highlight two general points that are worth expanding on.

First, as we noted in our discussion of party effects in Congress, reinterpretation sometimes takes the form of an omitted-variables bias critique that speaks to commensurability. Krehbiel, for instance, uses theory to show that earlier empirical work failed to account for ideological sorting when comparing Republicans and Democrats. The objection would evaporate if we could randomly assign members to parties. If we still saw systematic differences in behavior, they could not be due to ideological sorting. So a difference in behavior between Democrats and Republicans would not be a common

---

3. It is worth noting that this reinterpretation was built on the assumption that natural disasters, while random, have consequences that interact with policy. While that is true for many of the shocks used in the empirical literature, it is not the case in two prominent papers, one using shark attacks and the other college football losses (Achen and Bartels, 2004; Healy, Malhotra, and Mo, 2010). These findings, then, would constitute the most compelling evidence for the voter irrationality mechanism, as they are immune from the sort of reinterpretation just offered. However, careful empirical scrutiny calls into question the empirical findings in both papers (Fowler and Montagnes, 2015; Fowler and Hall, 2018), as we will discuss in Chapter 7.

implication of the party pressure mechanism and the ideological sorting mechanism under random reassignment.

But not all reinterpretations are of this form. Indeed, neither of the other two reinterpretations discussed in this chapter are critiques about omitted variables. We have already discussed this in the context of terrorist recruitment. It is even clearer in the case of disasters and elections. There, the appeal of the initial empirical papers was precisely that disasters are as-if randomly assigned. The reinterpretation shows that the meaning of a correlation between as-if random disasters and incumbent reelection is not as obvious as was initially thought.

Second, you don't necessarily need to invent a brand new mechanism to reinterpret. Reinterpretation often involves making new use of mechanisms that are already well understood. In the case of the literature on party effects in Congress, Krehbiel invokes the canonical model of ideological voting. His contribution is not creating this model, it is seeing its implications for the interpretation of a set of empirical results. Ashworth, Bueno de Mesquita, and Friedenberg's Bayesian learning model similarly builds on canonical models of voter learning due to Achen (1992) and Bartels (1993). The screening model of terrorist organizations is not standard in that literature. But it too invokes standard models of previously understood mechanisms—in this case, a model of positive selection—applying it in a new context.

Each of these illustrates a point that harkens back to our discussion of well-understood mechanisms in Chapter 4. Reinterpreting is about pointing out that models embodying different plausible mechanisms have common implications. You are more likely to spot a reinterpretation the more mechanisms you understand. This is not to say it is enough to simply pick any model from the theorist's toolkit that generates a common implication. Your new mechanisms must have a plausible claim of similarity to the target. Evaluating similarity is in large part a matter of substantive knowledge of the phenomenon in question. Hence, being good at reinterpreting depends both on being familiar with how to model many mechanisms and knowing enough substance to judge their applicability in particular settings. Finally, those pieces of background knowledge must be accompanied by the habit of always asking whether empirical findings can be understood through alternative, substantively plausible mechanisms other than those already on offer in a literature.

7

Elaborating

Our discussion of reinterpretation shows that agreement between an empirical finding and an implication of a theoretical model does not constitute definitive evidence that the model's mechanism is similar to the target. We should do more to strengthen the evidence we bring to bear. One important way to do this is to *elaborate*: to draw out many different implications of a theoretical model and empirically assess them in more than one way.

Sometimes elaboration results in agreement between multiple theoretical implications and empirical findings. Multiple instances of agreement make it more likely that the mechanism in question is at work in the target and less likely that some alternative mechanism (perhaps not as yet conceived) or some failure of similarity between the research design and the target explains all of the findings. The opposite is true if those elaborations do not find support.

While we have emphasized the possibility of reinterpretation, that is not the only concern that elaborating addresses. It also provides reassurance that a particular empirical finding is not a false positive. This is an especially important point in light of growing concerns over publication bias and the replication crisis in the social sciences. A couple of our examples in this chapter illustrate the use of elaborating to address to such concerns.

To get a sense of how elaborating works, let's return to Dell's (2015) study of the politics of the Mexican drug war. As we discussed in Chapter 5, Dell argues that PAN-instigated drug crackdowns led to increased territorial competition among gangs and thus to increased violence. Her main evidence comes from a regression discontinuity design showing that drug-related homicides increased following PAN victories in close mayoral races. But this is not all she does.

Dell further elaborates the crackdown mechanism, drawing out several additional implications. First, she shows that casualties from confrontations between police and criminals increased following close PAN victories, as did arrests of high-profile drug traffickers. This evidence lends support to the claim that PAN mayors are indeed associated with an increase in drug crackdowns. Second, she shows that violence increased more following close PAN victories in municipalities that are closer to the US border, consistent with the idea that the mechanism is territorial competition, as these municipalities are more valuable to drug traffickers. Third, she shows that violence increased more following close PAN victories in territories that border territory controlled by a rival drug trafficking organization. Each of these findings is consistent with the hypothesis that PAN victories created violence by increasing crackdowns that induced conflict between drug traffickers trying to take or maintain control of valuable territory.

Finally, Dell uses a theoretical model to predict the routes that would minimize the traffickers' costs of transporting their goods to the United States. Dell's mechanism implies that, following a PAN victory in a municipality located on a preferred route, traffickers will divert their goods to the cost-minimizing route that does not pass through a PAN-controlled municipality. In this way, the model suggests that crackdowns in PAN municipalities generate spillovers to other municipalities located on substitute routes. And, indeed, Dell shows that when a municipality becomes part of a predicted route, as a result of diversion from a PAN-controlled municipality, there is an increase in drug-related violence and an increase in drug interdiction on that new route. Taken together, the agreement between theoretical implications and empirical findings in these elaborations strengthens the evidence in favor of Dell's account.

In this chapter, we discuss several papers that productively elaborate. It will become clear as we go that elaboration can take many forms. It is not just about deriving additional theoretical implications and confronting them with data, but can also involve heterogeneous treatment effects, varying the research design, extrapolation, and structural modeling. We discuss these various approaches in greater depth after describing the papers.

7.1   Partisan Bias in Federal Prosecutions

Gordon (2009) asks if US attorneys in the Department of Justice (DOJ) have partisan motivations for pursing political corruption cases. It is plausible that they do because US attorneys are political appointees, and there is some anecdotal and descriptive evidence pointing in this direction. For example, Shields and Cragan (2007) show that Democrats were seven times more likely than Republicans to be investigated by the Bush DOJ.

Gordon studies the US attorneys' decisions about prosecution. A key institutional detail justifies this focus. US attorneys do not initiate investigations; instead, they choose which cases to charge from the pool of cases referred by investigative agencies, such as the FBI. As such, a US attorney's possible political bias is more likely to affect the decision to prosecute than to directly affect the cases and facts under consideration.

Let's consider a simplified version of Gordon's model of a prosecutor's choice over which cases to prosecute. Each politician i engages in a level of corruption, c_i. If $c_i = 0$, then politician i is not corrupt at all. Larger values of c_i represent greater levels of corruption. When a case against politician i is referred to the prosecutor, she observes c_i. If politician i engaged in corruption c_i and is prosecuted, she receives a punishment whose severity is $s(c_i)$, where s is an increasing function. The prosecutor benefits from prosecuting higher levels of corruption, but bears a cost, $k > 0$, for prosecuting a case. She also gets an idiosyncratic benefit $b_i \geq 0$ for prosecuting politician i. We can think of this idiosyncratic benefit as arising from bias against the politician, perhaps because the politician and prosecutor are from different political parties.

The prosecutor will prosecute politician i if her net benefit from doing so is positive, that is, if $c_i + b_i - k > 0$. Thus the prosecutor will use a cutoff strategy, prosecuting if

$$c_i > c^*(b_i) \equiv k - b_i.$$

Unsurprisingly, the cutoff c^* is decreasing in b_i—the larger is the idiosyncratic benefit the prosecutor gets from prosecuting politician i, the lower is the level of corruption by i needed to trigger prosecution.

Now suppose that the politicians are divided into two parties: Democrats, D, and Republicans, R. The division into parties manifests in two ways. First, the distribution of corruption might differ between the two parties. Denote the distribution of corruption in party P by F^P and write f^P for its probability density function. Second, the prosecutor is also a member of one of these two parties and is more biased against members of the other party than against her own. Formally, suppose that $b_i = \underline{b}$ if politician i is from the prosecutor's party and $b_i = \bar{b} > \underline{b}$ if politician i is from the other party.

Consider politicians from party D. Suppose first that the prosecutor is also from party D. Then she will prosecute all cases against party D politicians with $c > c^*(\underline{b})$. There will be $1 - F^D(c^*(\underline{b}))$ such prosecutions. The average severity of punishment in these cases is

$$\mathbb{E}^D[s(c) \mid c > c^*(\underline{b})] = \int_{c^*(\underline{b})}^{\infty} s(c) \frac{f^D(c)}{1 - F^D(c^*(\underline{b}))} \, dc.$$

Suppose next that the prosecutor is from party R. Then she will prosecute all cases against party D politicians with $c > c^*(\overline{b})$. There will be $1 - F^D(c^*(\overline{b}))$ such prosecutions. And the average severity of punishment in these cases is

$$\mathbb{E}^D[s(c) \mid c > c^*(\overline{b})] = \int_{c^*(\overline{b})}^{\infty} s(c) \frac{f^D(c)}{1 - F^D(c^*(\overline{b}))} \, dc.$$

Recall that $\overline{b} > \underline{b}$ and $c^*(\cdot)$ is decreasing. Thus the cutoff for prosecution of a party D politician by a party R prosecutor is less stringent than the cutoff for prosecution of a party D politician by a party D prosecutor: $c^*(\overline{b}) < c^*(\underline{b})$. Two theoretical implications follow from this inequality. First, all else equal, more party D politicians are prosecuted by party R prosecutors than by party D prosecutors:

$$1 - F^D(c^*(\underline{b})) < 1 - F^D(c^*(\overline{b})).$$

Second, all else equal, the average punishment severity for party D politicians who are prosecuted is greater when the prosecutor is from party D than when the prosecutor is from party R:

$$\mathbb{E}^D[s(c) \mid c > c^*(\underline{b})] > \mathbb{E}^D[s(c) \mid c > c^*(\overline{b})].$$

Analogous arguments show that more party R politicians are prosecuted by party D prosecutors than by party R prosecutors, and that the average punishment severity for a prosecuted party R politician is greater when the prosecutor is from party R than from party D.

Gordon's research design builds on these implications directly. He studies prosecutions and punishments before and after the changeover from the Clinton (Democratic) administration to the Bush (Republican) administration. If prosecutorial decisions in the model are similar to decisions made by federal prosecutors, then two things should be true. First, the changeover should increase the proportion of Democrats who are prosecuted, relative to Republicans. Second, the changeover should increase the average punishment of Republicans, relative to Democrats.

This second implication is a particularly valuable elaboration because it is somewhat counterintuitive. A first thought might be that prosecutorial bias

TABLE 7.1. Partisan Affiliations of Public Corruption Prosecution Defendants in the Bush and Clinton Administrations

	Bush Administration (2004–2005)	Clinton Administration (1998–2000)	Difference
Republican defendant	8	14	−6
Democratic defendant	49	36	13
Difference	−41	−22	**−19**

From Gordon (2009).

would result in harsher punishments for politicians from the opposing party. But the theoretical model shows that biased case selection implies exactly the opposite. All else equal, co-partisans who get prosecuted are expected to get harsher sentences, because the extra prosecutions of partisan opponents are of politicians with relatively low levels of corruption.

Gordon uses a difference-in-differences design to assess each of the implications. Recall from Chapter 5 that the key assumption is parallel trends— here, that the distributions of corruption within each party change in the same way between the two administrations. We evaluate the argument for that assumption later, but for the moment assume that it holds.

Table 7.1 reports the difference-in-differences assessing the first theoretical implication—politicians from one party are more likely to be prosecuted when the prosecutor is from the other party. The empirical findings agree with the implication. The switch from the Clinton to the Bush administration was associated with an increase in the prosecution of Democrats and a decrease in the prosecution of Republicans. While six times as many Democratic as Republican public officials were prosecuted during the Bush administration, even during the Clinton administration two and a half times as many Democrats were prosecuted. In other words, both administrations prosecuted more Democrats than Republicans. Gordon attributes this fact to greater opportunities for corruption in urban areas, where Democrats predominate. We could imagine other possible explanations, but the specific reason why Democrats are consistently overrepresented in corruption cases is not important for our discussion. It does, however, mean that it was an important part of the argument for similarity that the theoretical model allowed for politicians from different parties to have different underlying distributions of corruption. And it also shows why it is important that Gordon uses a difference-in-differences design, rather than just comparing prosecution rates in one administration. Contrary to the interpretation presented by Shields

TABLE 7.2. Difference-in-Differences for Sentence Length in Months (Inclusive of Probation) for Republican and Democratic Defendants Under the Clinton and Bush Administrations

	Bush Administration (2004–2005)	Clinton Administration (1998–2000)	Difference
Republican defendant	51.25	21.41	29.84
Democratic defendant	29.55	32.05	−2.5
Difference	21.7	−10.64	**32.34**

From Gordon (2009).

and Cragan, Democrats are more likely to be prosecuted even under a Democratic administration, so disproportionality in the number of prosecutions alone cannot be taken as evidence of anti-Democratic bias.

Gordon also highlights one further subtlety. The difference-in-differences provides evidence of partisan bias. But these results don't speak to which administration is the culprit. For instance, the data are equally consistent with the idea that the Bush administration is biased against Democrats (if the actual ratio of Democrats to Republicans in the referral pool is around 2.5), that the Clinton administration is biased against Republicans (if the actual ratio is around 6), or both (if the actual ratio is somewhere in between). So Gordon has shown evidence of partisan bias but cannot attribute it to either administration specifically.

The second theoretical implication that Gordon assesses concerns the average punishment received by partisan allies of the prosecutor relative to that received by opponents. We focus on the results that measure punishment as sentence length including probationary periods. Table 7.2 reconstructs his difference-in-differences analysis assessing this implication. The average sentence for Democratic defendants is lower than the average sentence for Republican defendants during the Bush administration. The reverse is true under the Clinton administration. The average sentence for a Democratic defendant was about 21.7 months lower during the Bush administration, whereas it was about 10.7 months higher under the Clinton administration. The difference-in-differences, then, is about 32 months.[1] This finding, then, also agrees with the theoretical implication—public officials receive longer

1. Our discussion of Gordon's sentencing results is based on a difference-in-differences using mean sentences under the Bush and Clinton administrations. In his paper, Gordon also presents analyses controlling for covariates using regression and matching. While we do not discuss those results here, we note that the difference-in-differences estimates are always in the ballpark of 30 months and always statistically significant.

sentences, on average, when prosecuted by a partisan ally than when prosecuted by a partisan opponent.

Gordon has shown that a prosecutor's partisan opponents are more likely to be prosecuted, but receive lower sentences conditional on conviction, than a prosecutor's partisan allies. The key assumptions for substantive identification are that the underlying partisan composition and the relative distribution of criminal severity across parties in the referral pool did not change between the Clinton and Bush administrations. Suppose this assumption doesn't hold. How might Gordon's analysis be threatened? Is there a way in which Gordon's results could be the product of a change in the referral pool in the absence of prosecutorial bias?

The answer is yes, but the necessary conditions strike us as unlikely. Gordon's design would be biased in favor of his results if Democratic officials committed fewer and less severe crimes relative to Republicans under Clinton than under Bush. This pattern seems contrary to expectation. One might expect that, knowing prosecutors have become partisan allies, elected officials would commit more or more severe crimes.

There is at least one other way in which the parallel trends assumption might be violated, however. Suppose that the composition of the referral pool changes across administrations not because of the changing criminal behavior of public officials, but rather because of partisan targeting by the investigative agencies. That is, Gordon's results are also consistent with partisan bias in the referral process. If investigators target partisan opponents in the manner predicted by Gordon's model, they would refer more partisan opponents, and for lesser offenses, which would be consistent with the difference-in-differences estimates from Gordon's paper. Note that this could hold even in the absence of prosecutorial bias, say if prosecutors chose cases at random from the referral pool. This is to say that Gordon has provided evidence of partisan bias in the federal prosecution process but not necessarily evidence that prosecutors themselves were biased. Gordon acknowledges this alternative interpretation.

Gordon's research design allows him to say something credible about partisan bias in the overall DOJ process leading to prosecution, but it does not allow him to apportion bias between the two administrations. On the surface, this may appear to be a limitation of his approach compared with that of Shields and Cragan, who confidently claim that US attorneys in the Bush administration are biased against Democrats. While Shields and Cragan's claim is more sensational, it is also unfounded, at least given their evidence.

Gordon's elaboration and research design leave us on more secure footing. In particular, a reinterpretation of the results would have to account for both the higher number of prosecutions and the shorter sentence lengths of partisan opponents.

7.2   Accountability and Information

One motivation for institutions that create electoral accountability is that giving citizens the right to retain or replace policymakers leads to outcomes that are better for citizen welfare. Theorists have proposed two mechanisms that work to link institutions of accountability and democratic functioning (Fearon, 1999). First, when voters have the formal right to retain or replace policymakers, the politicians' actions are shaped by how they expect the voters to respond. That is, accountability may create *electoral incentives*. Second, voters have the ability to elect and retain politicians whose characteristics are best aligned with their own interests. That is, accountability may create *electoral selection*.

Theory suggests that the effectiveness of these two mechanisms depends on the quality of voters' information. If voters have better information about governance outcomes, their electoral decisions will be more sensitive to those outcomes. This gives incumbents stronger incentives to devote costly effort to achieving good outcomes. And, if voters have better information, they are better able to learn about which politicians have characteristics they prefer, strengthening electoral selection.

Much of the theoretical literature uses models that capture the electoral incentives and electoral selection mechanism in a stripped-down way (see Ashworth, 2012, for a review). Those models have a single, representative voter. There are two policy-making periods with an election in between. In the first period, the politician in office takes an action, a, that affects a governance outcome. The voter observes some information (perhaps the action, perhaps the outcome, perhaps a noisy signal of one or both of these) and then decides to either reelect the incumbent or replace her with a challenger. The winner is then in office in the second policy-making period. She chooses an action that affects another governance outcome, after which the game ends (without another election). Figure 7.1 provides a timeline.

Three important facts about incumbents further characterize these models. First, an incumbent gets a benefit B if she is reelected. The benefit to reelection could represent personal glory, salary, opportunities for

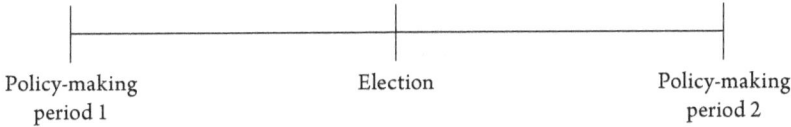

| Policy-making period 1 | Election | Policy-making period 2 |

FIGURE 7.1. Timeline of electoral accountability models.

corruption, or the fact that policy better reflects the politician's ideology when in office. Second, incumbents in the models vary in characteristics that matter for the quality of governance outcomes as perceived by the voter. We summarize these characteristics with a type, denoted θ. Type could represent how closely their ideological preferences align with voters' ideological preferences (Maskin and Tirole, 2004), how tempting they find corruption (Ferraz and Finan, 2011), their competence (Ashworth, 2005), or their ability to recognize good policy ideas (Canes-Wrone, Herron, and Shotts, 2001). Third, they care about what actions they take directly, and not only because of their desire for reelection. These preferences are represented by a utility $u(a, \theta)$, which could reflect personal policy priorities, a desire to avoid hard work, the need to conform to the demands of organized interests, and so on.

Two additional features of the model are critical. The first period governance outcome is informative about the incumbent's type. And the voters' payoff in the second period is increasing in the type of politician in office. As a consequence, the voter's decision about whether or not to reelect the incumbent will be influenced by past governance outcomes because those outcomes are informative about future governance outcomes.

For instance, suppose that in the first policy-making period, the voter observes some signal s that depends on some combination of the governance outcome, the incumbent's type, and the incumbent's actions. The voter's beliefs about the expected type of the incumbent and challenger after the first policy-making period are $\mathbb{E}[\theta_I \mid s]$ and $\mathbb{E}[\theta_C]$, respectively. The voter compares the difference between these two expectations to some threshold, τ, reelecting the incumbent if and only if:

$$\mathbb{E}[\theta_I \mid s] - \mathbb{E}[\theta_C] \geq \tau. \tag{7.1}$$

If the voter cares about nothing other than second-period governance outcomes, then $\tau = 0$—the voter just elects the candidate with the higher expected type. But the parameter τ lets us represent other facts pushing voters toward one or the other candidate (e.g., partisanship, warm glow incumbency effects, or discrimination). We can also represent uncertainty about, say, partisan swings or differential voter turnout by letting τ be the realization of a random variable.

The incumbent recognizes that her reelection probability can be affected by the action she takes, since this action affects the signal the voter sees in the first policy-making period. Let this probability (given a strategy for the voter of the sort just described) be $\Pr(\text{reelect} \mid a)$. Then the incumbent chooses her action to solve

$$\max_{a_1} \Pr(\text{reelect} \mid a_1)B + u(a_1, \theta_I). \tag{7.2}$$

We can now see the implications of varying voter information in a model embodying electoral incentives and electoral selection. If voter information changes in a way that makes reelection probabilities more sensitive to outcomes, the incumbent becomes more willing to change her action, sacrificing more of the immediate payoff captured by u to get an extra probability of the benefit B. That is, the improved voter information strengthens electoral incentives.

Snyder and Strömberg (2010) explore the relationship between voter information and electoral incentives in the context of the US Congress. A major part of Snyder and Strömberg's contribution involves improving measurement validity. They construct a new measure of voter information about congressional representatives, and employ a variety of measures of politicians' efforts on behalf of their constituents.

To measure voter information, Snyder and Strömberg use the geographic congruence between congressional districts and media markets. Here's the idea. Imagine a voter in a mid-sized city with a local daily newspaper. Suppose, further, that the city and the congressional district are basically the same. Snyder and Strömberg would say that the congressional district is highly congruent with its media market. By contrast, imagine another voter in a town thirty miles outside of that city, and in a different congressional district. That voter's daily newspaper may still be the city's paper. But that newspaper is not terribly interested in reporting on this voter's congressperson, since he or she represents relatively few of the newspaper's readers. That congressional district is not very congruent with its media market. Snyder and Strömberg claim that a locality's congruence is a good measure of voter access to information (i.e., is similar to voter information in electoral accountability models like those we discussed earlier). In highly congruent districts, the local media are likely to cover the local congressperson, whereas in noncongruent districts the local media are less likely to do so.

An important step in Snyder and Strömberg's analysis is to provide evidence for the similarity of the research design and the target. They do this in two steps. First, they provide evidence of measurement validity. Second, they provide evidence for the plausibility of some of the assumptions they will make to estimate commensurable estimands.

To bolster their claim of measurement validity, Snyder and Strömberg need to show that their congruence measure really does capture voter information. The first panel (reading clockwise from the top) of Figure 7.2 shows that the more readers of a given newspaper live in a particular congressional district, the more articles are written about the district's congressional representative. The next two panels show that the more congruent is a congressional district, the more informed voters are about their local representative in the sense of having read an article about the representative and recalling the representative's name.

With respect to the plausibility of assumptions for substantive identification, Snyder and Strömberg need to show that the relationship between congruence and voter information is not the consequence of some omitted variable that might also matter for the outcomes they study. They show three pieces of evidence to support this claim. First, congruence is not correlated with voter knowledge of statewide elected officials, making it unlikely that congruence is capturing knowledge of politics in general. Second, the relationship between congruence and voter knowledge does not hold for people who are not newspaper readers. Third, the relationship between individual voter knowledge and congruence holds in a difference-in-differences design that includes incumbent and state-by-year fixed effects. In this design, identification comes purely from the way redistricting changes the congruence of some voters, but not others, represented by a given incumbent.

Snyder and Strömberg then turn to assessing the relationship between voter information and electoral incentives. They use three different measures of the relevant endogenous outcomes. Two of those measures try to directly capture incumbent effort: how often a congressperson appears as a witness in a congressional committee and how often a congressperson votes in lock-step with his or her party. Both of these are actions that might affect the representative's reelection chances more when there is press coverage than when there is not. Finally, Snyder and Strömberg measure one outcome—federal spending flowing to the district—that is a consequence of incumbent effort.

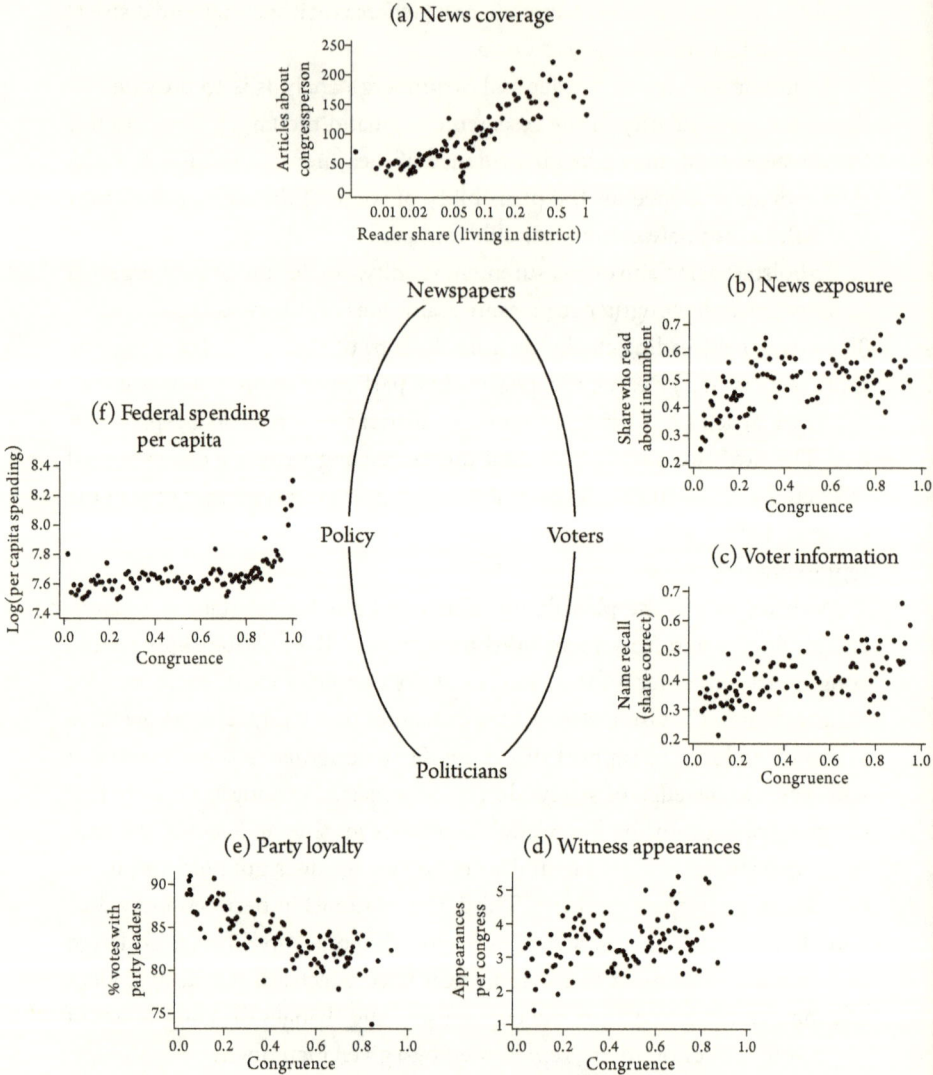

FIGURE 7.2. Media coverage and government performance in Congress. This figure uses Snyder and Strömberg's (2010) data to replicate analyses from their Figure 1.

With these measures in hand, Snyder and Strömberg attempt to estimate all-else-equal relationships between congruence and politician effort. These relationships are represented in the next three cells of Figure 7.2. The more congruent a congressional district, the more likely the representative from that district is to appear as a witness, the less likely the representative is to vote in lock-step with his or her party, and the more federal funds flow to the district.

But these relationships may not be all else equal. For instance, it's possible that more urban districts are both more congruent on average and more likely to receive federal funds for reasons unrelated to incumbent effort. To address such concerns, Snyder and Strömberg employ a difference-in-differences design.

For the regressions on the behavior of representatives (i.e., witness appearances and party-line voting) they use an empirical strategy that asks whether members from more congruent districts perform better than other members within the same state at the same time (specifically, by using member and year-by-state fixed effects). Substantive identification of the relevant all-else-equal relationships is not airtight here, since there could be other differences between more and less congruent districts even within the same state and year, something Snyder and Strömberg acknowledge. The qualitative results from Figure 7.2 all continue to hold.

Credibility is stronger for the results on federal spending. That data are measured at the county level, so Snyder and Strömberg can take two approaches to the difference-in-differences design, both with stronger substantive identification.

First, they consider an empirical strategy that compares spending received by different counties that are within the same congressional district but have different levels of congruence (specifically, by using district-by-year fixed effects). In this specification, the identifying variation comes from differences in congruence among counties that all have the same congressional representative in a given year. Second, they consider an empirical strategy based on changes in congruence resulting from redistricting, asking if the same county gets more federal money when it is redistricted into a more congruent district (specifically, by using state-by-year and county fixed effects). Again, the qualitative results from Figure 7.2 continue to hold.

All told, then, Snyder and Strömberg elaborate in two important ways. First, they use multiple measures of politician performance that are expected to respond to electoral incentives. Second, they use multiple research designs based on different assumptions for substantive identification. This elaboration bolsters confidence in the plausibility of the assumptions needed to identify the relevant all-else-equal relationships and confidence that the results are not due to chance. In addition, they propose a new approach to measuring voter information and assess multiple implications that should hold if that measure is valid. While the latter is not a theoretical elaboration in our sense, it bolsters confidence in measurement validity, which is key for establishing similarity of the research design to the target.

7.3   Elections and Consumption

Scholars of political behavior often assert that voters' beliefs about the state of the world are shaped by their partisan identification. This so-called perceptual screen leads supporters of different parties to interpret the same facts in different ways (Campbell et al., 1960). Since this mechanism bears on questions of democratic representation and accountability, there may be much at stake in assessing its similarity to particular targets.

Most of the evidence for the perceptual screen comes from surveys asking respondents to evaluate a common set of facts. Such studies have repeatedly found that, for instance, partisans evaluate the state of the economy at any point in time differently, with supporters of the governing party rating the economy more positively than supporters of the opposition party (Conover, Feldman, and Knight, 1986). Bartels (2002, p. 138) summarizes the findings, across a variety of factual areas, as showing that "partisan loyalties have pervasive effects on perceptions of the political world."

A key question for this interpretation is whether the partisan screen alters voters' actual beliefs or merely alters their answers to survey questions. That is, do supporters of a sitting president rate the economy more favorably than do opponents simply as a way of expressing support for their party, a form of partisan cheerleading? Some experiments support this view. Bullock, Gerber, Hill, and Huber (2015) and Prior, Sood, and Khanna (2015) show that paying respondents for accurate responses to factual questions significantly reduces partisan differences in reported economic evaluations.

Gerber and Huber (2010) investigate whether a partisan perceptual screen influences people's actual economic behavior. To do so, they use a model that combines the partisan screen mechanism with a well-known mechanism from economics, consumption smoothing (Friedman, 1957; Campbell and Mankiw, 1990). Let's see how it works.

The permanent income hypothesis suggests that people try to smooth their consumption over time. As a result, a voter spends more today when she expects her future income to be higher. Denote by y_i^R the income voter i expects in the event of a Republican victory and y_i^D the income voter i expects in the event of a Democratic victory. Let p be the ex ante probability the

Republican wins. Then the voter's preelection expectation of her postelection income is:

$$\bar{y} = p y_i^R + (1-p) y_i^D.$$

Suppose the Republican wins. Then the voter's expectation of her income changes by

$$y_i^R - \bar{y} = (1-p)(y_i^R - y_i^D). \qquad (7.3)$$

Suppose a voter believes that her party is better for the economy than the other party. This is meant to represent the partisan screen. Formally, if i is a Republican voter, $y_i^R > y_i^D$, and if i is a Democratic voter, $y_i^R < y_i^D$. So the partisan screen implies that a Republican voter's expectation of income goes up when the Republican wins, while a Democratic voter's expectation of income goes down when the Republican wins. One can see this in Equation (7.3). (The reverse is the case if the Democrat wins.)

An implication of the model combining the partisan screen and consumption smoothing is that, all else equal, in a district where the majority of voters are Republicans, a Republican victory results in an increase in expected future income and thus in current consumption for most consumers. And in a district where the majority of voters are Democrats, a Republican victory results in a decrease in expected future income and thus in current consumption for most consumers.

Gerber and Huber empirically assess this implication. Using data on county-level taxable sales from 1990 to 2006, they ask how consumption changes after presidential elections. They estimate the county-level change in consumption from the quarter before the election to the quarter after the election, controlling for the same quarter-to-quarter changes in nonelection years. Their key estimate is whether the change in consumption is greater in counties where the normal vote for the winning party is higher. (Here, the normal vote is measured in terms of share of the two-party presidential vote in 2000.) They find agreement with the implication of the theoretical model—alignment with the winner increases consumption. These results suggest that partisans not only report different evaluations of the economy in surveys, but also act on those beliefs when making economic decisions.

McGrath (2017) elaborates and assesses an additional implication of Gerber and Huber's theoretical model. She notes that the model implies heterogeneous treatment effects, since the magnitude of the consumption response to an election depends on how surprising the outcome is. For example, consumption changes less in response to a Republican victory if voters assigned

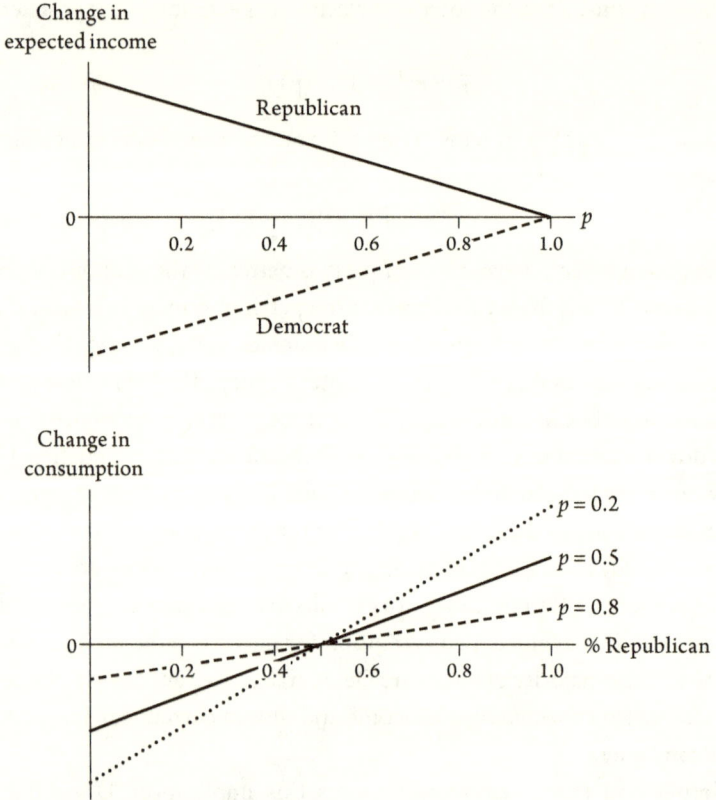

FIGURE 7.3. Effect of Republican victory on individual permanent income and district-level consumption.

a 90% probability to the Republican winning than if they assigned only a 10% probability to the Republican winning. The reason is that, before the election, voters already have factored expectations about the election outcome into their beliefs about their future income. As a result, if the election outcome isn't very surprising, expected future income changes very little, so consumption changes very little. But if the election outcome is surprising, expected future income changes a lot and so does consumption.

This implication is evident in Equation (7.3). The magnitude of the change in expected income when a Republican wins is decreasing in the probability of a Republican victory (p). Figure 7.3 illustrates the result. The top panel shows that the change in expected income from a Republican victory is largest in magnitude for p close to zero (it is positive for Republicans and negative for Democrats) and decreasing linearly to 0 as p goes to 1. The lower panel shows the effect of a Republican victory on consumption, depending on the partisan composition of the district and the ex ante probability of a Republican victory. For Democratic leaning districts (share Republican less than .5), consumption goes down with a Republican victory. For Republican leaning districts (share Republican greater than .5), consumption goes up with a Republican victory. The magnitude of these effects is greater the smaller the ex ante likelihood of a Republican victory (p).

McGrath empirically assesses this implication—examining whether the change in consumption in partisan counties is greater the more surprising was the election outcome. To do so, she replicates Gerber and Huber's analysis separately for each presidential election. Contrary to the theoretical implication, the results are largest for the 1996 election, when Bill Clinton's victory was arguably the least surprising outcome in all the elections under consideration. Indeed, McGrath cites Hibbs's (1996) predictive model to claim that Clinton had an ex ante estimated probability of winning between 94% and 98%. The estimates from all the other elections are small and insignificant.

The result is strongest for the election where the theory predicts it should be weakest and insignificant or wrongly signed in all other elections. This lack of agreement between the elaborated theoretical implication and the estimated relationship reduces the plausibility of the claim that the combination of the partisan screen and consumption smoothing mechanisms are a good representation of voters in US presidential elections.

McGrath does several other analyses. First, she shows that when 1996 is removed from the analysis, the estimates are close to zero and statistically insignificant. Next, McGrath shows that the 1996 results were driven entirely by one state, Texas, where the postelection change in consumption was an order of magnitude larger than in any other state. If Texas is removed from the analysis, Gerber and Huber's results are insignificant even for the 1996 election. These additional robustness checks, coupled with the lack of evidence for the second implication of the partisan screen mechanism, lead McGrath to conclude that Gerber and Huber's finding was likely a false positive, the result of sampling variation rather than a genuine relationship.

Note that McGrath does not challenge Gerber and Huber's research design or the commensurability of their estimand with the theoretical implication. McGrath also does not reinterpret their results by suggesting an alternative theoretical mechanism that generates their findings as a common implication.

Rather, her argument is by way of elaborating an additional implication of the partisan screen and consumption smoothing mechanisms and showing that it does not agree with the data. Even granting that the original results were well identified, the case that these mechanisms are at work is weakened in light of the failure to find support for the second implication. This highlights a dual role for elaborating: original authors can elaborate to bolster their own confidence in their conclusions; subsequent authors can elaborate to further assess interpretations supported by earlier findings.

7.4   Who Becomes a Terrorist?

In Chapter 6, we discussed a reinterpretation of the empirical finding that terrorist operatives are neither poor nor ill educated relative to their societies. In that reinterpretation, economic opportunity plays a role, but terrorist organizations screen recruits, seeking those with higher ability. Our earlier discussion emphasized the agreement between that reinterpretation's theoretical implications and the empirical evidence that motivated it. But the model also has a variety of features that might be assessed in an elaboration.

Here, we focus on two elaborations. First, the screening model assumes that higher socioeconomic status is associated with greater efficacy as a terrorist operative and that terrorist organizations know and care about this. Evaluating this is a way of directly assessing evidence that crucial features of the model appear similar to features of the world. Second, the screening model implies that wealthier individuals should be less willing to mobilize for terrorism. Third, the screening model implies that economic shocks will affect the efficacy of a terrorist organization. Evaluating this implication is a way of assessing agreement between an implication of the model and a commensurate empirical finding.

Each of these elaborations has been taken up by empirical scholars.

Using data on Palestinian suicide bombers between 2000 and 2005, Benmelech and Berrebi (2007) examine whether socioeconomic status is positively associated with efficacy as a terrorist operative and, if so, whether terrorist organizations are aware of this. They show that more highly educated operatives are more likely to be assigned to high value targets, suggesting terrorist organizations do in fact use information correlated with socioeconomic status in decision making. Further, they show that better educated operatives both successfully complete their missions more often and kill more people per attack, suggesting a positive association between educational attainment and effectiveness as a terrorist operative. Using data from the personnel records of members of the Islamic State of Iraq and Syria, Morris (2020) finds that recruitment officers make notes tying attributes of a recruit that are valuable in the economy to efficacy as a terrorist operative—noting, for instance, whether recruits have a background in chemistry or a visa to enter the United States. These results offer reasons to believe that the assumptions behind the screening mechanism do represent features of real-world terrorist organizations.

Using those same personnel data Morris (2020) provides evidence in support of the claim that wealthier individuals should be less willing to mobilize. In particular, she finds that, among those who wish to go to work for the Islamic State, wealthier individuals are less likely to volunteer to become a suicide terrorist, rather than a regular member of the armed group. (Of course, this doesn't tell us about the relationship between economic status and willingness to join the Islamic State at all.)

And again using data on Palestinian operatives, Benmelech, Berrebi, and Klor (2012) study the effect of economic shocks on terrorism. They use a difference-in-differences design exploiting changes in unemployment in Palestinian districts. They find that increased unemployment has two effects. First, the quality of suicide terrorist operatives coming from that district (as measured by education, age, and experience) increases. Second, this improvement in the quality of operatives translates into a more effective terrorist organization. During bad economic times, terrorist organizations, having recruited higher quality operatives, attack higher value targets and do so with greater success. Finally, it is worth noting that the finding that unemployment seems to cause an increase in terrorism directly contradicts the claim that the best explanation for the fact that terrorists are neither poor nor ill educated is that economic factors do not matter for terrorist recruitment.

Taken together, these empirical studies offer evidence in favor of an interpretation based on the economic opportunity costs and screening mechanisms. But this is not the end of the story. There is more elaboration to be done. New evidence or new research designs, perhaps from other conflicts, could certainly be brought to bear to shift our beliefs. Moreover, further reinterpretation is always possible.

For instance, Spaniel (2018) suggests a model representing a new mechanism that also has implications that agree with all of the empirical findings we have discussed. In Spaniel's model, mobilization depends on two factors: economic opportunity (poorer people are more willing to mobilize) and ideology (more extreme people are more willing to mobilize). Ideology matters for efficacy because more extreme terrorist operatives work harder. The terrorist organization has two kinds of tasks: nonsensitive and sensitive. There is a complementarity between operative effort and task sensitivity, so the effort–ideology link makes the terrorist organization wary of assigning members to sensitive tasks unless those members are sufficiently extreme.

Because wealthier people are less willing to mobilize, the model implies a positive association between wealth and extremism within the mobilized population. The terrorist organization observes wealth but not ideology. As such, the organization uses wealth as a proxy for extremism and assigns operatives to sensitive tasks only if they are sufficiently wealthy. Unlike in Bueno de Mesquita's model, no primitive link between socioeconomic status and skill as a terrorist is assumed. Instead, such a link arises endogenously in the mobilized population, because opportunity costs and ideology are substitutes in the decision to mobilize.

The empirical findings in the literature are common implications of Spaniel's and Bueno de Mesquita's models. But the models also have implications that distinguish between them. Bueno de Mesquita's model implies a monotone relationship between economic shocks and terrorism. But Spaniel's model has competing effects. On the one hand, as economic opportunity worsens, people become more willing to mobilize, which tends to increase violence. On the other hand, as this happens, the informational content of socioeconomic status is reduced (since lots of people are now willing to mobilize). This informational effect tends to decrease violence, because terrorist organizations will do a worse job at task assignment. Overall, as a result, Spaniel's model predicts a nonmonotone relationship between economic opportunity and terrorist violence. A future empirical literature might assess these two elaborations and thereby make further progress in understanding the mechanisms at work.

7.5   Football and Accountability

Scholars are increasingly aware that norms surrounding statistical significance have unintended consequences. Among the most concerning is publication bias—the phenomenon whereby, even when the authors of individual papers are following good practices, a disciplinary preference for publishing statistically significant results leads to published estimates that are disproportionately likely to be false positives and overestimates. As we saw in our discussion of elections and consumption, elaboration can be helpful in identifying instances where this might be the case. If many independent implications of the underlying mechanism being studied find empirical agreement, it is less likely that existing support for the mechanism is spurious. This, we think, is what Fisher had in mind when he said, "Make your theories elaborate." As Cochran (1965) explains, "when constructing a causal hypothesis one should envisage as many different consequences of its truth as possible." (Fisher's and Cochran's views are discussed by Rosenbaum, 2010, p. 329.)

To see how this works, consider an example from the literature on voter behavior and electoral accountability. In Chapter 6 we discussed a literature attempting to evaluate voter rationality by assessing whether electoral outcomes respond to events outside the control of incumbents. We pointed out that such evidence is, in general, not convincing because there is a ready reinterpretation available. That reinterpretation hinges on the events outside the incumbent's control interacting with policy in some way, so that their occurrence might affect the voters' opportunity to learn about the incumbent. Many kinds of events studied in this literature—for example, weather or economic shocks—do plausibly interact this way with policy. But not all do.

Healy, Malhotra, and Mo (2010) present evidence that cannot be reinterpreted in this way. They show that the local electoral performance of incumbent presidential, gubernatorial, and congressional parties is positively associated with the on-the-field performance of local college football teams. Going from a loss to a win in a game 10 days before the election seems to increase the incumbent party's vote share in the team's home county by 1–2 percentage points. Healy, Malhotra, and Mo interpret this as evidence for a nonrational mechanism—voters' mood in a domain that is uninformative about politics or policy bleeds over into the political domain and affects vote choice.

Without challenging the validity of the research design, Fowler and Montagnes (2015) elaborate the mechanism proposed by Healy, Malhotra, and Mo and provide evidence suggesting that their result is a false positive. How does this work?

Fowler and Montagnes's first elaboration concerns theoretically implied heterogeneous treatment effects. They argue that, if voters' moods really do transfer from the realm of sports fandom to voting, then the relationship between football outcomes and election outcomes should be stronger in counties where either college football is particularly popular or where the college football team is based.

Their second elaboration concerns the scope of the theoretical similarity claim. They argue that, since college football and professional football are similar, if the mechanism works with college football, it should also work with NFL football. As such, finding or failing to find the same negative relationship between NFL football losses and election outcomes should affect how much weight we give to the college football results in forming our beliefs about how representational the mechanism is.

Fowler and Montagnes find that the data do not agree with any of these additional implications. Indeed, the association between college football outcomes and incumbent party electoral fortunes is stronger in counties where there is less interest in college football (as measured by the number of people in the county who like football on Facebook), it is just as strong in other counties in the same state as in the team's home county, and there is no relationship between NFL outcomes and incumbent party electoral fortunes. Based on this elaboration, they argue that it is likely the association between college football losses and incumbent electoral success documented by Healy, Malhotra, and Mo is not the result of the voter mood mechanism, but rather a false positive, due to chance.

7.6   Deforestation and Corruption

We've seen that elaborating often involves generating and separately assessing multiple implications of a theoretical model. But we can sometimes go beyond just asking whether each implication separately is consistent with the evidence. We can ask whether several quantitative estimates relate to one another in a way that is consistent with the model. This extra step of elaboration is a move in the direction of the structural approach since, when we follow this approach, each of the model's "[a]ssumptions face immediate discipline by the data (individually or jointly) and often can be verified and rejected" (Bombardini and Trebbi, 2020, p. 397).

This more structural form of elaboration typically requires stronger assumptions than does simply assessing the qualitative implications of a theoretical model. The model must be sufficiently specific that we can feed quantitative estimates into it and check their consistency. This often requires additional functional form or distributional assumptions over and above those needed to derive the qualitative implications on their own. So if you find disagreement, a question remains about whether that is because the mechanisms in the model do not represent those in the target or because the auxiliary features of the model are insufficiently similar to the target.

This chapter's final example illustrates these ideas and shows how our approach relates to a more structural approach. The discussion is unavoidably more technical than what has come before. We think working through it pays dividends, but a reader who is uncomfortable with this level of technicality may want to skip to the end of the chapter.

Burgess et al. (2012) study local political officials' incentives to allow illegal deforestation in Indonesia. Since most tropical forests are owned and managed by governments, corruption in the permitting process for logging might be a first-order issue driving excessive deforestation. Indeed, this seems plausible based on some simple descriptive facts. For example, the World Bank estimates that 60% to 80% of the wood taken from Indonesian forests may involve illegal activity (Burgess et al., 2012, p. 1708).

Shleifer and Vishny (1993) argue that many instances of government corruption can be understood as the sale of an illegal good by a bureaucrat, where that bureaucrat can restrict the quantity of the good to be sold. This quantity restriction allows the bureaucrat to charge a higher price, in the tradition of the standard economic analysis of monopoly. We call this the *market power mechanism*.

Burgess et al. point out that if this market power mechanism is at work, greater jurisdictional fragmentation will increase illegal deforestation. They formally develop this intuition in a model that features a large number of firms, each of which wants to buy permits to log. In each jurisdiction, a bureaucrat controls the permitting process. Each bureaucrat independently sets the price for these permits in their jurisdiction. Burgess et al. assume there is free entry into the market for buying permits, so the local bureaucrats capture all of the surplus (i.e., they charge prices such that firms make zero profits). As a result, their theoretical model is formally identical to the canonical Cournot model of oligopoly (Tirole, 1988, Chapter 5). Since the bureaucrat gets all the surplus, we simplify the analysis of Burgess et al. by modeling the bureaucrats as directly choosing how much logging is done in their jurisdiction, abstracting away from firms completely.

There are n jurisdictions, each governed by one bureaucrat. Each bureaucrat, i, chooses how much logging to allow in their jurisdiction, q_i. Write the total amount of logging as $Q = \sum_i q_i$ and the total amount of logging in jurisdictions other than i's as $Q_{-i} = \sum_{j \neq i} q_j$.

The market price of timber is determined by the total quantity logged according to a decreasing function $P(\cdot)$. So if total logging is Q and bureaucrat i's logging is q_i, bureaucrat i's revenue is

$$P(Q)q_i.$$

Logging comes with two costs. First, there is the direct cost, which is c per unit cut. Second, there is the risk of being caught and punished by national officials. That risk is increasing in the amount of logging allowed in a bureaucrat's jurisdiction. Specifically, if bureaucrat i allows logging q_i, then she suffers expected punishment κq_i. So her total cost from logging q_i is $(c+\kappa)q_i$. To simplify notation, we will define $K \equiv c + \kappa$, so that bureaucrat i's total costs are Kq_i.

Putting all of this together, bureaucrat i's best response to Q_{-i} solves

$$\max_{q_i} \left(P(q_i + Q_{-i}) - K \right) q_i.$$

The first-order condition for the maximum is

$$P'(q_i + Q_{-i})q_i + P(q_i + Q_{-i}) - K = 0.$$

To ensure that this first-order condition is sufficient for a maximum, we assume that $P'(q + Q_{-i})q + P(q + Q_{-i})$ is a decreasing function of q for any Q_{-i}.[2]

Each term of this first-order condition can be interpreted as an effect on the bureaucrat's payoff from an increase in logging. The first two terms, together, represent the net effect on revenue. The first term comes from the fact that the per-log price decreases when she increases logging. This tends to decrease revenue. The second term comes from the fact that she has more logs to sell when she increases logging. This tends to increase revenue. The third term represents the costs of logging, both direct production costs and expected punishment from being caught engaged in illegal activity.

The symmetry of the model makes it natural to look for a symmetric equilibrium in which each bureaucrat chooses the same q, and the total number of permits sold is just $Q = nq$. In a symmetric equilibrium, the level of logging, Q^*, is given by the following condition (which comes from substitution into the first-order condition):

---

2. A sufficient condition for this is that P be concave, but some convex P also satisfy it, a fact we exploit in what follows.

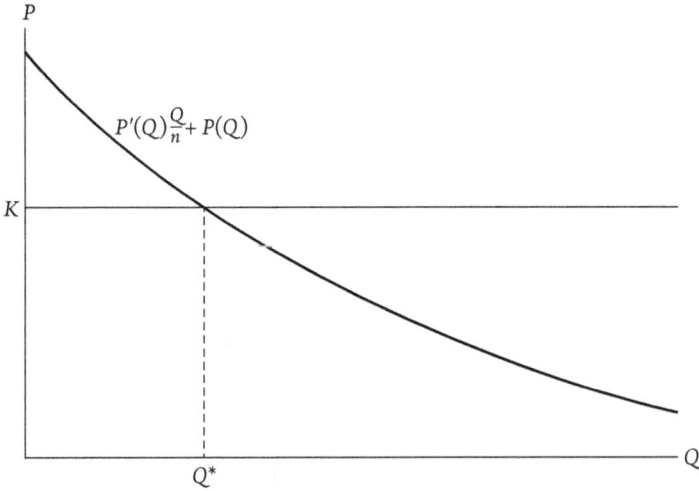

FIGURE 7.4. The unique symmetric equilibrium of the logging game.

$$P(Q^*) + P'(Q^*) \cdot \frac{Q^*}{n} = K. \qquad (7.4)$$

The left-hand side of Equation (7.4) is a decreasing function of Q and the right-hand side is constant in Q. This implies that Q^* is unique, as illustrated in Figure 7.4.

A first implication of the model now follows straightforwardly. Increasing the number of jurisdictions (n) has no effect on the right-hand side of Equation (7.4), but increases the left-hand side (since P' is negative). Hence, as illustrated in Figure 7.5, the amount of timber cut is increasing in the number of jurisdictions. That is, the equilibrium level of logging is an increasing function, $Q^*(n)$. We call this the *monotonicity implication* because it is about a qualitative feature (monotonicity) of the relationship between the number of jurisdictions and logging.

To get an intuition for why the monotonicity implication holds, compare the cases of $n = 1$ and $n = 2$. When there is only one jurisdiction, Equation (7.4) says that the equilibrium total amount of logging, Q_1^*, satisfies

$$P(Q_1^*) + P'(Q_1^*) \cdot Q_1^* = K.$$

Now consider the case of two jurisdictions and ask whether it is an equilibrium for each of them to choose an amount of logging equal to $\frac{Q_1^*}{2}$, so that total logging stays the same. The answer is no. When one bureaucrat is only

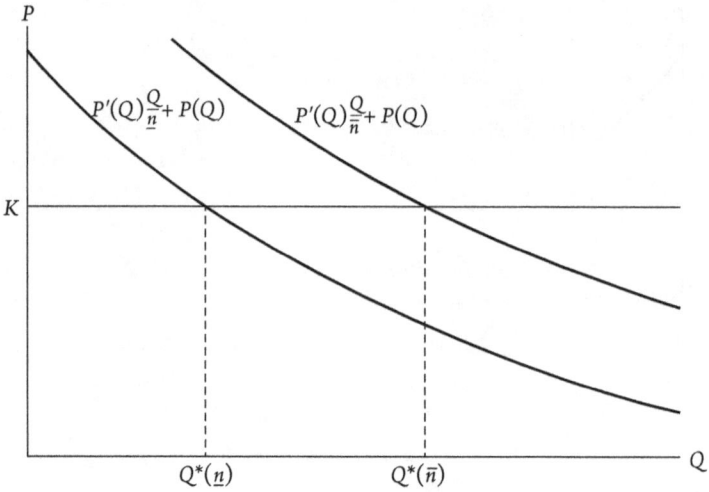

FIGURE 7.5. Increasing number of jurisdictions from $\underline{n}$ to $\bar{n} > \underline{n}$ increases the amount of logging.

responsible for half of the logging, the effect of a price decrease on her revenue is smaller than when she is responsible for all of the logging. Hence, total logging must be higher when $n = 2$ than when $n = 1$. Formally, this follows from the observation that, because P' is negative,

$$P(Q_1^*) + P'(Q_1^*) \cdot \frac{Q^*}{2} > P(Q_1^*) + P'(Q_1^*) \cdot Q_1^*.$$

Equation (7.4) shows that this intuition holds beyond the comparison of $n = 1$ and $n = 2$.[3]

We can get a second implication about the number of jurisdictions by making a more specific assumption about the relationship between the amount of logging and the price of timber. That implication will be quantitative, in contrast to the qualitative monotonicity implication already discussed.

Assume the following functional form, which is common in empirical economics:

$$P(Q) = \frac{1}{Q^\lambda}. \tag{7.5}$$

3. Readers who are still thinking about our claim from Section 4.4 that one value of thinking about mechanisms is reasoning by analogy should note that this result can be thought of in terms of externalities and, indeed, this model exhibits a "law of $\frac{1}{N}$," though here it is a law of $\frac{1}{n}$.

Note that with this specific functional form, P is still decreasing in Q. And the first-order condition in Equation (7.4) still characterizes the maximum so long as $0 < \lambda < 1$. This functional form is more restrictive than needed to derive the monotonicity implication. However, there is some flexibility left through the parameter λ. This parameter is an *elasticity*: if we increase logging by x percent, we decrease the price of timber by λx percent.

Let's use the specific functional form to get an expression relating the effect on logging of increasing the number of jurisdictions to two parameters: the baseline number of jurisdictions (n) and the elasticity (λ). Substituting in the functional form lets us rewrite Equation (7.4) as follows:

$$-\left(\frac{1}{Q^*(n)^\lambda}\right)\frac{\lambda}{n} + \frac{1}{Q^*(n)^\lambda} = K. \tag{7.6}$$

Rearranging Equation (7.6), taking logs, and differentiating yields

$$\frac{d}{dn}\log Q^*(n) = \frac{1}{n^2 - n\lambda}. \tag{7.7}$$

Call this the *elasticity-formula implication.*

Before turning to a research design, it is worth reflecting on a difference between the monotonicity and elasticity-formula implications. The monotonicity implication is a standard, qualitative comparative static of the sort we are accustomed to by now. Moreover, it is a robust implication of the market power mechanism. By contrast, the elasticity-formula implication is more quantitative or structural—it gives us a formula that, if the model is similar to the world, will be approximately satisfied when we substitute in separately estimable quantities. But the elasticity-formula implication also rests on a different construal of the functional form of P. That functional form—with its implication that the elasticity is constant in Q—is now being treated as a representational feature of the model.

Burgess et al. empirically assess both the monotonicity implication and the elasticity-formula implication using data from Indonesia. They argue that two institutional facts make their model a good representation of the timber industry in an Indonesian province.

First, in the post-Suharto period, Indonesia devolved significant administrative powers to district governments. Crucially, this involved the decentralization of both substantial authority over and royalty rights to natural resource extraction, making "the district forest office . . . the key gatekeeper for illegal logging" [p. 1717]. Thus a district forest office is similar to a bureaucrat in the model.

Second, raw logs cannot be exported from Indonesia. Instead, they must be transported, typically by river, to mills for processing. Since province boundaries tend to follow geographic features that constrain shipping of raw logs, each province is essentially a separate market. Thus a province's market for timber is similar to the entire model. Since there are many provinces, Burgess et al. get to observe multiple units, each hypothesized to be similar to the model.

Both of the theoretical implications concern what happens when the number of jurisdictions increases. To get at these implications, Burgess et al. use a difference-in-differences design that exploits a substantial fragmentation of districts that followed the decentralization of power. Between 2000 and 2008, the number of districts covering the key forest areas approximately doubled. The splitting of districts was staggered over time, and Burgess et al. argue that the timing was driven by ethnic divisions and the size of government, rather than anything to do with logging.

A concern when studying an illegal market is that official statistics are unlikely to be trustworthy. To improve measurement validity, Burgess et al. use satellite data to get a direct measure of the deforestation in each district— a count of pixels deforested in each year.

Burgess et al. first assesses the monotonicity implication. Consistent with this implication, their difference-in-differences analysis finds that increasing the number of jurisdictions within a province increases the amount of illegal logging. Specifically, adding one extra district to a province increases deforestation by 3.85%.

Market power is not the only mechanism that would yield the monotonicity implication. For example, suppose that a district is split into two. One of these successor districts will contain the old capital, and that successor district might have more efficient administration than the other. If the less efficient administration were unable to stop un-permitted logging, then the jurisdictional split would increase logging even without corruption. To rule out this alternative interpretation, Burgess et al. estimate their model allowing for different effects between old and new district capitals and find no difference. This is one of many analyses they do to build confidence in their research design.

Burgess et al. also assess the elasticity-formula implication. Notice that their estimate of the effect of increasing the number of jurisdictions on the amount of logging is commensurable with the derivative on the left-hand side of Equation (7.7). So, if they can separately estimate n and λ, Burgess et al. can substitute these into the right-hand side of Equation (7.7) to see whether their various estimates hold together quantitatively, as implied by the model.

Estimating n is straightforward: at the beginning of the sample period, there are 116 districts spread over 21 provinces. Thus the average province contains 5.5 districts.

To estimate λ, Burgess et al. use the fact that, in the model, changes in the number of districts lead to moves along the demand curve. That is, for any n, the equilibrium price, $P^*(n)$, is determined by the equilibrium quantity according to $P^*(n) = \frac{1}{Q^*(n)^\lambda}$. Taking logs on both sides and differentiating with respect to n yields

$$\lambda = -\frac{\frac{d}{dn}\log P^*(n)}{\frac{d}{dn}\log Q^*(n)}.$$

The denominator again corresponds to the estimate of the effect of the number of jurisdictions on the amount of logging from the original difference-in-differences. And another difference-in-differences allows them to estimate the effect of the number of jurisdictions on price, which corresponds to the numerator.[4]

Using these two estimates, Burgess et al. calculate $\frac{1}{n^2-n\lambda}$ and find an answer strikingly similar to their direct estimate of the left-hand side. Specifically, their original difference-in-differences yielded an estimate of 0.038, while their calculation of $\frac{1}{n^2-n\lambda}$ yields an estimate of 0.034.

Finding support for the elasticity-formula implication is evidence that the market-power mechanism is at work in illegal logging in Indonesian timber markets. But rather than simply asserting a qualitative similarity, the elasticity-formula implication says that, for one specific way of fleshing out the model, the model's quantitative implications agree with the actual quantities found in the empirical exercise. This test suggests support for a more fine-grained kind of similarity than does the test of the monotonicity implication. Even if quantities of logging increase in the number of bureaucrats, it would still be possible that no plausible choice of functional form for P would lead to a formula that matched the world so closely. But finding support for the elasticity-formula implication shows that, for a sensible instantiation of the

---

4. The price data come from the official statistics. Unlike the quantity data, official price data are probably reliable, since legal and illegal timber are close substitutes for buyers.

model, all of the quantitative estimates fit together in a way that is consistent with the model.

The flip side of this stronger similarity claim is that, had the results gone the other way, we would have had a weaker conclusion. That is because a failure of the elasticity-formula implication would be evidence against the similarity of the version of the model filled in with the specific functional form for demand. Even if that version of the model is not similar to the target, the market-power mechanisms might still be at work. Thus, the strength of this sort of test depends on whether you have good reasons, based on substantive knowledge or other information, to believe that your particular functional form assumption is a good one.

7.7   Gleanings

The examples we've discussed illustrate a variety of different ways to elaborate the implications of a model. Each approach is productive both for assessing similarity and for guarding against false positives.

Benmelech, Berrebi, and Klor; Morris; and Gordon each do the most straightforward form of elaboration—assessing multiple implications of the same model. Benmelech and Berrebi do something similar, but instead of assessing implications derived from the model, they assess the assumptions of the model.

Sometimes elaboration involves implications that go beyond just the sign of some relationship. For instance, theory may have implications about moderators, which can be assessed by looking for heterogeneous treatment effects, as in McGrath's and Fowler and Montagnes's papers. Or theory may imply something more structural, as in Burgess et al.'s derivation of a formula that describes a quantitative relationship that should hold between quantities they have estimated, along with an evaluation of whether that relationship does hold.

A third form of elaboration uses a variety of different research designs to assess a theoretical implication. This strengthens our confidence about the plausibility of the assumptions required to identify a commensurable estimand. This is one of the approaches Snyder and Strömberg take to elaborating when they are using variation in media congruence that comes both from within-district variation and from redistricting to identify the effects of voter information.

Snyder and Strömberg's work also illustrates yet a fourth kind of elaboration, namely, relating an implication to empirical findings based on multiple different measures. For instance, they note that the model object "governance outcomes" might be similar to a variety of measurable behaviors or outcomes in the world. Hence, they elaborate by empirically assessing a series of relationships—better voter information leads to more district spending, less party line voting, and more legislative effort—each of which should hold if the mechanisms embodied in the electoral agency model are at work.

Fowler and Montagnes elaborate in one final way. Using the logic of extrapolation, they argue that if the voter mood mechanism is at work for college football games, it should also be at work for NFL games, since the two targets are similar. Thus, finding that there is no relationship between NFL losses and incumbent electoral fortunes should change our beliefs about whether we think the estimated relationship between college football losses and incumbent electoral fortunes is the result of the voter mood mechanism being at work versus a false positive.

These approaches surely do not exhaust the possibilities of how one might elaborate. But they illustrate the broad point that it is important to take as many approaches as possible to deriving and assessing the implications of a model.

8

Distinguishing

The previous chapter discussed one way to shore up inference about a mechanism—identifying as many implications as possible and assessing them in as many ways as possible. But it is more than just the number of implications and assessments that matters. Suppose two models, each embodying different mechanisms, each generates the same implications. Then the elaboration cannot adjudicate among the mechanisms. Assessing common implications only helps assess whether at least one of the mechanisms is at work. Any stronger claim is open to immediate reinterpretation.

How can we better assess whether a particular mechanism is at work? We can identify and evaluate implications that are not common implications of the alternatives on offer. We call such an implication a *distinguishing implication*.

Many mechanisms are at work in most real-world targets. So it's important not to overinterpret a claim about distinguishing. Distinguishing is rarely about arguing for one mechanism and against others. Rather, it is about increasing how much we know about whether a particular mechanism is at work. In some circumstances, good news for one mechanism may indeed be bad news for another. But distinguishing is essentially about the question: "How convincing is the case that this mechanism plays a role in explaining what's going on in the target?" This is an importantly different question from: "Which mechanism explains what's going on in the target?"

To get a feel for how distinguishing works, let's return once again to Dell's (2015) work on the Mexican drug war. She shows an association between PAN election victories and increases in drug-related violence. Her interpretation points to increased crackdowns by the PAN. These crackdowns weakened incumbent drug traffickers, creating opportunities for other organizations to try to wrest control of territory through violence. But other mechanisms might be at work as well. To take just one example, the mere fact of a change in political power might lead to violence. Recall that the PAN was mostly the challenger party. So PAN victories are associated with the instability that accompanies a change in political control. As an alternative mechanism, this could be the explanation for increased violence in places where the PAN won the mayoral election.

Dell identifies an implication of her interpretation that distinguishes it from this alternative. On her account, violence should increase more when there is a crackdown than when there is not. Only the PAN implemented a crackdown policy. Thus we should expect an increase in violence when a PAN challenger wins a close election over a non-PAN incumbent, but not when a non-PAN challenger wins a close election over a PAN incumbent. The alternative account implies an increase in both cases because both cases result in a change in political control. Dell compares the change in violence following turnovers in which PAN mayors displace incumbents of other parties to those in which PAN incumbents themselves are displaced. She finds that violence increases when the party in control switches to the PAN but not when it switches away from the PAN. This bolsters her claim that the crackdown mechanism is at work.

In this chapter, we discuss several papers that distinguish between alternative models. As was the case for elaborating, distinguishing can take many forms. After describing the papers, we discuss some strategies that are specific to distinguishing over and above elaborating.

8.1 Accountability and Term Limits

The family of accountability models introduced in Chapter 7 represents two mechanisms: electoral incentives and electoral selection. An incumbent who will stand for reelection shapes her actions with an eye toward convincing the voter she is a good type. And candidates who have won past elections differ systematically from those who have not had to face a process that selectively filters out lower types.

The electoral incentives mechanism is intimately related to classical questions about accountability from democratic theory. As such, distinguishing the electoral incentives mechanism from the electoral selection mechanism has become particularly salient in the literature.

To distinguish the electoral incentives mechanism, we need a way to compare politicians with different electoral incentives. A first thought is that term limits provide that comparison. Incumbents who are term limited cannot stand for reelection and so have weaker electoral incentives than incumbents who are not term limited and can stand for reelection.

Unfortunately, most comparisons of term-limited and non-term-limited incumbents fail to hold all else equal. Imagine comparing senators, who are never term limited, to governors in a state that has gubernatorial term limits. Too much differs between the two offices for a reasonable interlocutor to accept that all else has been held equal. Similarly, comparing incumbent legislators in states with and without legislative term limits would not provide a credible estimate of electoral incentive effects. Too much else differs across states.

The obvious solution is to compare term-limited and non-term-limited incumbents in the same political office, in the same political system. For example, a scholar could study a legislature with term limits, and compare members for whom the limit did and did not bind. This comparison does hold equal significantly more than the governor–senator or cross-state comparisons. But it does not hold electoral selection equal. To see the problem, imagine a simple setting in which no one can serve more than two terms. Electoral incentives imply that first-term incumbents should behave differently than second-term incumbents. But electoral selection implies that second-term incumbents are, on average, better than first-term incumbents. So differences in performance between term-limited and non-term-limited incumbents are a common implication of both mechanisms.

There are ways forward here. The two papers we discuss next try, in different ways, to combine term limits with a research design that also holds equal electoral selection.

8.1.1 Mayors in Brazil

Ferraz and Finan (2011) study the electoral incentives mechanism in the context of Brazilian mayors. For measurement, they exploit an anticorruption policy implemented in 2003. Starting that summer, the central government used lotteries to select municipalities for audits. These lotteries were staggered, with fifty or sixty municipalities audited in most months. All of these audits covered the period from 2001 to 2003. The program was unanticipated, so the actions taken prior to the announcement of the audits were unlikely to be affected by the possibility of random audits.

Ferraz and Finan use the corruption uncovered by these audits as a measure of whether incumbent politicians take costly actions that benefit voters. They compare the corruption of first-term mayors (who were eligible for reelection) to that of second-term mayors (who were not eligible for reelection). All else equal, the incentives created by electoral accountability imply that first-term mayors should engage in less corruption.

The model that Ferraz and Finan have in mind to motivate their study is as follows. Suppose there are corruptible and incorruptible types. The corruptible types make up a share $\lambda \in (0, 1)$ of politicians, while the incorruptible types make up a $1 - \lambda$ share. In each period, corruptible types choose to engage in an amount $a \in [0, 1]$ of corruption, while incorruptible types do not engage in corruption. The voter observes a noisy signal of corruption.

Suppose the equilibrium level of corruption by corruptible types in their first term in office is $a^* \in (0, 1)$ and the equilibrium level of corruption by corruptible types in their second term is 1, reflecting the absence of electoral incentives in the second period. Moreover, electoral selection implies that the share of corruptible types among second-term incumbents is $\underline{\lambda} < \lambda$.

A comparison of corruption by second-term mayors to corruption by first-term mayors includes both electoral selection and electoral incentives. The expected level of corruption in the first period is λa^* and the expected amount of corruption in the second period is $\underline{\lambda}$. The electoral selection component is reflected in the fact that second-term mayors are less likely to be corruptible types ($\underline{\lambda} < \lambda$). The electoral incentives component is reflected in the fact that, conditional on being a corruptible type, second-term incumbents engage in more corruption than do first-term incumbents ($1 > a^*$).

Ferraz and Finan estimate that second-term incumbents divert between 2 and 3 percentage points more resources to corruption than do first-term incumbents.

As we've already noted, this difference does not isolate the effect of electoral incentives. If the electoral selection mechanism works as in the model, some of the difference reflects the fact that second-term incumbents are, on average, less corruptible than first-term incumbents. As such, this finding may be an underestimate of the true effect of electoral incentives.

But it is also possible that selection works in the opposite direction. For instance, corruptible incumbents might be more willing to engage in corrupt election practices, and that could lead to positive selection for corruption. So the simple comparison does not distinguish the mechanisms as clearly as we would like.

To address this worry, Ferraz and Finan compare second-term incumbents to just those first-term incumbents who will go on to win reelection. All of these incumbents, first- and second-termers alike, won reelection at the conclusion of their first term. As such, the distribution of types is likely more similar between the first- and second-term mayors in this restricted sample than in the simple comparison of all first- and second-term mayors.

To see this in the model, note that the share of corruptible types among first-term incumbents who win reelection is the same as among second-term incumbents, λ. But they differ in their effort due to differing electoral incentives. A comparison of the amount of corruption by second-term incumbents and first-term winners yields the quantity $\lambda(1 - a^*)$. This quantity reflects the effect of electoral incentives $(1 - a^*)$ weighted by the share of corruptible types among those who win reelection (λ).

The empirical analysis finds that first-term incumbents who go on to win reelection behave 3–4 percentage points less corruptly than do second-term incumbents. This estimate is consistent with our argument, earlier, that the simple comparison of second- to first-term mayors underestimated the incentive effect. Moreover, it supports the distinguishing implication, bolstering the claim that electoral incentives are at work.

8.1.2   State Legislatures

Fouirnaies and Hall (2018) study electoral incentives in the context of US state legislatures. They collect data on bill sponsorship, roll-call voting, and committee assignments, covering legislatures in fourteen states that have legislative term limits. They use principal components analysis to construct a one-dimensional measure of legislative productivity out of these data.

Their main analysis regresses productivity on an indicator variable for being term limited, with individual legislator and chamber-by-year fixed effects. Intuitively, this research design compares, for members of a particular legislature, the change in productivity from year t to year $t + 1$ for those who are term limited in year $t + 1$ to the change for those who are not term limited.

A virtue of this difference-in-differences type design is that it controls for fixed legislator attributes that may be the target of electoral selection. For example, suppose that each legislator's competence stays the same over

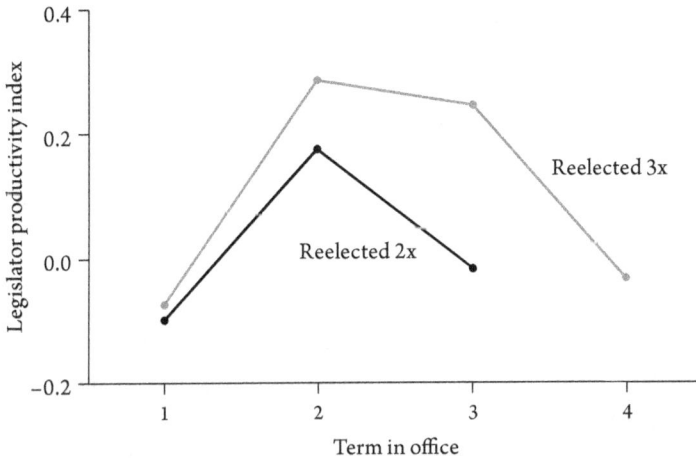

FIGURE 8.1. Term-limited legislators are less productive in their final term. Based on Fouirnaies and Hall (2018), Figure 1.

time. Electoral selection implies that the legislators who make it to their final allowed term have a better distribution of competences than do those who lose an election along the way. But, as long as an individual's competence isn't changing systematically over time, the fixed effects account for this difference, because the analysis is within-legislator. In other words, Fouirnaies and Hall are asking whether the same legislator behaves differently when she is able to run again or not.

Figure 8.1 illustrates the design. The gray curve represents the productivity over time for legislators who left office via term limits. The black curve represents the productivity over time for legislators who do not win reelection into the last term allowed by the term limit. Both graphs show a decline between the penultimate and final terms, but the decline is greater in the gray curve. Fouirnaies and Hall interpret this to mean that term limited, but not other, incumbents lose electoral incentives for effort.

Although the design controls for differences in incumbent characteristics that are fixed over time, we still might worry about Fouirnaies and Hall's comparison of term-limited incumbents to incumbents who have won fewer elections. Even without differences in legislator characteristics, this comparison may not hold all else equal.

One example, which Fouirnaies and Hall emphasize, is that there may be learning by doing in the legislature, and the magnitude of that learning may change over a career. It is plausible, for example, that legislators learn less between their third and fourth terms than between their first and second. If this is the case, then Fouirnaies and Hall's comparison overstates the effect of electoral incentives.

To partially address such concerns, Fouirnaies and Hall replicate their analysis with cohort-year fixed effects in place of chamber-year fixed effects. This means that they compare changes in productivity for legislators who have served the same number of terms, some who face binding term limits and others who do not. Although this analysis now makes comparisons between states, if state legislatures that differ in the number of terms they allow are otherwise comparable, then learning on the job should be similar for term-limited and non-term-limited incumbents. The results of this analysis are very similar to the primary specification.

Another concern is that the results might be explained by reversion to the mean in legislative performance. To examine this possibility, Fouirnaies and Hall elaborate two additional implications of the electoral incentives mechanism that are not subject to concerns about reversion to the mean. First, incentives should be stronger the higher is the salary of a member of the legislature. Second, incentives for term-limited legislators are not completely absent if they can run again after a term out of office. And, indeed, Fouirnaies and Hall find that states with higher legislative salaries or lifetime bans on returning to the legislature have larger declines in productivity for term-limited legislators. These patterns are implications of the electoral incentives mechanism, but do not seem to be implications of learning or of reversion to the mean, bolstering the case that the incentives mechanism is at work.

8.2 Party Effects in Congress

In Chapter 6, we left the debate over the role of parties versus ideology in determining legislative behavior at something of an impasse. Rohde (1991) argued that over-time increases in party-unity voting suggest parties matter. But Krehbiel showed that such increases are a common implication of two different mechanisms, one based on party influence and the other on ideological sorting.

Krehbiel (1993) also pointed out a distinguishing implication of the party influence mechanism. If there is party influence ($\beta > 0$ in the model from Chapter 6), then two congresspeople with the same ideal point, but belonging to different parties, will vote differently on some bills. By contrast, if there is no party influence, these two members will vote the same way on every bill. If there is overlap in the distribution of ideal points, so that there are congress-people with the same ideal points who belong to different parties, it is possible to empirically evaluate this distinguishing implication.

The ideological voting mechanism also has an implication that distinguishes it from the party influence mechanism. Ideological voting implies that two congresspeople in the same party, but who have different ideologies, will vote differently on some bills, even though both face the same party pressure.

Ansolabehere, Snyder, and Stewart (2001) set out to assess these distinguishing implications. A first challenge in doing so is measurement validity. The theory makes a distinction between the preferences of the members and the positions they take in response to party pressure. So it is crucial that the measure of ideological preferences not be tainted by party influence. That means measures based on roll-call votes (e.g., NOMINATE) are inappropriate. Instead, Ansolabehere, Snyder, and Stewart use data from a survey called the National Political Awareness Test (NPAT). The NPAT asked all congressional candidates in 1994, 1996, and 1998 a battery of questions on a wide range of topical political issues. Fifty-seven percent of all members of Congress completed the NPAT at least once.

Are the NPAT scores a good measure of ideology, in the sense of being similar to the ideal points in our model? In general, a member's vote depends on many factors—party pressure, the member's own personal beliefs, the policies desired by constituents, pressure from donors, and so on. In the model, the ideal point stands in for all of these, except for party pressure. From this perspective, it is okay that the responses to the NPAT are unlikely to be pure reflections of the respondent's personal beliefs. Indeed, we don't want them to be. Instead, measurement validity rests on two key claims. First, NPAT scores are less likely to be affected by party pressure than is roll-call voting. Second, since the NPAT responses were public, the respondents would reasonably want to shape their answers to please their voters, donors, and so on. As such it might be reasonable to treat the NPAT answers as similar to the ideal points in the model. But if the NPAT responses reflect party influence or do not reflect constituent or donor demands, but only the representative's personal ideology, then the analysis will not succeed in holding all else equal in the comparison of Democrats and Republicans.

Ansolabehere, Snyder, and Stewart distill the NPAT answers into a single ideological score for each candidate using a simple scaling technique. Comparing roll-call voting records to the NPAT-based ideological scores, they can assess the extent to which Republicans and Democrats with similar measured ideologies vote differently. This allows an assessment of the

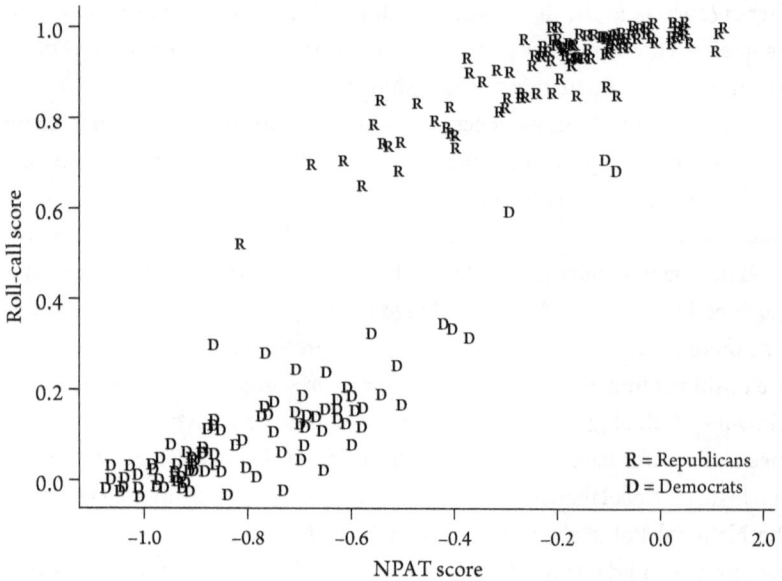

FIGURE 8.2. Replication of Ansolabehere, Snyder, and Stewart's (2001) Figure 2, show-ing the ideology and roll-call voting behavior of individual Democratic and Republican congressional representatives for the 105th Congress.

distinguishing implication of the party influence mechanism—represen-tatives of different parties, but with the same ideology, will sometimes vote differently.

Figure 8.2 shows Ansolabehere, Snyder, and Stewart's analysis in a nutshell. The horizontal axis represents the scaled NPAT ideology scores, while the vertical axis represents scaled roll-call voting scores. In other words, the hor-izontal axis represents the candidates' stated ideological positions, while the vertical axis represents how they actually voted in Congress. The "D"s and "R"s on the graph represent individual Democrats and Republicans.

There are Democrats and Republicans with similar ideological positions in the middle range of the horizontal axis. The gap between the Democrats and Republicans in this region reflects the difference in voting records between members of different parties, but similar scaled NPAT responses. To the extent that we believe the NPAT score is a reasonable measure of ideology in our model, the gap shows that ideological sorting cannot account for the data on its own—Democrats and Republicans with the same ideology vote differently on average. This agrees with the distinguishing implication of the party influence mechanism.

At the same time, the data show that voting records of members of each party are positively correlated with ideology. This evidence is consistent with the distinguishing implication of the ideological mechanism, although this is not the authors' main focus.

While it takes an important step forward in the literature, the Ansolabehere, Snyder, and Stewart study is not without its own limitations. Candidates may respond to voter influence differently on the NPAT and in actual roll-call voting. If candidates attempt to appear, say, moderate on the NPAT, but then vote their true ideology once in Congress, then the results of Figure 8.2 could arise without any party influence. On the other hand, suppose that candidates who are more moderate than the party overall attempt to appear to be in line with the party by giving NPAT answers that reflect the standard party platform even when they disagree with it. Then Figure 8.2 would underestimate the extent of party influence because party influence would already be at play in the NPAT scores themselves.

A second measurement concern is that the roll-call voting measure, NOM-INATE, may not capture the same issues that are covered in the NPAT survey. If the issues that received roll-call votes were more polarizing than the NPAT questions, then the differences evident in Figure 8.2 could simply reflect the differing nature of the issues considered rather than party influence. In principle, it should be possible to match NPAT questions to roll-call votes on the same issues, but to our knowledge this has not been done.

Measurement concerns aside, let's take stock of the progression from Rohde to Krehbiel to Ansolabehere, Snyder, and Stewart. Rohde claims that increased party-line voting indicates that party influence has increased in Congress over time. Krehbiel reinterprets, suggesting that evidence of increased party-line voting is consistent with a purely ideological mechanism and increased ideological sorting. But Krehbiel doesn't only reinterpret. He also suggests a distinguishing implication of the party influence mechanism. Evidence agreeing with that implication would constitute more compelling evidence of party effects. Ansolabehere, Snyder, and Stewart do not engage the question about change over time. Instead, they pick up Krehbiel's distinguishing challenge and attempt to provide evidence about party-line voting not confounded by ideology. By reducing the plausibility of the claim that the evidence can be entirely explained by ideological differences between Democrats and Republicans, Ansolabehere, Snyder, and Stewart make it harder for a reasonable interlocutor to claim that parties don't matter for roll-call voting in Congress.

But this is not the end of the story. Members of the same party do not all vote the same way on every roll call. We have identified several factors that could account for this heterogeneity—personal preferences, constituent or donor demands, and so on. Although this relationship is not Ansolabehere, Snyder, and Stewart's main focus, a future researcher with a compelling research design might be able to assess the importance of these more fine-grained mechanisms.

8.3   Social Pressure and Political Behavior

An important strand of literature on political behavior contrasts two different visions of what motivates people to act politically. To what extent are people motivated by their intrinsic individual interests or values and to what extent are they motivated by the desire to conform to extrinsic social norms? To start approaching this question, it is useful to be able to distinguish the two different theoretical mechanisms.

Empirically assessing the influence of these mechanisms on political behavior in a way that holds all else equal is challenging. Suppose individuals who vote express a higher sense of civic duty, for instance in a survey. It would not be obvious whether the relationship is causal or whether there are other factors—perhaps related to an individual's upbringing—that lead to both a sense of duty and a propensity to vote. Similarly, if people in the same social network were observed to vote for similar candidates, the similarity could be due to social pressure imposed by the network or it could be the result of homophily, the tendency for birds of a feather to flock together. Given these concerns about unobservable confounders, a just-controlling research design is unlikely to uncover credible evidence about the all-else-equal implications of the intrinsic or extrinsic mechanisms in question.

As such, experiments have come to play an important role in this literature. Here we discuss two contributions, both of which use experiments to assess distinguishing implications of the social pressure mechanism. One focuses on voter turnout and the other on racial solidarity in politics.

8.3.1   Social Pressure and Voting

The question of why people vote has received considerable attention from both theorists and empiricists (Feddersen, 2004; Blais, 2006). A leading explanation is that people vote, at least in part, out a sense of civic duty (see

Riker and Ordeshook, 1968, for an early formulation). Gerber, Green, and Larimer (2008) set out to distinguish two possible mechanisms that might underlie such a sense of duty. The first is intrinsic: the reward that the voter obtains from the act of voting, or the guilt she would feel from sitting at home on election day. The second is extrinsic: the reward that the voter obtains when others observe her voting, or the shame she would feel from others learning that she failed to perform her civic duty. A priori, it is plausible that both mechanisms are at work.

Gerber, Green, and Larimer conduct a large-scale experiment in which some participants received a treatment that is meant to activate the intrinsic sense of duty to vote, and other participants received one of several other treatments that primed both intrinsic and extrinsic considerations to varying degrees. The setting is in the weeks prior to the August 2006 statewide primary election in Michigan. The authors sent mailings to 80,000 households, divided into four treatment groups. (Another 100,000 households received no mailing and constituted an untreated group.) All of the treated households received postcards that reminded them of the date of the upcoming election. The first treatment group's postcards primed the intrinsic duty to vote with a reminder to "DO YOUR CIVIC DUTY AND VOTE" [capitalization in original]. The three remaining treatment groups received postcards that included that intrinsic duty prime along with an additional message meant to prime feelings of social pressure to vote, with each consecutive treatment meant to produce increasing degrees of social pressure. One group received a postcard noting that voting is a matter of public record and "YOU ARE BEING STUDIED"; another group received a postcard displaying the voting records of those within the household and reading "WHO VOTES IS PUBLIC INFORMATION"; and the final group received a mailing displaying both the household's turnout history and neighbors' turnout history, with the question "WHAT IF YOUR NEIGHBORS KNEW WHETHER YOU VOTED?" These last two treatments indicated that a follow-up mailing after the election would report to either the household or the neighborhood the subject's turnout in the upcoming election. Importantly, each of the three social pressure treatment groups also received the message to "DO YOUR CIVIC DUTY—VOTE!" So we can think of the social pressure mailings as priming the combined sense of intrinsic and extrinsic motivations.

How does Gerber, Green, and Larimer's experiment distinguish extrinsic from intrinsic motivations for voting? Comparing the first treatment group to the untreated group provides evidence about the combination of the

TABLE 8.1. Voting Rates Under Various Treatments from Gerber, Green, and Larimer's (2008) Experiment on Social Pressure and Voting

	Experimental Group				
	No Mailer	Civic Duty	Being Studied	Voting Public	Neighbors
Percent voting	29.7	31.5	32.2	34.5	37.8
Observations	191,243	38,218	38,204	38,218	38,201

reminder of the election and intrinsic motivations, since it only primes the sense of civic duty. The remaining three treatments prime various extrinsic considerations in addition to reminding voters about the election and priming intrinsic motivations. Thus, an increase in turnout for any of these three treatment groups—relative to the stand-alone civic duty treatment—is an implication of the extrinsic mechanism but not the intrinsic mechanism. In addition, because each of the three remaining treatments are meant to prime an increasingly strong sense of extrinsic motivation, an increase in turnout across the three remaining treatment groups is also an implication of the extrinsic mechanism but not the intrinsic mechanism. Thus, we can see Gerber, Green, and Larimer as assessing two distinguishing implications of the extrinsic mechanism.

Table 8.1 shows the turnout rates Gerber, Green, and Larimer report for each treatment group. In additional analyses not reproduced here, the authors show that all of the pairwise differences between groups are statistically significant. Each treated group turned out at a higher rate than the untreated. Individuals in the civic duty treatment were roughly 2 percentage points more likely to vote than those in the untreated group, and the treatment effects increased with the strength of the social pressure message for the three remaining groups. Of particular note, individuals in the fourth treatment group, who saw both their own and their neighbors' turnout history, had the highest turnout rate and were roughly 8 percentage points more likely to vote than those in the untreated group. This is a very large treatment effect in the context of the get-out-the-vote literature (see Gerber, Green, and Larimer, 2008, Table 4).

The results of the experiment provide support for two implications that distinguish the extrinsic mechanism from the intrinsic mechanism: turnout is higher for all of the social pressure treatment groups relative to the civic duty treatment group, and turnout rates increase with the intensity of the social pressure treatments. Taken together, these results provide support for the claim that the extrinsic mechanism is at work in explaining voter turnout.

8.3.2 *Social Pressure and Racial Solidarity*

Questions about the role of social norms are particularly important in the context of the political behavior of Black Americans. As White, Laird, and Allen (2014) argue, Black Americans' political behavior is highly uniform even though the considerable economic and religious heterogeneity in the Black community might suggest substantial divergence of individual policy interests. Is this because Black Americans, while primarily motivated by private interest, use group interest as an informative proxy for private interest (Dawson, 1995)? Or is it because social pressure and social norms, in addition to private interests, play a major role in shaping political behavior?

White, Laird, and Allen seek to distinguish the private interest mechanism and the social pressure mechanism in an experiment on college students who attend a historically Black college or university (HBCU). The particular behavior they study is political donations during the 2012 presidential election between Barack Obama and Mitt Romney.

They divide students into an untreated group and two treated groups. Each member of the untreated group is simply asked to choose a division of $100 into an amount to be donated to Obama and an amount to be donated to Romney. While no actual political donations get made, the study participants are not made aware of this until the end of the experiment.

Members of the first treated group are given this same task. But they are also told that the computer will randomly give them an incentive— identifying one of the candidates and offering them $1 in personal compensation for every $10 that they donate to that candidate. In actuality, the computer always identifies Romney as the incentivized candidate. The idea is to induce private incentives to support the candidate opposed by the social norms of the student's community at the HBCU. Unlike the political donations, subjects actually receive these personal incentive payments.

Members of the second treated group are given the same task and the same incentives as the members of the first treated group. But, in addition, they are told that their names and donations will be published in the campus newspaper. The idea here is to induce students to consider the possibility that they will face social sanctions for behaving against social norms.

TABLE 8.2. Donations to Obama Under Various Treatments from White, Laird, and Allen's (2014) Experiment

	Experimental Group		
	No Incentive	Incentive	Incentive and Newspaper
Average Obama donation	$90.22	$68.10	$85.98
Observations	48	50	50

How does this experiment distinguish the private interests from the social norms mechanism? An implication of the private interests mechanism is that, all else equal, a person with a private interest in donating to one candidate should be more inclined to donate to that candidate. The social norms mechanism has no such implication. So, the first treated group donating more to Romney and less to Obama than the untreated group is a distinguishing implication of the private interests mechanism. Similarly, an implication of the social norms mechanism is that, all else equal, a person whose actions will be made public should behave more in conformity with social norms than a person whose actions will remain private. The private interest mechanism has no such implication. So, the second treated group donating less to Romney and more to Obama than the first treated group is a distinguishing implication of the social norms mechanism.

White, Laird, and Allen's findings are reported in Table 8.2 (which is based on their Figure 3). The table shows the average donation to Obama for each of the three groups. (Students had to donate the full amount, so donations to Romney are the balance.) Students in the control group donated an average of about $90 to Obama. Students in the group that were incentivized to donate to Romney decreased their donations to Obama to about $68. This suggests the private interest mechanism is at work. Making donation behavior public increased donations to Obama back up to $86, almost the unincentivized level. This suggests the social norms mechanism is also at work.

8.4   Gleanings

Distinguishing requires elaborating. So all the approaches described in Chapter 7 are relevant here. This chapter illustrates some additional strategies that are particularly useful for distinguishing. All of them boil down to controlling away the effects of other mechanisms to isolate the mechanism in question. But there are some interesting nuances that are worth drawing attention to.

One approach is to construct comparison groups in a way that plausibly holds constant the effects of other mechanisms. To get a distinguishing implication of the party influence mechanism, Ansolabehere, Snyder, and Stewart compare voting records of representatives with the same ideology but different party affiliations. The studies by Ferraz and Finan and by Fouirnaies and Hall compare politicians with the same degree of electoral selection, but who face different electoral incentives.

An experimental setting opens up additional possibilities, since the researcher, at least in part, constructs the environment being studied. Gerber, Green, and Larimer's field experiment and White, Laird, and Allen's lab experiment both exploit this opportunity by designing experiments with multiple treatments. In each case, one treatment is designed to activate one mechanism, and the other treatment adds to the initial design a feature that activates the second mechanism. Comparing the two distinguishes the second mechanism from the first.

9

Disentangling

Credible estimates of all-else-equal relationships often represent the net effect of several mechanisms. This does not always provide enough information to answer important questions. We often want to know how each mechanism separately contributes to the overall effect. When that is so, we need to *disentangle*—breaking the estimated relationship down into its constituent parts.

For an example of why disentangling might be important, return to the debate about the role of Congressional parties we discussed in Chapters 6 and 8. Rohde (1991) suggested that parties exercised increasing influence over roll-call voting. Krehbiel (1993) countered that increased partisan sorting might instead explain increased party-unity voting. This dispute is normatively charged. Rohde's account raises concerns about a decline in democratic representation. Are members reducing the attention they pay to their constituents' preferences in order to do the party's bidding? Krehbiel's explanation does not suggest such a conclusion. How normatively troubling the over-time trends are depends, at least in part, on what caused them. How much of the increase in party-line voting is due to increased party discipline, and how much to increased ideological sorting? That question calls for disentangling quantitatively comparable estimates of the influence of these two mechanisms.

Disentangling involves distinguishing multiple mechanisms from one another. Assessing a distinguishing implication of a mechanism requires only one research design. But disentangling asks for more. We want to use implications of each mechanism to figure out how it is contributing to an empirical relationship. This requires multiple research designs, commensurable with multiple distinguishing implications.

To see the distinction, think back to the study by Ansolabehere, Snyder, and Stewart (2001) that we discussed in Chapter 8. They show evidence of party influence by comparing members from different parties with the same NPAT scores. Those members vote differently, which they would not do were voting purely ideological. So this analysis distinguishes the party discipline mechanism. But it cannot speak to the relative importance of party influence and representative ideology. That would require disentangling these mechanisms, something their approach was not designed to do.

At first glance, disentangling seems like it might require the tools of causal mediation analysis (Imai et al., 2011). That might be worrying, since the identification assumptions for such an analysis are so strong (Green, Ha, and Bullock, 2010). But, while causal mediation analysis is one useful tool for disentangling, it is not the only one. Indeed, our examples in this chapter all involve disentangling through methods other than causal mediation analysis, though mediators do sometimes play a role.

9.1 Accountability and Competence in Elections

As we discussed in Chapter 8, an extensive literature uses term limits as a device to home in on the electoral incentives mechanism. Across a pair of papers studying the effect of term limits on incentives, Besley and Case (1995, 2003) uncover a puzzle. In their first paper, Besley and Case find evidence of an effect of term limits on electoral incentives. In a difference-in-differences analysis using data from the American states between 1950 and 1986, they show that per capita spending and taxes were higher under term-limited governors than non-term-limited governors. In their 2003 follow-up paper, Besley and Case repeat the analysis on a sample that extends through the mid-1990s and find that the effect of term limits has gradually disappeared over time. They conclude that "it seems likely that some omitted variable is responsible for the change in behavior observed for governors working under a term limit. This is an area ripe for future research" (Besley and Case, 2003, p. 55).

Alt, Bueno de Mesquita, and Rose (2011) argue for a resolution of the puzzle that combines a version of the model of electoral accountability we discussed in Chapter 7 with some institutional knowledge about the nature of gubernatorial term limits in the United States. Recall that the accountability model suggests two ways in which elections affect the quality of governance—not only the incentive mechanism that is Besley and Case's focus, but also an electoral selection mechanism. The key institutional fact is a change over time in the number of terms allowed. In the early postwar years, the majority of term-limited governors served under so-called "no succession" laws, limiting them to a single term. By the mid-1980s, virtually every state with gubernatorial term limits had a two-term limit, with most of the changes coming in the late 1960s and later. Today, Virginia alone retains a one-term limit.

How does combining the two mechanisms with the institutional fact offer a potential resolution of the puzzle? Let's start by thinking about the identifying variation in Besley and Case's difference-in-differences studies. They regress their outcome variables against an indicator variable for whether the governor was term limited in a given year along with state and year fixed effects. So their estimates reflect how the outcome differed, on average, under a term-limited governor versus a non-term-limited governor within a state. To get a sense of what's going on, think about a state that switched from a one-term to a two-term limit (which is typical). In such a state, governors who aren't term limited are in their first term. Governors who are term limited are a mix of first-term governors (from before the policy change) and second-term governors (from after the policy change). So the difference-in-differences compares a weighted average of outcomes under first- and second-term governors who are term limited to the average outcome under first-term governors who are not term limited.[1]

In Besley and Case's first study, where the data go through only the mid-1980s, most term-limited governors are in their first term because states didn't change policy until late in the sample period. So that study is primarily comparing outcomes under first-term governors who are term limited (combined with a smattering of second-term governors who are term limited) to outcomes under first-term governors who are not term limited. These two groups of governors are differentiated by electoral incentives, but since both are in their first term, they are not differentiated by electoral selection. In Besley and Case's second study, which extends the data through the 1990s, many more term-limited governors are in their second term. So that study primarily compares outcomes under second-term governors who are term limited (along with some first-term governors who are term limited) to outcomes under first-term governors who are not term limited. Those governors are differentiated by both electoral incentives and electoral selection.

1. Things are actually somewhat more complicated than this because there are states that never switch, states that switch from no term limits to a two-term limit, and so on. But this discussion gives the general sense of what is going on.

This means that in their first study, Besley and Case's estimates primarily reflect electoral incentives. But in the second study, the estimates reflect two mechanisms pushing in opposite directions. Governors who are term limited have weaker incentives than governors who are not. This should make term-limited governors tend to perform worse. But governors who are term limited also happen to be in their second term and so have undergone electoral selection. This should make term-limited governors tend to perform better.

This situation is illustrated by the directed acyclic graph (DAG) in the top of Figure 9.1. Electoral incentives work through edge 2, while electoral selection works through edge 1, as a confounder. Moreover, those two mechanisms pull in opposite directions. So maybe the electoral incentive effect of term limits has not disappeared, but instead is being masked by electoral selection. To know if this is the case, we need to disentangle the two mechanisms, to see how much each is contributing to the estimated effect of term limits.

Alt, Bueno de Mesquita, and Rose disentangle by shutting down one mechanism at a time to see how the other operates. Their empirical strategy exploits variation in the length of gubernatorial term limits. To see the idea, suppose two otherwise identical states differ in how many terms a governor can serve. In state A governors can serve only one term, while in state B they can serve two terms. This sets up two different comparisons, one to identify each effect.

Compare first-term governors in each state. Each governor has been elected to office only once, so they have withstood the same level of electoral selection. However, the governor from state A cannot seek reelection, while the governor from state B can. Hence, the two governors differ in their electoral incentives, and comparing these two governors provides an estimate of the incentive effect, purged of electoral selection.

This comparison is illustrated in the bottom left DAG in Figure 9.1. The treatment of interest is whether or not a governor is term limited, since term limits affect incentives. The problem is that, when term limits apply at the second term, electoral selection says that politician quality is a confounder for identifying the incentive effect because higher quality politicians are more likely to make it to a second term. However, restricting attention to first-term governors, some of whom are term limited and some who are not, eliminates the confounding by eliminating the edge between term in office and term limits.

Next compare a first-term governor in state A to a second-term governor in state B. Both governors are term limited, so neither has electoral incentives.

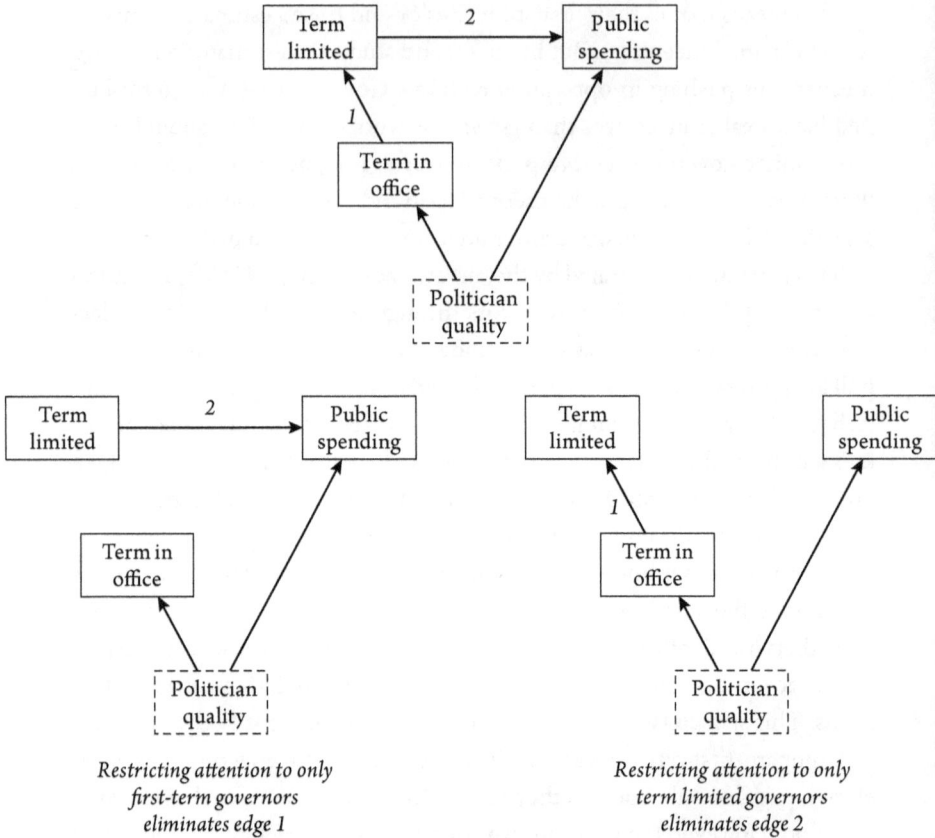

FIGURE 9.1. A DAG illustrating Alt, Bueno de Mesquita, and Rose's (2011) strategy for estimating the incentive effect by comparing first-term governors who are and are not term limited.

However, the second-term governor in state B has withstood a reelection challenge and thus has been subject to more electoral selection than the first-term governor in state A. Hence, comparing their performance provides an estimate of the electoral selection effect, purged of incentives.

This comparison is illustrated in the bottom right DAG of Figure 9.1. Here the idea is not to identify a treatment effect at all. Rather, the argument is that comparing governors who are all term limited breaks the causal link (running through the mediator of incentives) from term limits to performance. Hence, what is left is the bias due to electoral selection.

Alt, Bueno de Mesquita, and Rose make these comparisons within a difference-in-differences framework, while also controlling for a variety of time varying state characteristics. This means the variation exploited in estimation comes from states that change term limit laws. They drop the governor in office at the time the term limit law was changed, to avoid the risk that the change in the law was related to that specific governor. In addition to studying the outcomes Besley and Case studied (i.e., per capita spending and per capita taxes), they also study borrowing costs for the state government and state economic growth (relative to national economic growth).

For all outcomes, Alt, Bueno de Mesquita, and Rose find both an electoral incentive effect and an electoral selection effect. Recall, to estimate incentives, they compare first-term eligible to first-term ineligible governors. Reelection eligible first-term governors have spending that is 6.5% lower, taxes that are 4% lower, borrowing costs that are 14 basis points lower, and economic growth that is .8 percentage points higher than term-limited first-term governors. To estimate electoral selection, they compare first-term term-limited to second-term term-limited governors. They find that second-term term-limited governors have spending that is 5% lower, taxes that are 3% lower, borrowing costs that are 14.5 basis points lower, and economic growth that is .5 percentage points higher than term-limited first-term governors. These empirical results suggest that both incentives and selection play a role in determining governance outcomes.

This disentangling indeed resolves the puzzle posed by Besley and Case. The effects of the electoral incentives and electoral selection mechanisms are roughly equal in magnitude, but pull in opposite directions. So when term limits switched from one to two terms, what appeared to be a vanishing effect of electoral incentives was actually the negative incentive effect of term limits being offset by the positive selection effect associated with being in the second term.

It is worth nothing that while Alt, Bueno de Mesquita, and Rose have an argument for having disentangled the effects of differences in incentives and differences in selection, there may still be more disentangling to do. For instance, the comparison of first-term term-limited to second-term term-limited governors estimates a quality difference that might reflect both electoral selection and learning-by-doing that occurs during a term in office. To disentangle these two mechanisms, future researchers would need some new research design.

9.2 Economic Shocks and Violence

Let's now take a more detailed look at one of the examples we discussed in Chapter 1, about how economic factors affect the likelihood of violent conflict. Early empirical studies on the topic used a just-controlling design on a sample of country-years, regressing some measure of civil conflict (e.g., whether or not a civil war began, or the number of battle deaths) against a measure of the state of the economy (e.g., lagged GDP per capita, or unemployment), plus controls such as population, measures of rough terrain, whether the state was an oil exporter, measures of democracy, ethnic or religious fractionalization, natural resource endowments, and so on (see, for example, Fearon and Laitin, 2003; Collier and Hoeffler, 2004, and many others). These studies typically find a significant negative relationship between civil conflict and economic performance.

At least two issues complicate such studies. Most straightforwardly, the state of the economy cannot be treated as exogenous to civil conflict. This is especially true because of the clear reverse causality problem—the anticipation of civil conflict will affect the economy through (among many other pathways) investment and migration decisions.

Scholars have employed a variety of creative research designs in an attempt to more credibly estimate the all-else-equal relationship between economic factors and conflict. An early example was Miguel, Satyanath, and Sergenti's (2004) use of rainfall shocks in sub-Saharan Africa as an instrument for income. But probably the most prominent research design in this literature is a difference-in-differences design exploiting shocks to the value of a country's commodities.

Here's the basic idea. Start by measuring a fairly deep lag of each country's commodity exports. Take this bundle of commodities to represent the underlying natural commodity endowment of the country. For each commodity, calculate the world price each year. For most commodities, most countries are price takers. Hence, the interaction of the underlying commodity endowment of a country and the world prices of the commodities provides a year-to-year measure of exogenous economic shocks. This interaction can thus be used as a source of variation to credibly estimate the relationship of interest. Using this approach, Bazzi and Blattman (2014) find little evidence of a systematic relationship between economic shocks and civil conflict.

This takes us to the second complication, one that is particularly important for highly aggregated studies of the economy and civil conflict. Economic factors might affect conflict via many mechanisms (Fearon and Laitin, 2003; Humphreys, 2005; Bazzi and Blattman, 2014). So even a credibly identified all-else-equal relationship is difficult to definitively interpret. This is especially so since not all of the mechanisms linking economic factors to conflict pull in the same direction.

A model will help think through these complications. A mass of citizens, with size N, is deciding whether to join a rebel organization that is fighting for control of some territory or resource. To keep things simple, suppose that each citizen can create a fixed amount of violence, v. So if the proportion of citizens mobilizing is η, the amount of violence is $\eta \cdot N \cdot v$. Moreover, assume that the rebels win with probability η when η percent of citizens mobilize. This represents the idea that the more people who rise up against a government, the more likely that government is to fall.

The total spoils are B, evenly divided among the participants in the event of success. If individual i joins the rebels, her expected payoff is $p \cdot B_i$, where p is the probability the rebel group wins and B_i is her share of the spoils of victory. So if η percent of the people participate and the rebels win, each participant gets a benefit of $B_i = \frac{B}{\eta N}$.

If, instead, citizen i does not join the rebel group, she makes a payoff equal to her wage, w_i. The distribution of wages in the society is F.

B represents the economic and political returns from participating in a winning rebellion. So changes in B represent economic shocks that change the value of the economic spoils of conquest. And w_i represents a citizen's wages in the regular economy. Thus, changes to the distribution of the w_is represent economic shocks that affect wages.

Suppose citizen i believes a fraction η of other citizens will participate in the rebellion. Then citizen i's best response is to participate if

$$\eta \cdot \frac{B}{\eta N} > w_i,$$

or

$$w_i < \frac{B}{N}.$$

Because of the linearity assumptions in this simple model, a citizen's participation decision turns out to be independent of her belief about others' participation. This is because others' participation decisions enter both the probability of winning and the share of the rewards in ways that cancel with one another. (This is obviously not a robust feature of the model, but it is also not essential for the key results and is not meant to be representational.) Hence, the share of the population that participates in rebellion is the fraction of citizens with wage less than this participation threshold:

$$F\left(\frac{B}{N}\right).$$

The amount of violence is proportional to this quantity.

Two implications follow. First, suppose a shock increases the economic value of the prize, B. More people participate and there is more violence. Second, suppose a shock improves the distribution of wages, F, so that fewer people have wages below any fixed cutoff.[2] Then fewer people participate and there is less violence.

This model embodies two mechanisms by which economic shocks might affect violence. On the one hand, a weaker economy might diminish conflict by reducing the value of territorial conquest, weakening incentives for predation. On the other hand, a weaker economy might increase conflict by reducing wages, thereby reducing the opportunity costs of mobilization. So even a credible estimate of the all-else-equal relationship between the state of the economy and civil conflict might be estimating a mixture of these competing effects.

As Bazzi and Blattman point out, these mechanisms pull in opposite directions, so there are at least two ways one might interpret the null result. One possibility is that the putative mechanisms linking economic factors to civil conflict are unimportant. Maybe there really is nothing to see here. But another possibility is that multiple mechanisms are doing important work, with their offsetting effects resulting in a null net effect. To assess which of these accounts is more plausible, we need to disentangle the mechanisms.

Dal Bó and Dal Bó (2011) study a theoretical model that helps structure such a disentangling. They augment a canonical model of trade to include predatory conflict. The model differentiates between two different types of commodities: *labor intensive* and *capital intensive*. Negative shocks to the price of labor-intensive goods have a big effect on wages—that is, they are similar to a worsening of the distribution of wages, F. Consequently, such shocks primarily activate the opportunity costs mechanism and thus lead to an increase in conflict. Negative shocks to the price of capital-intensive goods have little effect on wages, but do affect the value of the prize over which people fight—that is, they are similar to a decrease in the value of the resource being fought over, B. Consequently, such shocks primarily activate the predation mechanism and thus decrease conflict.

Since shocks to labor- and capital-intensive goods primarily activate different mechanisms, they should affect conflict in opposite directions. This is an instance of the worry we noted earlier: if a country's economy is made up

---

2. Formally, consider an improvement in the sense of first-order stochastic dominance.

of a mix of capital- and labor-intensive goods, then finding that the average effect of a commodity price shock is zero might reflect these offsetting effects, rather than reflecting that the economy doesn't matter for conflict outcomes. But this way of stating the worry also suggests a path forward: disaggregate and look at labor-intensive and capital-intensive goods separately.

Dube and Vargas (2013) use this insight to take a step in the direction of disentangling, using data on the conflict in Colombia. They start by arguing that two of Colombia's primary exports—oil and coffee—fit Dal Bó and Dal Bó's distinction between capital- and labor-intensive goods, respectively. They then follow the approach described earlier for cross-country studies exploiting commodity price shocks, but at the subnational level. That is, they measure the coffee and oil intensivity of each municipality in Colombia. They interact these fixed municipal endowments with the world prices of coffee and oil. They also have municipality-level data on conflict events. They can now study the effect of commodity price shocks in a difference-in-differences framework. That is, they ask how changes to world coffee prices affect conflict outcomes in coffee-intensive municipalities relative to non-coffee-intensive municipalities, and likewise for oil. The argument is that the differential response of violence to coffee price shocks in coffee-intensive versus non-coffee-intensive municipalities provides an estimate that primarily (though perhaps not exclusively) reflects the opportunity costs mechanism. Similarly, the differential response of violence to oil price shocks in oil-intensive versus non-oil-intensive municipalities provides an estimate that primarily reflects the predation mechanism.

This idea is illustrated in Figure 9.2. The left-hand side of the figure illustrates the argument that coffee price shocks affect violence through the opportunity-cost mechanism (i.e., by changing wages) but not through the predation mechanism, while oil price shocks do the opposite.

The evidence supports both mechanisms. When world coffee prices rise, violent events decrease in coffee intensive municipalities relative to non-coffee-intensive municipalities. And when world oil prices rise, violent events increase in oil-intensive municipalities relative to non-oil-intensive municipalities.

Dube and Vargas also elaborate, looking for further ways to assess whether their research designs are in fact identifying the effects of the different economic mechanisms. For instance, they look at a key mediator, showing that shocks to coffee prices are associated with changes in wages in coffee intensive-municipalities relative to non-coffee-intensive municipalities, while

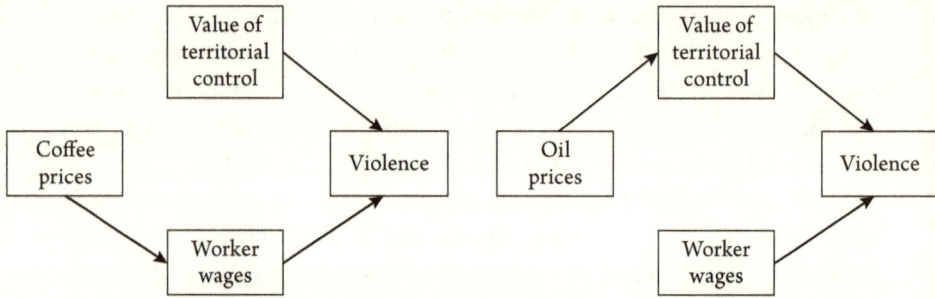

FIGURE 9.2. DAGs illustrating Dube and Vargas's (2013) strategy for disentangling the opportunity cost and predation mechanisms.

shocks to oil prices are not associated with changes in wages in oil intensive municipalities relative to non-oil intensive municipalities. Hence, the data from Colombia agree with Dal Bó and Dal Bó's underlying model of the economy, as well as with the interpretation that economic shocks matter for conflict. Moreover, the results reveal the off-setting effects of the two mechanisms, providing a possible explanation for why those effects can't be seen in regressions that pool together the effects of shocks to many different commodities.

It is worth noting that Dube and Vargas's strategy may not provide a complete disentangling. Figure 9.2 presents an idealized version of the world. But shocks to coffee prices, while working primarily through opportunity costs, may have at least some effect on the value of predation. And shocks to oil prices, while working primarily through predation, may have at least some effect on opportunity costs. So, while these research designs are informative about the competing effects, we can't, in any simple way, compare the magnitudes of the estimates they provide to ask whether the two mechanisms are exactly offsetting.

A possible concern about Dube and Vargas's study as a general explanation of Bazzi and Blattman's null result is that its geographic scope is limited to Colombia. So it is important to note that a subsequent literature has combined Dube and Vargas's empirical strategies for disentangling with newly available data. These studies expand the geographic scope, without giving up commensurability with the distinct implications of the opportunity-cost and predation mechanisms. For instance, Berman et al. (2017) combine fine-grained data at the 50 km by 50 km grid-cell level on violence and mining intensity for fourteen different minerals across all of Africa with data on mineral price shocks to show evidence consistent with the predation mechanism. And Berman and Couttenier (2015), again at the grid-cell level, use measures of agricultural production to show that commodity price shocks lead to increased conflict in sub-Saharan Africa in ways consistent with the opportunity-cost mechanism. So this literature also illustrates how well-identified studies, combined with both theory and the availability of new data, can help spur the ideas and machinery needed to broaden the settings to which accumulated knowledge can be applied.

9.3   Sources of Incumbent Success

In an agenda-setting paper, Erikson (1971) pointed out that incumbents win reelection at strikingly high rates. This observation raised a normative concern: Do high reelection rates indicate that incumbents use the perquisites of office—for example, greater access to campaign resources, gerrymandering, or public attention—to insulate themselves from electoral threat? If so, elections may be ineffective at generating good governance outcomes. Cox and Katz (2002, p. 7) nicely summarize the worry:

> Whenever the resources of public office are used to insulate individual politicians from electoral risk, their accountability to their constituents is weakened. . . . Thus, insulation from electoral risk of the kind suspected would, at a single stroke, debilitate the two fundamental accountability relationships of a democratic system of government.

This normative concern has attracted the attention of journalists, pundits, and activists, and has sparked an enormous empirical literature attempting to estimate the so-called incumbency advantage.

The literature on the incumbency advantage discusses several mechanisms that might underlie incumbent success. First, districts have partisan leanings and incumbents are often from the party the district favors. This *party match* mechanism naturally gives rise to high reelection rates for incumbents (Gelman and King, 1990). Second, high incumbent reelection rates may reflect *electoral selection*. Incumbents become incumbents by appealing to voters. Thus, the average incumbent may have characteristics that appeal to voters more than those of the average challenger (Samuelson,

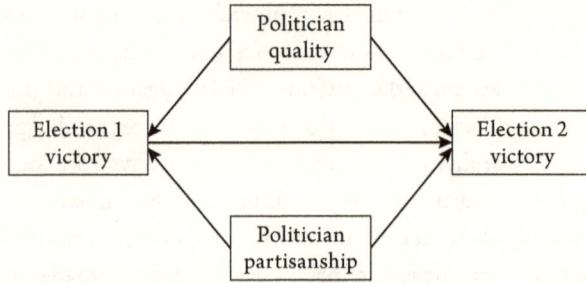

FIGURE 9.3. A DAG illustrating three sources of the incumbency electoral success.

1984; Zaller, 1998; Ashworth and Bueno de Mesquita, 2008). Third, incumbents may be *insulated* from electoral challenges through the perquisites of office.[3]

This insulation mechanism motivates the normative concerns we discussed earlier. The first two mechanisms do not have the same kind of normative implications—indeed, it might be normatively appealing if incumbents win reelection at high rates because voters tend to like them, whether because of partisan affinity or positively valued characteristics.

We illustrate the basic ideas in the theoretical literature with the DAG in Figure 9.3. The treatment is winning a first election (i.e,. becoming an incumbent) and the outcome is vote share in the next election. The direct effect runs through the insulation mechanism. The other two mechanisms appear as confounders. The partisanship of a politician affects both whether they win a first election and how they perform in the second election. This is the party match mechanism. Similarly, the quality of a politician affects whether they win a first election and how they perform in the second election. This is the electoral selection mechanism.

Fowler (2016) develops an empirical strategy to disentangle these sources of incumbent electoral success. Specifically, he estimates the extent to which incumbent electoral success can be attributed to three mutually exclusive factors: party match; candidate quality, which is defined as those fixed attributes of candidates that make them more appealing to voters than nonincumbents

---

3. The literature also highlights the possibility that incumbents scare off high-quality challengers (Cox and Katz, 1996). Such scare-off could arise as a consequence of any of the three mechanisms already discussed and so are not separately featured in our discussion.

of the same party (capturing electoral selection); and the electoral benefits obtained by holding office (capturing insulation).[4]

Fowler uses a multistep empirical analysis to disentangle these three components of the incumbency advantage. He starts by regressing Democratic vote share on an incumbency variable, coded to take the value of 1 if a Democratic incumbent seeks reelection, 0 if no incumbent runs, and -1 if a Republican incumbent seeks reelection. The regression also includes year fixed effects to account for national trends in partisanship. The estimated coefficient on the incumbency variable, β_1, is the average additional vote share that incumbents receive relative to nonincumbents from the same political party. This difference is an omnibus measure of incumbents' electoral advantage, capturing the sum all three factors just defined.

We have emphasized that disentangling requires multiple research designs. In this case, the three effects sum to β_1, by construction. Thus, Fowler needs two research designs above and beyond his estimate of β_1—having estimated any two of the component effects, the third can be deduced by subtracting the other two from β_1. Note that this last step in the decomposition is possible only because of the assumption that no other mechanism is at work. We return to this point.

Fowler's first research design augments the cross-sectional regression with state-by-decade fixed effects, to account for the district's normal vote. That is, the state-decade fixed effects capture the average performance of Democratic candidates in the state during a particular decade. This strategy removes the party match component of incumbent success and recovers a parameter, β_2, that is the sum of electoral selection and insulation.[5] Subtracting β_2 from β_1 thus reveals the size of the party match component.

Fowler's second research design uses a fuzzy regression discontinuity. This aims to estimate insulation alone, purged of electoral selection and party

4. Fowler refers to these three mechanisms as party match, characteristic selection, and officeholder benefits, respectively.

5. Gelman and King (1990) estimate the incumbency advantage purged of district partisan leanings by regressing candidate vote share on a dummy for incumbency and a measure of the normal vote—that is, the expected vote of a candidate's party in a district. This strategy estimates the extent to which an incumbent candidate from a given party in a given district performs better than would be expected for a candidate from the same party in an open-seat election in the same district. Such an estimate includes both the insulation and electoral selection mechanisms. Fowler's β_2 is roughly comparable to the estimate from Gelman and King's regression, though it makes use of fixed effects rather than a direct measure of the normal vote.

match. Following Lee (2008), he uses Democratic share of the two-party vote as the running variable. There is a discontinuity in the likelihood of having a Democratic incumbent at 50%. Fowler uses a close election outcome in the previous election as an instrument for incumbency in the next election. (The design is fuzzy because some incumbents do not run for reelection.)

Fowler's regression discontinuity delivers a coefficient, β_3, which is the difference in next-election Democratic vote share between races with barely elected Democratic incumbents and races with barely elected Republicans incumbents. Recall that the incumbency variable is 1 for Democratic incumbents and -1 for Republican incumbents, so the difference between Democratic and Republican incumbents is 2. Thus Fowler interprets the estimate as twice the insulation component of the incumbency advantage, purged of party match and electoral selection.

There is an important caveat to this RD analysis regarding commensurability. Continuity of potential outcomes at the election threshold implies that, in the limit, winners and losers of close elections do not differ systematically *from one another* in terms of individual quality or party match. However, for the RD approach to identify insulation purged of electoral selection and party match, it must be that winners of close elections do not differ systematically in terms of individual characteristics or party match *from those they could subsequently face as challengers.*[6] As we discuss in Chapter 10, this condition is not an implication of the standard continuity assumption for RD but requires additional assumptions. For now, we simply take such additional assumptions as granted, returning to them in the next chapter.

With the estimates of β_1, β_2, and β_3 in hand, Fowler can disentangle the incumbency advantage into its three components as follows:

$$\text{Party match} = \beta_1 - \beta_2$$

$$\text{Electoral selection} = \beta_2 - \beta_3 \qquad (9.1)$$

$$\text{Insulation} = \beta_3.$$

Fowler's estimates suggest that all three factors play an important role in explaining incumbent success in elections. His primary analysis is for US

---

6. There is a subtlety here—insulation includes scare-off effects. As such, it is important to distinguish between the pool of politicians who could run as challengers from those who actually choose to do so.

Senate elections between 1926 and 2010, though he also extends the analysis to other offices covering more than 90,000 elections. In the Senate, the total incumbency effect is estimated at 12.3 percentage points, of which party match accounts for 5.3 percentage points, electoral selection accounts for 3.3 percentage points, and insulation accounts for 3.7 percentage points. Looking beyond the Senate to seven different electoral settings, he finds that the share of incumbent success due to each component varies but that party match is typically the largest factor, with the lone exception of gubernatorial elections.

With this disentangling, Fowler can speak to the larger normative debate that motivates much of the literature. Notably, according to Fowler's analysis, insulation explains less than half of incumbent success, suggesting that the presence of an incumbency advantage is not as damning of the US political system as previously thought.

As we've discussed, the regression discontinuity design Fowler uses requires additional assumptions to purge electoral selection. If electoral selection is not purged from β_3, then not only is the estimate of insulation called into question, but so is the estimate of electoral selection, threatening the overall validity of the disentangling. Even if such concerns about β_3 are valid, however, Fowler has still disentangled the party match component, which he shows to be the most important factor in the overall incumbency advantage.

There is one more potential issue with Fowler's strategy for disentangling electoral selection and insulation. His approach assumes that those mechanisms operate in an additively separable way. But there could be an interaction between incumbent quality and the perquisites of office. To be concrete, let θ be a measure of the incumbent's quality, and suppose that the increase in vote share due to officeholder benefits is equal to $\gamma\theta$. Substantively, this would represent a situation in which higher quality incumbents can more effectively take advantage of the various perquisites of office.

If there is such an interaction, the average increase in vote share due to officeholder benefits in the population of incumbents is $\gamma\mathbb{E}(\theta \mid \text{incumbent})$. But this is not what the RD estimates. The RD analysis only includes incumbents who barely won office, a group likely to have a different distribution of quality than the full population of incumbents. Hence, the RD estimates a LATE, namely $\beta_3 = \gamma\mathbb{E}(\theta \mid \text{close election})$. Since electoral selection is estimated as the difference $\beta_2 - \beta_3$, the difference between the LATE and the population average of the officeholder benefit affects the estimate of the effect of both mechanisms. In particular, the estimate of electoral selection will also include the quantity $\gamma[\mathbb{E}(\theta \mid \text{incumbent}) - \mathbb{E}(\theta \mid \text{close election})]$.

This potential difference between the RD estimand and the average effect of insulation reflects a broader issue. The three analyses in Fowler's disentangling are based on coefficients identified off of different subpopulations of districts: β_1 is identified off of all races, β_2 is identified off of offices that changed hands within state-decades, and β_3 is identified off of races that follow close elections. Even if there are no interactions across the mechanisms, these different subpopulations may not be comparable. Fowler addresses this concern with an analysis that reweights the fixed-effect and RD portions, to correct for the differences in subpopulations. His results are not sensitive to this reweighting.

9.4   Gleanings

Disentangling makes sense when two things are true. First, you have good reason to believe that an existing estimate reflects the combined impact of multiple mechanisms. Second, understanding the relative contribution of those mechanisms is of interest. When both of these conditions are met, you face a challenge. Disentangling involves distinguishing multiple times. So it is feasible only when you have multiple research designs.

The papers we've discussed exemplify two different motivations for understanding the relative contribution of different mechanisms.

The studies by Alt, Bueno de Mesquita, and Rose and by Dube and Vargas both start with a surprising existing finding. While it was possible no mechanism of interest was at work, it was also possible that two mechanisms had offsetting effects. For Dube and Vargas, the puzzling fact was the absence of a relationship between commodity price shocks and conflict. This left open the possibility that economic factors were unimportant for conflict outcomes. By studying the effects of shocks to labor-intensive and capital-intensive commodities, Dube and Vargas showed that it is likely that those null results were a consequence of two substantively important but offsetting economic mechanisms—opportunity costs and predation. Both of these mechanisms are reflected in a measure of shocks to the aggregate value of a country's commodity bundle. Something similar is going on in Alt, Bueno de Mesquita, and Rose's effort to understand Besley and Case's surprising null result.

Fowler's motivation was normative. Some of the mechanisms that might lead incumbents to win at high rates are normatively troubling. Others are potentially desirable. Knowing how much of the incumbency advantage is due to each is thus important for our overall take on democratic performance.

These papers also differ in the extent to which they fully disentangle the mechanisms. Alt, Bueno de Mesquita, and Rose disentangle mechanisms using the same data that generated the aggregate findings. As such, it makes sense to add up their component estimates and compare them to the aggregate estimates. Fowler's estimates have an even more direct relationship with aggregate estimates, since replicating them is the first step in his disentangling. The situation for Dube and Vargas is different. The cross-country results they are responding to are about shocks to countries' aggregate commodity bundles. There is no reason to think that Dube and Vargas's estimates of the effect of coffee shocks and oil shocks on conflict in Colombia will add up to any quantity directly derived from the estimated effects of aggregate commodity shocks across countries. In this sense, they have not literally disentangled those prior results. Nonetheless, their exercise is in the spirit of disentangling. We can make better sense of the existing aggregate null findings once we see evidence that the opportunity cost and predation mechanisms, both of which can be activated by commodity shocks, pull in opposite directions.

Finally, it is worth noting an interesting feature that differentiates Fowler's analysis from the other two. Fowler estimates three quantities with three different research designs. But those research designs are not independent of one another. The research designs for party match and electoral selection both involve the quantity β_2, and the research designs for electoral selection and insulation both involve the quantity β_3. There is a trade-off here. By cleverly combining estimates, Fowler is able to maximally exploit the data to disentangle several mechanisms. But this comes with a risk. Any problem in estimating either one of β_2 or β_3 compromises the credibility of his method to disentangle two of the mechanisms of interest.

10

Modeling the Research Design

In Chapter 6 we discussed one way that we can use theory to offer a new understanding of an empirical result—reinterpreting by offering an alternative mechanism. In this chapter, we explore another approach. *Modeling the research design* involves representing a research design itself within a model that embodies the mechanisms in question. The goal is a better understanding of which theoretical implications are commensurable with the estimand of the research design.

In some sense, our approach to linking theory and empirics through all-else-equal claims suggests that much theorizing already implicitly involves a model of a research design. In particular, any comparative static can be thought of as a model of a just-controlling design with no omitted confounders. Modeling the research design becomes more interesting, and worth consideration as a distinct approach, when multiple mechanisms interact in potentially complicated ways or when a more complicated research design makes thinking about commensurability conceptually difficult.

In such circumstances, studying an analog of the research design within a theoretical model can be of help. This involves an additional step of theorizing beyond simply making a model of the phenomenon under study, but it is a step that can be particularly illuminating if the goal is to construct theoretical models with implications that speak very directly to empirical research. The key is to build a model that is both plausibly similar to the world and in which we can faithfully represent the research design.

10.1   Close Elections and the Incumbency Advantage

In Chapter 9, we discussed several mechanisms that help explain incumbent success in elections—party match, electoral selection, and insulation. We also discussed Fowler's (2016) empirical strategies for disentangling these mechanisms. A key step in the disentangling involved using a regression discontinuity design to separate the insulation mechanism from the electoral selection mechanism.

This election regression discontinuity approach was pioneered by Lee (2008), who studied the effect of incumbency status on Democratic vote share in US House elections. The running variable in such an analysis is the Democratic share of the two-party vote in the previous election. If it is just below 50%, the winner is a Republican. If it is just above 50%, the winner is a Democrat. So in the subsequent election, whether the incumbent is a Democrat or Republican depends on where the running variable lies relative to this 50% threshold. Such a regression discontinuity design returns an estimate of the difference in Democratic vote share in districts where the Democrat barely won versus barely lost the previous election. Under the assumption that potential Democratic vote shares are continuous in lagged Democratic vote share at the 50% threshold, such a difference cannot be the result of other systematic differences between the winners and losers of the preceding election.

A common claim is that the estimates from such a regression discontinuity design isolate the insulation mechanism. For example, Erikson and Titiunik (2015, p. 102), in their discussion of the personal incumbency advantage, interpret the estimand from an election regression discontinuity as

> the votes a candidate gains upon becoming an incumbent due to the direct and indirect benefits of office-holding.

Similarly, Fowler and Hall (2014, p. 507) characterize the personal incumbency advantage as the answer to the question

> Holding all factors fixed, including the underlying quality and talent of the candidate and the incumbency status of the party, how much better will she perform in an election as an incumbent compared to the counterfactual scenario where she is a non-incumbent?

In our terminology, these quotes suggest that finding a nonzero incumbency effect in a regression discontinuity is a distinguishing implication of the insulation mechanism relative to other mechanisms (say, party match or electoral selection). Or, more specifically, in a model embodying both the insulation mechanism and some other mechanism, the claim is that the election RD yields an estimate that is commensurable with the effect of insulation on reelection purged of all other effects.

While the claim that the regression discontinuity isolates (or, is commensurable with) the pure insulation mechanism is a common one, Eggers (2017) shows that assumptions above and beyond the usual RD assumption of continuity of potential outcomes are required to justify this interpretation. As we alluded to in Chapter 9, continuity of potential outcomes at the election threshold implies that, in the limit, winners and losers of close elections do not differ systematically from one another in terms of individual characteristics. For some quantities—for example, the effect of incumbency on the decision to run again—this is enough. But for commensurability with a pure insulation effect, we need more. The all-else-equal condition for commensurability with the pure insulation effect is that winners of close elections must not differ systematically (other than through their incumbency status) from the challengers they might face in subsequent elections.[1] If they do differ systematically, then the RD is not commensurable with pure insulation—a non-zero RD estimate reflects a combination of insulation and those other systematic differences. By modeling the research design, Eggers shows that, even in the RD sample, incumbents and challengers do indeed systematically differ, except under a knife-edge condition, so that the RD estimand does not isolate the insulation mechanism.

We illustrate Eggers's argument with a model inspired by his. There are many districts. Each district has two elections—first an open-seat election and second an election in which the incumbent from the first election runs against a new challenger. There is always a candidate from each party (L and R) in each election, and the incumbent always seeks reelection.

Each politician has a characteristic that some voters care about. To keep things as simple as possible, each politician is either high quality ($\overline{\theta}$) or low quality ($\underline{\theta}$). A politician is high quality with probability $p \in (0, 1)$, and qualities are independent across candidates. Candidates are randomly paired against each other in elections.

Voters observe candidates' quality perfectly. Each district has a unit mass of voters, divided into two kinds. To capture insulation, we assume there is a group of voters who always vote for the incumbent when one is available and otherwise vote for whichever candidate is of the higher quality. This group of

---

1. As we mentioned in Chapter 9, scare-off effects are part of the insulation mechanism. Scare-off plays no role in the discussion that follows.

R Candidate

	High	Low
High	$\frac{1}{2}, \frac{1}{2}$	$1, 0$
Low	$0, 1$	$\frac{1}{2}, \frac{1}{2}$

L Candidate (labels rows High and Low)

FIGURE 10.1. Vote shares in an open-seat election. In each cell, the first number is the vote share of the *L* candidate and the second number is the vote share of the *R* candidate.

R Candidate

	High	Low
High	p^2	$p(1-p)$
Low	$(1-p)p$	$(1-p)^2$

L Candidate (labels rows High and Low)

FIGURE 10.2. Electoral match frequencies in open-seat elections.

voters is of size λ. The remaining $1 - \lambda > 0$ voters vote for the higher quality candidate in all elections. When a voter is indifferent, she flips a coin.

The vote shares in an open-seat election in this model are in Figure 10.1. When both candidates are of the same quality, they win an equal number of votes; when the candidates are of different quality, the high-quality one gets the support of every voter.

A regression discontinuity design focuses on districts that had close open-seat elections and compares the vote share for one party in districts that just barely do and do not have incumbents from that party. Close elections are represented in the model by those situations where the voters split their votes evenly between the two candidates, that is, open-seat elections where the left- and right-party candidates were the same quality. These elections are the diagonal elements in Figure 10.1.

To start to see the problem that Eggers identifies, think about the distribution of high- and low-quality types among incumbents in districts that had a close open-seat election. The frequency of different open-seat match-ups is represented in Figure 10.2. There is a high-quality incumbent following a close open-seat election if and only if the open seat election matched two high-quality candidates against each other. And there is a low-quality incumbent following a close open-seat election if and only if the open seat election matched two low-quality candidates against each other. (It wouldn't have been a close election unless the two candidates were of the same quality.) So, the distribution of quality among incumbents in the RD sample is

$$\Pr(\overline{\theta} \mid \text{inc}, \text{RD}) = \frac{p^2}{p^2 + (1-p)^2}$$

$$\Pr(\underline{\theta} \mid \text{inc}, \text{RD}) = \frac{(1-p)^2}{p^2 + (1-p)^2}.$$

(10.1)

There is an important point to notice here. Conditional on there being a close open-seat election, it is true that the candidates *in that election* are not different from one another. But this is not the condition we need to isolate insulation. Rather, we need that the incumbents in the RD sample do not systematically differ from their challengers *in the next election*. And this, quite generally, is not the case.

The probability a challenger is high quality is just p. But in the RD sample, the probability an incumbent is high quality is determined by the number of close elections that involved two high-quality candidates compared to the number that involved two low-quality ones: $\Pr(\overline{\theta} \mid \text{inc}, \text{RD}) = \frac{p^2}{p^2+(1-p)^2}$. Comparing these, we find that incumbents in the RD sample are more likely to be high quality than are their challengers if $p > \frac{1}{2}$ and are less likely to be high quality than are their challengers if $p < \frac{1}{2}$. The RD sample of incumbents has the same distribution of quality as the pool of challengers if and only if $p = \frac{1}{2}$—that is, only under a knife-edge symmetry condition. Hence, for any $p \neq \frac{1}{2}$ the distribution of incumbent quality in the RD sample differs systematically from the distribution of challenger quality. The fact that each open-seat election in the RD sample is determined by a coin flip doesn't mean that restricting attention to close elections purges systematic differences between incumbents and future challengers.

What is going on? Voters flip coins only when the candidates have the same quality. If there are more high-quality than low-quality types in the population of candidates $(p > \frac{1}{2})$, then most of those coin-flip elections are between two high-quality candidates. As a result, the RD sample overrepresents high-quality candidates. If there are fewer high-quality than low-quality types in the population of candidates $(p < \frac{1}{2})$, then most of those coin-flip elections are between two low-quality ones. As a result, the RD sample overrepresents low-quality types. In either case, the regression discontinuity does not achieve what is needed to isolate insulation.[2]

2. Eggers shows that this result extends beyond the case of two quality types.

To see how this matters, it will be helpful to ask exactly what it would mean to isolate insulation. The ideal way to isolate insulation would be to experimentally randomize incumbency status. Under randomization, the distribution of abilities among incumbents is the same as the distribution of abilities among candidates in general (and therefore, among challengers).

What would the incumbent's expected vote share in the second election be in this ideal experiment? The incumbent would win the support of the λ voters who always support incumbents. And, since the abilities of incumbents and challengers would have the same distribution, on average the incumbent would win half the votes of the remaining $1 - \lambda$ voters who vote based on quality. As such, the incumbent's expected vote share under random assignment of incumbency is

$$\lambda + (1 - \lambda) \cdot \frac{1}{2}.$$

The expected vote share of any candidate in the open seat election is $\frac{1}{2}$. Call the extra votes a candidate expects to win by virtue of being an incumbent the *incumbency differential*. Under random assignment of incumbency, the incumbency differential is

$$\lambda + (1 - \lambda) \cdot \frac{1}{2} - \frac{1}{2} = \frac{\lambda}{2}. \tag{10.2}$$

So, if the regression discontinuity isolates the insulation effect, we should find that the incumbency differential is equal to $\frac{\lambda}{2}$ in our model with a first election rather than random assignment of incumbency. Let's see if it does.

Write $\mathbb{E}[\text{VS} \mid \theta, \text{inc}]$ for the expected vote share of an incumbent of type θ. The expected vote share of an incumbent in the RD sample is

$$\Pr(\overline{\theta} \mid \text{inc}, \text{RD}) \cdot \mathbb{E}[\text{VS} \mid \overline{\theta}, \text{inc}] + \Pr(\underline{\theta} \mid \text{inc}, \text{RD}) \cdot \mathbb{E}[\text{VS} \mid \underline{\theta}, \text{inc}]. \tag{10.3}$$

We calculated $\Pr(\overline{\theta} \mid \text{inc}, \text{RD})$ and $\Pr(\underline{\theta} \mid \text{inc}, \text{RD})$ in Equation (10.1). The other two terms are straightforward. Regardless of the incumbent's quality, the λ voters who value incumbency vote for her in the second election. If the incumbent is high quality, of the $1 - \lambda$ remaining voters, all vote for her in the event that the challenger is low quality and half vote for her in the event that the challenger is high quality. So the expected vote share of a high-quality incumbent is

$$\mathbb{E}[VS \mid \overline{\theta}, \text{inc}] = \lambda + (1 - \lambda) \left((1 - p) \cdot 1 + p \cdot \frac{1}{2} \right)$$

$$= \lambda + (1 - \lambda) \left(1 - \frac{p}{2} \right).$$

If the incumbent is low quality, of the $1 - \lambda$ remaining voters, half vote for her in the event that the challenger is low quality and none vote for her in the event that the challenger is high quality. So the expected vote share of a low-quality incumbent is

$$\mathbb{E}[VS \mid \underline{\theta}, \text{inc}] = \lambda + (1 - \lambda) \left((1 - p) \cdot \frac{1}{2} + p \cdot 0 \right)$$

$$= \lambda + (1 - \lambda) \frac{1 - p}{2}.$$

Substituting these into Equation (10.3), we find that the expected vote share of an incumbent in the RD sample is

$$\lambda + (1 - \lambda) \left(\frac{p^2}{p^2 + (1 - p)^2} \left(1 - \frac{p}{2} \right) + \frac{(1 - p)^2}{p^2 + (1 - p)^2} \left(\frac{1 - p}{2} \right) \right)$$

$$= \lambda + (1 - \lambda) \left(\frac{1 - 3p + 5p^2 - 2p^3}{2 - 4p + 4p^2} \right).$$

And since the expected vote share of any candidate in the open seat election is $\frac{1}{2}$, the incumbency differential in the RD sample is

$$\lambda + (1 - \lambda) \left(\frac{1 - 3p + 5p^2 - 2p^3}{2 - 4p + 4p^2} \right) - \frac{1}{2}. \tag{10.4}$$

Comparing Equations (10.2) and (10.4), it is clear that the regression discontinuity isolates the insulation mechanism only if the term $\frac{1 - 3p + 5p^2 - 2p^3}{2 - 4p + 4p^2}$ is equal to $\frac{1}{2}$. We plot the incumbency differential from the RD as a function of p in Figure 10.3. Not surprisingly, as we've already discussed, the RD incumbency differential equals $\frac{\lambda}{2}$ only if $p = \frac{1}{2}$. (Recall we assume there are at least some high- and low-quality types, so p is not equal to 0 or 1.) For any other distribution of high- and low-quality types, the RD returns an estimate made up of a combination of the insulation mechanism and systematic differences in quality between incumbents and future challengers.

How should we think about this kind of result? It tells us that the regression discontinuity isolates the insulation effect only under a strong symmetry

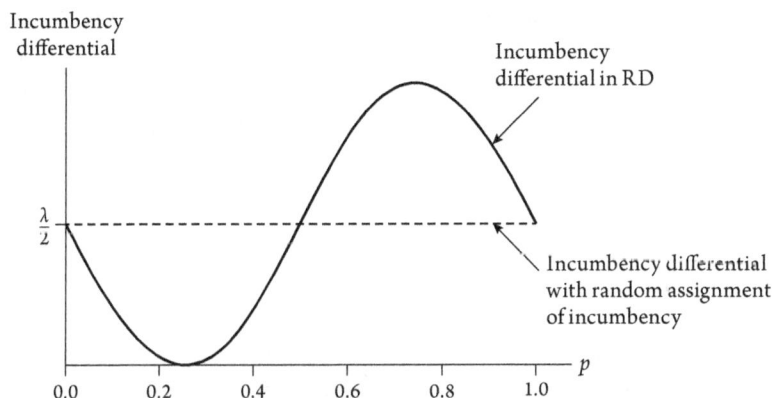

FIGURE 10.3. The RD isolates the insulation mechanism only if $p = \frac{1}{2}$.

assumption. So, if we make that symmetry assumption and it is representational, then a pertinent implication of our model is that the RD is commensurable with the pure insulation effect. But if we either don't make that symmetry assumption or don't believe it is representational, then we are not entitled to interpret the RD as isolating the insulation effect. One could also imagine separately assessing whether symmetry is representational. In this sense, Eggers's model of the research design offers some of the same benefits as a structural approach that provides "rigorous consideration of the theoretical assumptions which need actual empirical validation to deliver sensible parameter estimates" (Bombardini and Trebbi, 2020, p. 397).

10.2   The Efficacy of Protests

Scholars of political behavior and social movements want to understand how mass actions, such as protests or riots, affect policy decisions taken by the government. The literature posits a number of mechanisms by which such mobilization might yield a government response. For example, a protest may affect policy decisions by communicating information about the level of antiregime sentiment in the population (Lohmann, 1993, 1994), contributing to an extortionary strategy to extract concessions (Tilly, 2003), working as a tool of accountability to unseat an unpopular government (Fearon, 2011), attracting media attention (Wasow, 2020), or disrupting policy implementation. Mobilization might also spark a backlash, leading the government to increase repression or decrease its willingness to make concessions.

Empirical work on the relationship between mass mobilization and government actions thus addresses at least two possible questions. How does an increase in protest behavior affect government policy? And which mechanisms drive any such relationship? Answering either question credibly is difficult because mass mobilization results from choices that are likely to be endogenous to the government's behavior. For example, mobilization might not be worthwhile if the government already shares the policy goals of the mobilizable population, while mobilization might be a good tactic if the government is not already supportive of those goals.

A popular strategy to deal with these endogeneity problems uses weather shocks as a source of variation in mobilization in an IV analysis (e.g., Madestam et al., 2013; Ritter and Conrad, 2016; Wasow, 2020). There are concerns you might have about the validity of these instruments—for example, in some settings weather may directly affect the government's ability to respond. But let's put these concerns aside and grant that these studies have done a pretty good job of holding all-else-equal. (They certainly do a better job on this dimension than the prior literature.)

A commensurability question still looms: what exactly do we mean theoretically when we ask about the effect of the protesters' mobilization on the government's behavior? And how does this relate to the estimands of the empirical research designs?

This question is complicated because the treatment is itself a behavior, and people change their behavior for reasons. This is a particularly important point for informational mechanisms, in which the government's belief about the level of antiregime sentiment is a mediator for the effect of protest on policy choices. The informational content of a change in the citizens' behavior may well depend on the reasons for these changes.

Bueno de Mesquita and Tyson (2020) model the research design to clarify what we learn about the mechanisms underlying the efficacy of protest from such studies. To see the idea, consider a model of protest with two players: a government and a group of citizens. The group first decides whether to protest and then the government responds.

The group has one of two types, $\theta \in \{\underline{\theta}, \overline{\theta}\}$. Think of the group's type as representing its level of antigovernment sentiment. The prior probability that $\theta = \overline{\theta}$ is $p \in (0, 1)$. There is a cost to protesting, which can take one of two values: $\underline{c} < \overline{c}$, each of which is equally likely. High costs can be thought of as representing, for example, bad weather.

The group protests if and only if $\theta > c$. Assume $\overline{\theta} > \overline{c} > \underline{\theta} > \underline{c}$, so that a high type always protests and a low type protests if and only if the costs of protesting are low. This represents the idea that people who are more strongly antigovernment are willing to bear higher costs to protest that government.

The government observes protest behavior and forms a posterior belief, $\hat{p}$, about the probability that $\theta = \overline{\theta}$. The government's response is described by a function r that takes as an input whether or not there was a protest and the government's posterior belief. Let $\mathbb{I}$ be an indicator function that takes the value 1 if there was a protest and 0 if there was not. The government's response function is as follows:

$$r(\mathbb{I}, \hat{p}) = \begin{cases} \overline{\alpha} + \overline{\beta} \cdot (\hat{p})^{\gamma} & \text{if } \mathbb{I} = 1 \\ \underline{\alpha} + \underline{\beta} \cdot (\hat{p})^{\gamma} & \text{if } \mathbb{I} = 0, \end{cases}$$

with $\overline{\alpha} > \underline{\alpha} > 0$, $\overline{\beta} \geq \underline{\beta} > 0$, and $\gamma > 0$.

What does this response function represent? We can break it down into two components. Start by imagining moving from no protest $\mathbb{I} = 0$ to a protest $\mathbb{I} = 1$, but hold fixed the government's beliefs about antiregime sentiment at $\hat{p}$. The government's response changes by $\overline{\alpha} - \underline{\alpha} + (\overline{\beta} - \underline{\beta}) (\hat{p})^{\gamma}$. This is the government's *direct response* to protestors in the streets—for instance, holding fixed their beliefs about what citizens think, the government may be willing to make concessions or engage in repression to end a disruptive protest.

Second, imagine changing the government's beliefs about antiregime sentiment, say from $\hat{p}_0$ to $\hat{p}_1$, but without actually changing whether there was a protest. If we assume there is no protest, this will change the government's response by $\underline{\beta}(\hat{p}_1^{\gamma} - \hat{p}_0^{\gamma})$. And if we assume there is a protest it will change the government's response by $\overline{\beta}(\hat{p}_1^{\gamma} - \hat{p}_0^{\gamma})$. This is the government's *informational response*—for instance, the government's willingness to make concessions or engage in repression may depend on how disgruntled it believes its citizens are. The parameter γ allows flexibility in the shape of the informational response. (If $\gamma < 1$, the function is concave, if $\gamma = 1$ it is linear, and if $\gamma > 1$ it is convex.)

Finally, the comparison of $\overline{\beta}$ and $\underline{\beta}$ determines whether or not the direct and informational responses are additively separable. If $\overline{\beta} = \underline{\beta} \equiv \beta$, then the direct response is just $\overline{\alpha} - \underline{\alpha}$, which doesn't depend on the government's beliefs at all. And the informational response is $\beta(\hat{p}_1^{\gamma} - \hat{p}_0^{\gamma})$, regardless of whether or not there was a protest. By contrast, if $\overline{\beta} > \underline{\beta}$, then the direct and informational responses are not additively separable. The size of the direct response depends on the government's beliefs and the size of the informational response depends on whether there was a protest. The responses might not be additively separable because, for example, the government might be more willing to engage in repression to end a disruptive protest when it is particularly convinced citizens are highly disgruntled.

10.2.1   Representing the Ideal Experiment: Unobservable Costs

What does the literature have in mind when it asks about the efficacy of protesting? Presumably, it wants to know something like whether protests are an effective strategy for a group of citizens attempting to change government policy. In other words, are a group of aggrieved citizens more likely to achieve their goals if they protest than if they don't?

Bueno de Mesquita and Tyson argue that, inside the model, the ideal experiment for an empiricist trying to answer this question involves a shock to some feature of the world that influences citizens' protest behavior, but that is not observable by the government. Such unobservable shocks induce a change in the citizens' behavior whose reason is unknown by the government. As such, from the government's perspective, such a change in behavior might well result from a genuine shift in antigovernment sentiment. Hence, such unobservable shocks activate both the direct and informational mechanisms associated with protest in a way that gets at the effects that are of interest for substantive questions about the efficacy of protest.

To get at the key commensurability question, they first represent this ideal experiment in the model and derive the implications. They then represent actual research designs used in the literature and compare their implications to the implications of the ideal experiment.

To represent the ideal experiment, consider a situation in which c cannot be observed by the government but can be observed by the citizen group.

Let's start by calculating the government's posterior beliefs. Using Bayes' rule, if a protest occurs, the government has beliefs:

$$\Pr(\overline{\theta} \mid \text{protest}) = \frac{2p}{1+p}.$$

If a protest does not occur, the government is certain the group is a low type:

$$\Pr(\bar{\theta} \mid \text{no protest}) = 0.$$

What is the average effect on the government's response of a decrease in the cost of protesting?

If costs are low, then a protest occurs for sure and the government's response is $r\left(1, \frac{2p}{1+p}\right)$. If costs are high, then a protest occurs with probability p. If a protest occurs, the government's response is again $r\left(1, \frac{2p}{1+p}\right)$. But if a protest does not occur, the government's response is $r\left(0, 0\right)$. So the average effect of reducing costs is

$$r\left(1, \frac{2p}{1+p}\right) - \left[pr\left(1, \frac{2p}{1+p}\right) + (1-p)r\left(0,0\right)\right]$$

$$= (1-p)\left[\bar{\alpha} - \underline{\alpha} + \bar{\beta} \cdot \left(\frac{2p}{1+p}\right)^{\gamma}\right]. \tag{10.5}$$

Equation (10.5) represents the reduced-form causal relationship between the costs of protesting and the government's behavior. (This is analogous to the reduced form in our discussion of instrumental variables in Chapter 5.) Of course, lowering the cost does not always result in a change in protest behavior. With low costs there is always protest, whereas with high costs, there is protest with probability p. Consequently, a shock that lowers the costs has effect $1 - p$ on the probability of protest. Dividing the reduced-form relationship in Equation (10.5) by this first stage gives the local total average effect of increased protest on government response that results from lowering the cost of protest in a way that is unobservable to the government (this is the theoretical analog of the IV estimand). We label this τ_u:

$$\tau_u = \bar{\alpha} - \underline{\alpha} + \bar{\beta} \cdot \left(\frac{2p}{1+p}\right)^{\gamma}. \tag{10.6}$$

We can decompose this total effect into two substantive components: a direct effect and an informational effect. The direct effect of an increase in protest behavior is the effect of increasing protest behavior holding beliefs fixed (here we hold them fixed at $\frac{2p}{1+p}$):

$$\delta_u = \bar{\alpha} - \underline{\alpha} + \left(\bar{\beta} - \underline{\beta}\right) \cdot \left(\frac{2p}{1+p}\right)^{\gamma}. \tag{10.7}$$

The informational effect is the effect of changing the government's beliefs from what they would be if no protest occurs (0) to what they would be if a protest occurs $(\frac{2p}{1+p})$, holding protest behavior fixed (here, fixed at a protest not occurring):

$$\iota_u = \underline{\beta}\left(\frac{2p}{1+p}\right)^{\gamma}. \tag{10.8}$$

The total effect (τ_u) is equal to the sum of the direct effect (δ_u) and informational effect (ι_u). Notice, we could have defined the direct effect holding beliefs fixed instead at 0 and then redefined the information effect of a protest occurring. Nothing hinges on this choice.

Importantly, τ_u, δ_u, and ι_u do not necessarily represent quantities whose analogs are observable by an empirical researcher. Rather, these are representations of effects of theoretical interest in the ideal experiment, which an empirical researcher might never encounter. The key question is whether some actual research design generates estimates that are commensurable with any of these.

10.2.2   Representing an Actual Research Design: Observable Costs

A research design using weather as an instrument differs from the ideal experiment because weather is observable to the government. So the next step in modeling the research design is to study the effect of an observable shock to the cost of protesting. Then we assess commensurability by asking whether the theoretical quantity that represents the estimand of the actual research design corresponds to a theoretical quantity of interest from the ideal experiment.

So let's think about the same model, but now assume that the costs are observable to the government. Using Bayes' rule again, we now have to calculate the government's beliefs conditional on both whether or not a protest occurs and whether costs are high or low. If costs are low, both types protest, so the government learns nothing and its posterior equals its prior:

$$\Pr(\overline{\theta} \mid \text{protest}, \underline{c}) = p.$$

By contrast, if costs are high, one type protests and the other doesn't, so the government learns everything:

$$\Pr(\overline{\theta} \mid \text{protest}, \overline{c}) = 1.$$

$$\Pr(\overline{\theta} \mid \text{no protest}, \overline{c}) = 0.$$

What is the average effect on the government's response of the increased probability of protest associated with a decrease in the cost of protesting when costs are observable?

If costs are low, then a protest occurs for sure and the government's response is $r\left(1,p\right)$. If costs are high, then a protest occurs with probability p. If a protest occurs, the government's response is $r\left(1,1\right)$, but if a protest does not occur, the government's response is $r\left(0,0\right)$. So the average effect of reducing observable costs is

$$r\left(1,p\right) - \left[pr\left(1,1\right) + (1-p)r\left(0,0\right)\right] = (1-p)\left(\overline{\alpha} - \underline{\alpha}\right) + \overline{\beta}\left(p^{\gamma} - p\right).$$

Just as before, we divide this reduced form by the first stage $(1-p)$ to get the effect of the change in protest behavior due to a change in costs (τ_o):

$$\tau_o = \overline{\alpha} - \underline{\alpha} + \overline{\beta} \cdot \frac{p^{\gamma} - p}{1-p}.$$

If an empirical researcher uses a research design that corresponds to this nonideal experiment (i.e., one with observable cost shocks), then τ_o is commensurable with the resulting IV estimate.

10.2.3 Comparing the Actual Research Design and the Ideal Experiment

It is now straightforward to think about what we learn from weather shocks about the mechanisms underlying the efficacy of protest. An empirical researcher using a research design with observable cost shocks observes an estimate that is commensurable with τ_o. But the theoretical quantity most closely related to substantive questions about the overall efficacy of protest is τ_u. Also of interest are the theoretical quantities decomposing the two mechanisms, δ_u or ι_u. The question is whether the research design's estimand is commensurable with any of these. Since we know the research design's estimand is commensurable with τ_o, we can figure this out by asking whether τ_o is equal to any of the quantities of theoretical interest from the ideal experiment.

A first observation is that the total effect of the change in protest induced by a shock to costs is not the same when that shock is observable as when it is not. One can see this by checking whether $\tau_o = \tau_u$. They are equal if and only if

$$\left(\frac{2p}{1+p}\right)^{\gamma} = \frac{p^{\gamma} - p}{1-p},$$

which never holds. The left-hand side is greater than the right-hand side for any $p \in (0, 1)$ and $\gamma > 0$. This means that the research design using observable weather shocks is not commensurable with the total effect in the ideal experiment (i.e., an experiment with unobservable shocks).

Why do the actual research design and the ideal experiment yield different total effects for the same shock to costs? In both cases, the shock induces the same change in protest behavior—the probability of protest increases by $1 - p$. But there are different effects of that change on the government's beliefs in the actual research design and the ideal experiment. When costs are observable, the informational content of a protest depends on what the costs are—the government understands that a large protest means something different on a sunny day and on a rainy day. When costs are low, there is no informational content—holding a protest on a nice sunny day is too easy for the government to conclude anything about citizen attitudes. But when costs are high, there is considerable informational content because only deeply aggrieved citizens protest in the rain. By contrast, with unobservable shocks the government has to average across these possibilities, leading to different beliefs in the two scenarios.

We can see that the same change in average protest behavior has different effects on government behavior in the ideal experiment (represented in the model with unobservable shocks) and the actual research design (represented in the model with observable shocks). As a result, the model indicates that standard research designs are not commensurable with the total effect of protest in the ideal experiment.

A thought you might have is that, while the estimate generated by a research design with observable shocks does not correspond to the total effect of increased protest in the ideal experiment, maybe it corresponds to just the direct effect in the ideal experiment. The intuition is that when the government observes the cost shock, it knows those shocks are causing a change in protest behavior. Hence, it won't mistakenly think that increased protest size due to lower costs is the result of a genuine change in antigovernment sentiment. So, maybe, once it takes the shock into account, there is no informational content left in the change in protest behavior. If this is the case, perhaps the effect being estimated by a research design using observable shocks to protest costs captures the direct effect in the ideal experiment, purged of any informational effect. That is, maybe this research design distinguishes the direct mechanism from the informational mechanism.

We can explore this possibility in our model of the research design as well. Comparing the total effect in the model with observable shocks (representing the quantity estimated by the actual research design) to the direct effect in the model with unobservable shocks (i.e., the direct effect in the ideal experiment), and rearranging, we see that $\tau_o = \delta_u$ if and only if

$$\frac{(1+p)^\gamma(p^\gamma-p)}{(2p)^\gamma(1-p)} = \frac{\overline{\beta}-\underline{\beta}}{\overline{\beta}}.$$

The left-hand side of this condition is strictly decreasing in γ. The right-hand side is constant in γ. As such, for any $p \in (0,1)$, this condition holds for at most one value of γ, which is to say that the estimand of the actual research design is commensurable with the direct effect in the ideal experiment only in a knife-edge condition.

To start to get some intuition for what is going on, think about the case in which the direct and informational effects of protest on government behavior are additively separable (i.e., $\overline{\beta}=\underline{\beta}$). In this case, the right-hand side is zero and the unique γ for which the condition holds is $\gamma=1$. That is, if the direct and informational effects of protest on government behavior are additively separable, then the total effect in the actual research design equals the direct effect in the ideal experiment if and only if the government's behavior is linear in its beliefs. Why is this true?

Additive separability implies that the direct effect is the same regardless of beliefs. This means that the direct effect in the actual research design and the ideal experiment are the same, even though the government always has different beliefs in those two settings. As such, for the total effect in the actual research design to equal the direct effect in the ideal experiment, there must be no information effect in the actual research design. It might seem that this is impossible, since the government does learn from observing protest size. But, as must be the case for a Bayesian actor, on average the government's posterior beliefs equal its prior beliefs.[3] And so the information effect, which averages across the possible shocks, is zero if and only if beliefs enter linearly, so that the average is all that matters.

If there is not additive separability (i.e., $\overline{\beta} \neq \underline{\beta}$), then there is in fact heterogeneity in the direct effect itself, since it depends on the government's beliefs.

---

3. This is the Law of Iterated Expectations.

So now the direct effects in the actual research design and the ideal experiment are not equal. As such, for the total effect in the actual research design to equal the direct effect in the ideal experiment, it must be that the information effect in the actual research design is of precisely the right size and sign to exactly offset the difference between the direct effects in the actual research design and in the ideal experiment. This is obviously a knife-edge condition, reflected in the fact that it holds for one and only one value of γ.

The key idea in this example is that rainfall is observable to the government just as it is to the analyst (and the protestors). Even though weather may be random, the government will potentially respond differently to protests that occur in good and bad weather, since a protest on a sunny day conveys different information about antigovernment sentiment than a protest on a rainy day. The estimated effect of a protest on government policy always reflects both the direct effect of the protest and the indirect effect of the protest that operates through the government's beliefs. Estimates from research designs that exploit weather shocks capture the effect on the government's beliefs inclusive of the government's ability to adjust its interpretation of the protest in light of the weather. Such estimates differ from the theoretical ideal experiment, which exploits an unobservable shock, where the government can't reinterpret the meaning of the protest in light of the shock (since the government doesn't know the shock occurred).

10.3   Gleanings

As we said at the outset of this chapter, any comparative static can be thought of as a model of a just-controlling research design. The papers discussed in this chapter show how modeling the research design can become more interesting and productive when the research design in question is itself more complex. As Eggers shows, to understand which components of the incumbency advantage are and are not disentangled by a regression discontinuity design, it is not sufficient to simply study the incumbency advantage in a model of elections. One needs to directly analyze the incumbency advantage among those politicians in the model who become incumbents in a prior close election. Similarly, Bueno de Mesquita and Tyson show that there is not a univocal concept of the effect of increased protest activity. That effect depends on the source of variation in protest behavior and, as such, it is productive to model and compare the effects of different sources of variation.

The model of the research design in each of these papers sheds light on whether it is possible to disentangle or distinguish some particular mechanisms. And, in both cases, it turns out that the required commensurability is present only under knife-edge conditions. Eggers shows that a regression discontinuity analysis disentangles insulation and electoral selection only if the distribution of politician quality types is perfectly symmetric. Bueno de Mesquita and Tyson show that an observable shock isolates the direct effect of protests only if beliefs enter the government's response in just the right way.

Finally, Bueno de Mesquita and Tyson point out that when the treatment of interest is itself endogenous behavior, responses to that treatment may depend on the source of the variation in behavior. So different research designs, which exploit different sources of variation, estimate different treatment effects. This is particularly relevant for thinking about the interpretation of experimental findings where the source of variation is manipulation of behavior that subjects may perceive as endogenously determined.

11

Conclusion

Formal theory and the credibility revolution are natural partners that, together, can support a richer and more productive dialogue between theory and empirics than has ever before been possible. The first part of this book presented a framework for how this partnership works. The second part showed how that framework supports a variety of productive and interesting interactions between theory and empirics.

The practice of both theoretical and empirical political science will surely continue to advance in coming years. But we believe that our framework for linking theory and empirics, and the variety of interactions it supports, will continue to provide conceptual guidance, even as methods evolve.

Our ambition is for this book to be both useful and encouraging—especially to younger scholars. Anyone engaged in the hard work of research has had the experience of feeling stymied. It often seems that everything interesting has already been done or is unachievable. We hope that having a framework for thinking about the relationship between theory and empirics, and seeing the exciting opportunities it reveals, will give scholars the perspective and confidence needed to make their greatest contribution. There is always good work waiting to be done.

BIBLIOGRAPHY

Abadie, Alberto, Susan Athey, Guido W. Imbens, and Jeffrey M. Wooldridge. 2020. "Sampling-Based versus Design-Based Uncertainty in Regression Analysis." *Econometrica* 88(1):265–296.

Abney, F. Glenn, and Larry B. Hill. 1966. "Natural Disasters as a Political Variable: The Effect of a Hurricane on an Urban Election." *The American Political Science Review* 60(4): 974–981.

Acemoglu, Daron, Simon Johnson, and James A. Robinson. 2001. "The Colonial Origins of Comparative Development: An Empirical Investigation." *American Economic Review* 91(5):1369–1401.

Acemoglu, Daron, and James A. Robinson. 2001. "A Theory of Political Transitions." *American Economic Review* 91(4):938–963.

Acharya, Avidit, Matthew Blackwell, and Maya Sen. 2016. "The Political Legacy of American Slavery." *Journal of Politics* 78(3):621–641.

Achen, Christopher H. 1992. "Social Psychology, Demographic Variables, and Linear Regression: Breaking the Iron Triangle in Voting Research." *Political Behavior* 14(3):195–211.

Achen, Christopher H., and Larry M. Bartels. 2004. "Blind Retrospection: Electoral Responses to Drought, Flu, and Shark Attacks." http://web.international.ucla.edu/media/files/PERG.Achen.pdf. Unpublished paper.

Adcock, Robert, and David Collier. 2001. "Measurement Validity: A Shared Standard for Qualitative and Quantitative Research." *American Political Science Review* 95(3):529–546.

Alt, James E., Ethan Bueno de Mesquita, and Shanna Rose. 2011. "Disentangling Accountability and Competence in Elections: Evidence from US Term Limits." *Journal of Politics* 73(1):171–186.

Andrews, Isaiah, Matthew Gentzkow, and Jesse M. Shapiro. 2020. "Transparency in Structural Research." *Journal of Business & Economic Statistics* 38(4), 711–722.

Angrist, Joshua D., and Jörn-Steffen Pischke. 2008. *Mostly Harmless Econometrics: An Empiricist's Companion.* Princeton, NJ: Princeton University Press.

Angrist, Joshua D., and Jörn-Steffen Pischke. 2010. "The Credibility Revolution in Empirical Economics: How Better Research Design Is Taking the Con out of Econometrics." *Journal of Economic Perspectives* 24(2):3–30.

Ansolabehere, Stephen, James M Snyder, Jr., and Charles Stewart, III. 2001. "The Effects of Party and Preferences on Congressional Roll-Call Voting." *Legislative Studies Quarterly* 26(4):533–572.

Anzia, Sarah F., and Christopher R. Berry. 2011. "The Jackie (and Jill) Robinson Effect: Why Do Congresswomen Outperform Congressmen?" *American Journal of Political Science* 55(3):478–493.

Ashworth, Scott. 2005. "Reputational Dynamics and Political Careers." *Journal of Law, Economics and Organization* 21(2):441–466.

Ashworth, Scott. 2012. "Electoral Accountability: Recent Theoretical and Empirical Work." *Annual Review of Political Science* 15:183–201.

Ashworth, Scott, Christopher R. Berry, and Ethan Bueno de Mesquita. 2020. "Sources of Women's Underrepresentation in US Politics: A Model of Election Aversion and Voter Discrimination." Typescript.

Ashworth, Scott, and Ethan Bueno de Mesquita. 2006. "Monotone Comparative Statics for Models of Politics." *American Journal of Political Science* 50(1):214–231.

Ashworth, Scott, and Ethan Bueno de Mesquita. 2008. "Electoral Selection, Strategic Challenger Entry, and the Incumbency Advantage." *Journal of Politics* 70(4):1006–1025.

Ashworth, Scott, Ethan Bueno de Mesquita, and Amanda Friedenberg. 2018. "Learning about Voter Rationality." *American Journal of Political Science* 62(1):37–54.

Banks, Jeffrey S., and Rangarajan K. Sundaram. 1993. Moral Hazard and Adverse Selection in a Model of Repeated Elections. In *Political Economy: Institutions, Information, Competition, and Representation*, eds. William A. Barnett, Melvin J. Hinich, and Norman J. Schofield. New York: Cambridge University Press.

Banks, Jeffrey S., and Rangarajan K. Sundaram. 1998. "Optimal Retention in Agency Problems." *Journal of Economic Theory* 82:293–323.

Baqir, Reza. 2002. "Districting and Government Overspending." *Journal of Political Economy* 110(6):1318–1354.

Bartels, Larry M. 1993. "Messages Received: The Political Impact of Media Exposure." *American Political Science Review* 87(2):267–285.

Bartels, Larry M. 2002. "Beyond the Running Tally: Partisan Bias in Political Perceptions." *Political Behavior* 24(2):117–150.

Bates, Robert H. 1996. "Letter from the President: Area Studies and the Discipline." *APSA-CP: Newsletter of the APSA Organized Section on Comparative Politics* 7(1):1–2.

Bazzi, Samuel, and Christopher Blattman. 2014. "Economic Shocks and Conflict: Evidence from Commodity Prices." *American Economic Journal: Macroeconomics* 6(4): 1–38.

Bechtel, Michael M., and Jens Hainmueller. 2011. "How Lasting Is Voter Gratitude? An Analysis of the Short- and Long-Term Electoral Returns to Beneficial Policy." *American Journal of Political Science* 55(4):852–868.

Bendor, Jonathan, and Adam Meirowitz. 2004. "Spatial Models of Delegation." *American Political Science Review* 98(2):293–310.

Benmelech, Efraim, and Claude Berrebi. 2007. "Human Capital and the Productivity of Suicide Bombers." *Journal of Economic Perspectives* 21(3):223–238.

Benmelech, Efraim, Claude Berrebi, and Esteban F. Klor. 2012. "Economic Conditions and the Quality of Suicide Terrorism." *Journal of Politics* 74(1):113–128.

Berman, Nicolas, and Mathieu Couttenier. 2015. "External Shocks, Internal Shots: The Geography of Civil Conflicts." *Review of Economics and Statistics* 97(4):758–776.

Berman, Nicolas, Mathieu Couttenier, Dominic Rohner, and Mathias Thoenig. 2017. "This Mine Is Mine! How Minerals Fuel Conflicts in Africa." *American Economic Review* 107(6): 1564–1610.

Berrebi, Claude. 2007. "Evidence About the Link Between Education, Poverty and Terrorism Among Palestinians." *Peace Economics, Peace Science and Public Policy* 13(1):18–53.

Berry, Christopher R., and Anthony Fowler. 2016. "Cardinals or Clerics? Congressional Committees and the Distribution of Pork." *American Journal of Political Science* 60(3):692–708.

Berry, Christopher R., and Anthony Fowler. 2018. "Congressional Committees, Legislative Influence, and the Hegemony of Chairs." *Journal of Public Economics* 158:1–11.

Bertrand, Marianne, Esther Duflo, and Sendhil Mullainathan. 2004. "How Much Should We Trust Differences-in-Differences Estimates?" *Quarterly Journal of Economics* 119(1):249–275.

Besley, Timothy, and Anne Case. 1995. "Does Electoral Accountability Affect Economic Policy Choices? Evidence from Gubernatorial Term Limits." *Quarterly Journal of Economics* 110(3):769–798.

Besley, Timothy, and Anne Case. 2003. "Political Institutions and Policy Choices: Evidence from the United States." *Journal of Economic Literature* 41(1):7–73.

Binder, Sarah. 2019. "How We (Should) Study Congress and History." *Public Choice* 185:415–427.

Blair, Graeme, Jasper Cooper, Alexander Coppock, and Macartan Humphreys. 2019. "Declaring and Diagnosing Research Designs." *American Political Science Review* 113(3):838–859.

Blais, André. 2006. "What Affects Voter Turnout?" *Annual Review of Political Science* 9:111–125.

Blattman, Christopher. 2009. "From Violence to Voting: War and Political Participation in Uganda." *American Political Science Review* 103(2):231–247.

Bombardini, Matilde, and Francesco Trebbi. 2020. "Empirical Models of Lobbying." *Annual Review of Economics* 12(1):391–413.

Bordignon, Massimo, Tommaso Nannicini, and Guido Tabellini. 2016. "Moderating Political Extremism: Single Round versus Runoff Elections under Plurality Rule." *American Economic Review* 106(8):2349–2370.

Bueno de Mesquita, Ethan. 2005. "The Quality of Terror." *American Journal of Political Science* 49(3):515–530.

Bueno de Mesquita, Ethan, and Scott Tyson. 2020. "The Commensurability Problem: Conceptual Difficulties in Estimating the Effect of Behavior on Behavior." *American Political Science Review* 114(2):375–391.

Bullock, John G., Alan S. Gerber, Seth J. Hill, and Gregory A. Huber. 2015. "Partisan Bias in Factual Beliefs about Politics." *Quarterly Journal of Political Science* 10(4):519–578.

Burgess, Robin, Matthew Hansen, Benjamin A. Olken, Peter Potapov, and Stefanie Sieber. 2012. "The Political Economy of Deforestation in the Tropics." *Quarterly Journal of Economics* 127(4):1707–1754.

Burrell, Barbara C. 1994. *A Woman's Place Is in the House: Campaigning for Congress in the Feminist Era*. Ann Arbor: University of Michigan Press.

Callaway, Brantly, and Pedro HC Sant'Anna. 2020. "Difference-in-Differences with Multiple Time Periods." *Journal of Econometrics*, https://doi.org/10.1016/j.jeconom.2020.12.001.

Calvert, Randall L. 1985. "Robustness of the Multidimensional Voting Model: Candidate Motivations, Uncertainty, and Convergence." *American Journal of Political Science* 21(1):69–95.

Cameron, Charles, and Rebecca Morton. 2002. Formal Theory Meets Data. In *Political Science: The State of the Discipline, Vol. III*, eds. Ira Katznelson, and Helen Milner. New York: W. W. Norton, pp. 755–783.

Campbell, Angus, Philip E. Converse, Warren E. Miller, and Donald E. Stokes. 1960. *The American Voter*. New York: John Wiley & Sons.

Campbell, John Y., and N. Gregory Mankiw. 1990. "Permanent Income, Current Income, and Consumption." *Journal of Business & Economic Statistics* 8(3):265–279.

Canes-Wrone, Brandice, Michael C. Herron, and Kenneth W. Shotts. 2001. "Leadership and Pandering: A Theory of Executive Policymaking." *American Journal of Political Science* 45(3):532–550.

Chen, Jowei. 2013. "Voter Partisanship and the Effect of Distributive Spending on Political Participation." *American Journal of Political Science* 57(1):200–217.

Clark, William Roberts, and Matt Golder. 2015. "Big Data, Causal Inference, and Formal Theory: Contradictory Trends in Political Science? Introduction." *PS: Political Science & Politics* 48(1):65–70.

Clarke, Kevin A., and David M. Primo. 2012. *A Model Discipline: Political Science and the Logic of Representations*. New York: Oxford University Press.

Coate, Stephen, and Brian Knight. 2011. "Government Form and Public Spending: Theory and Evidence from US Municipalities." *American Economic Journal: Economic Policy* 3(3):82–112.

Cochran, William G. 1965. "The Planning of Observational Studies of Human Populations." *Journal of the Royal Statistical Society. Series A (General)* 128(2):234–266.

Cole, Shawn, Andrew Healy, and Eric Werker. 2012. "Do Voters Demand Responsive Governments? Evidence from Indian Disaster Relief." *Journal of Development Economics* 97(2): 167–181.

Collier, Paul, and Anke Hoeffler. 2004. "Greed and Grievance in Civil War." *Oxford Economic Papers* 56(4):563–595.

Conover, Pamela Johnston, Stanley Feldman, and Kathleen Knight. 1986. "Judging Inflation and Unemployment: The Origins of Retrospective Evaluations." *Journal of Politics* 48(3):565–588.

Cox, Gary W., and Jonathan N. Katz. 1996. "Why Did the Incumbency Advantage in US House Elections Grow?" *American Journal of Political Science* 40(2):478–497.

Cox, Gary W., and Jonathan N. Katz. 2002. *Elbridge Gerry's Salamander: The Electoral Consequences of the Reapportionment Revolution*. New York: Cambridge University Press.

Dal Bó, Ernesto, and Pedro Dal Bó. 2011. "Workers, Warriors, and Criminals: Social Conflict in General Equilibrium." *Journal of the European Economic Association* 9(4):646–677.

Darcy, Robert, and Sarah Slavin Schramm. 1977. "When Women Run Against Men." *Public Opinion Quarterly* 41(1):1–12.

Davidson, Donald. 1963. "Actions, Reasons, and Causes." *Journal of Philosophy* 60(23):685–700.

Dawson, Michael C. 1995. *Behind the Mule: Race and Class in African-American Politics*. Princeton, NJ: Princeton University Press.

de Figueiredo, Rui. 2002. "Electoral Competition, Political Uncertainty, and Policy Insulation." *American Political Science Review* 96(2):321–333.

Dell, Melissa. 2015. "Trafficking Networks and the Mexican Drug War." *American Economic Review* 105(6):1738–1779.

Delli Carpini, Michael X., and Scott Keeter. 1996. *What Americans Know About Politics and Why It Matters*. New Haven, CT: Yale University Press.

Dennett, Daniel C. 1989. *The Intentional Stance*. Cambridge: MIT Press.

Downs, Anthony. 1957. *An Economic Theory of Democracy*. New York: Columbia University Press.

Dray, William H. 1957. *Laws and Explanation in History*. New York: Oxford University Press.

Dube, Oeindrila, and Juan F. Vargas. 2013. "Commodity Price Shocks and Civil Conflict: Evidence from Colombia." *Review of Economic Studies* 80(4):1384–1421.

Duerst-Lahti, Georgia. 1998. The Bottleneck: Women Becoming Candidates. In *In Women and Elective Office*, eds. Sue Thomas and Clyde Wilcox. New York: Oxford University Press, pp. 15–25.

Dunning, Thad. 2012. *Natural Experiments in the Social Sciences: A Design-Based Approach*. Cambridge: Cambridge University Press.

Ebeid, Michael, and Jonathan Rodden. 2006. "Economic Geography and Economic Voting: Evidence from the US States." *British Journal of Political Science* 36(3):527.

Eggers, Andrew C. 2017. "Quality-Based Explanations of Incumbency Effects." *Journal of Politics* 79(4):1315–1328.

Elster, Jon. 1986. Introduction. In *Rational Choice*, ed. Jon Elster. New York: NYU Press.

Elster, Jon. 1998. A Plea for Mechanisms. In *Social Mechanisms: An Analytical Approach to Social Theory*, eds. Richard Swedberg and Peter Hedström. New York: Cambridge University Press, pp. 45–73.

Epstein, David, and Sharyn O'Halloran. 1999. *Delegating Powers: A Transaction Cost Politics Approach to Policy Making Under Separate Powers*. New York: Cambridge University Press.

Erikson, Robert S. 1971. "The Advantage of Incumbency in Congressional Elections." *Polity* 3(3):395–405.

Erikson, Robert S., and Rocío Titiunik. 2015. "Using Regression Discontinuity to Uncover the Personal Incumbency Advantage." *Quarterly Journal of Political Science* 10(1):101–119.

Erskine, Hazel. 1971. "The Polls: Women's Role." *The Public Opinion Quarterly* 35(2): 275–290.

Esteban, Joan, and Debraj Ray. 2001. "Collective Action and the Group Size Paradox." *American Political Science Review* 95(3):663–672.

Fair, Ray C. 1978. "The Effect of Economic Events on Votes for President." *The Review of Economics and Statistics* 60(2):159–173.

Fearon, James D. 1998. Commitment Problems and the Spread of Ethnic Conflict. In *The International Spread of Ethnic Conflict: Fear, Diffusion, and Escalation*, eds. David Lake and Donald Rothchild. Princeton, NJ: Princeton University Press, pp. 107–126.

Fearon, James D. 1999. Electoral Accountability and the Control of Politicians: Selecting Good Types versus Sanctioning Poor Performance. In *Democracy, Accountability, and Representation*, eds. Adam Przeworski, Susan Stokes, and Bernard Manin. New York: Cambridge University Press, pp. 55–97.

Fearon, James D. 2011. "Self Enforcing Democracy." *Quarterly Journal of Economics* 126(4): 1661–1708.

Fearon, James D., and David D. Laitin. 2003. "Ethnicity, Insurgency, and Civil War." *American Political Science Review* 97(1):75–90.

Feddersen, Timothy J. 2004. "Rational Choice Theory and the Paradox of Not Voting." *Journal of Economic Perspectives* 18(1):99–112.

Ferejohn, John. 1986. "Incumbent Performance and Electoral Control." *Public Choice* 50:5–26.

Ferejohn, John, and Debra Satz. 1995. "Unification, Universalism, and Rational Choice Theory." *Critical Review* 9(1–2):71–84.

Ferraz, Claudio, and Frederico Finan. 2011. "Electoral Accountability and Corruption: Evidence from the Audits of Local Governments." *American Economic Review* 101(4):1274–1311.

Ferree, Myra Marx. 1974. "A Woman for President? Changing Responses: 1958–1972." *The Public Opinion Quarterly* 38(3):390–399.

Føllesdal, Dagfinn. 1979. "Hermeneutics and the Hypothetico-Deductive Method." *Dialectica* 33(3–4):319–336.

Fouirnaies, Alexander, and Andrew B. Hall. 2018. "How Do Electoral Incentives Affect Legislator Behavior?" Stanford University typescript.

Fowler, Anthony. 2016. "What Explains Incumbent Success? Disentangling Selection on Party, Selection on Candidate Characteristics, and Office-Holding Benefits." *Quarterly Journal of Political Science* 11(3):313–338.

Fowler, Anthony, and Andrew B. Hall. 2014. "Disentangling the Personal and Partisan Incumbency Advantages: Evidence from Close Elections and Term Limits." *Quarterly Journal of Political Science* 9(4):501–531.

Fowler, Anthony, and Andrew B. Hall. 2018. "Do Shark Attacks Influence Presidential Elections? Reassessing a Prominent Finding on Voter Competence." *Journal of Politics* 80(4):1423–1437.

Fowler, Anthony, and B. Pablo Montagnes. 2015. "College Football, Elections, and False-positive Results in Observational Research." *Proceedings of the National Academy of Sciences of the USA* 112(45):13800–13804.

Fox, Richard L., and Jennifer L. Lawless. 2005. *It Takes a Candidate: Why Women Don't Run for Office.* New York: Cambridge University Press.

Fox, Richard L., and Jennifer L. Lawless. 2011. "Gendered Perceptions and Political Candidacies: A Central Barrier to Women's Equality in Electoral Politics." *American Journal of Political Science* 55(1):59–73.

Frey, Frederick W. 1985. "The Problem of Actor Designation in Political Analysis." *Comparative Politics* 17(2):127–152.

Friedman, Jeffrey. 1996. *The Rational Choice Controversy: Economic Models of Politics Reconsidered.* New Haven, CT: Yale University Press.

Friedman, Milton. 1957. *A Theory of the Consumption Function.* Princeton, NJ: Princeton University Press.

Frigg, Roman, and James Nguyen. 2020. Scientific Representation. In *The Stanford Encyclopedia of Philosophy*, ed. Edward N. Zalta. Spring 2020 ed. Metaphysics Research Lab, Stanford University.

Fulton, Sarah A. 2012. "Running Backwards and in High Heels: The Gendered Quality Gap and Incumbent Electoral Success." *Political Research Quarterly* 65(2):303–314.

Gangl, Markus. 2013. Partial Identification and Sensitivity Analysis. In *Handbook of Causal Analysis for Social Research*, ed. Stephen L. Morgan. New York: Springer Science + Business Media, pp. 377–402.

Gasper, John T., and Andrew Reeves. 2011. "Make It Rain? Retrospection and the Attentive Electorate in the Context of Natural Disasters." *American Journal of Political Science* 55(2):340–355.

Gelman, Andrew, and Eric Loken. 2013. "The Garden of Forking Paths: Why Multiple Comparisons Can Be a Problem, Even When There Is No 'Fishing Expedition' or 'p-Hacking' and the Research Hypothesis Was Posited Ahead of Time." Department of Statistics, Columbia University.

Gelman, Andrew, and Eric Loken. 2014. "The Statistical Crisis in Science." *American Scientist* 102:460–465.

Gelman, Andrew, and Gary King. 1990. "Estimating Incumbency Advantage without Bias." *American Journal of Political Science* 34(4):1142–1164.

Gerber, Alan S., and Donald P. Green. 2000. "The Effects of Canvassing, Telephone Calls, and Direct Mail on Voter Turnout: A Field Experiment." *American Political Science Review* 94(3):653–663.

Gerber, Alan S., and Donald P. Green. 2012. *Field Experiments: Design, Analysis, and Interpretation.* New York: W. W. Norton.

Gerber, Alan S., Donald P. Green, and Edward H. Kaplan. 2014. The Illusion of Learning from Observational Research. In *Field Experiments and Their Critics: Essays on the Uses and Abuses of Experimentation in the Social Sciences*, ed. Dawn Langan Teele. New Haven, CT: Yale University Press, pp. 9–32.

Gerber, Alan S., Donald P. Green, and Christopher W. Larimer. 2008. "Social Pressure and Voter Turnout: Evidence From a Large-Scale Field Experiment." *American Political Science Review* 102(1):33–48.

Gerber, Alan S., and Gregory A. Huber. 2010. "Partisanship, Political Control, and Economic Assessments." *American Journal of Political Science* 54(1):153–173.

Giere, Ronald N. 1988. *Explaining Science: A Cognitive Approach.* Chicago: University of Chicago Press.

Giere, Ronald N. 2006. *Scientific Perspectivism.* Chicago: University of Chicago Press.

Gilligan, Thomas W., and Keith Krehbiel. 1989. "Asymmetric Information and Legislative Rules with a Heterogeneous Committee." *American Journal of Political Science* 33(2):459–490.

Glaeser, Edward L., Rafael La Porta, Florencio Lopez-de Silanes, and Andrei Shleifer. 2004. "Do Institutions Cause Growth?" *Journal of Economic Growth* 9(3):271–303.

Godfrey-Smith, Peter. 2006. "The Strategy of Model-Based Science." *Biology and Philosophy* 21(5):725–740.

Goodman-Bacon, Andrew. 2018. "Difference-in-Differences with Variation in Treatment Timing." NBER Working Paper No. 25018. Cambridge, MA: National Bureau of Economic Research.

Gordon, Sanford C. 2009. "Assessing Partisan Bias in Federal Public Corruption Prosecutions." *American Political Science Review* 103(4):534–554.

Granato, Jim, Melody Lo, and M. C. Wong. 2010. "A Framework for Unifying Formal and Empirical Analysis." *American Journal of Political Science* 54(3):783–797.

Green, Donald, and Ian Shapiro. 1994. *Pathologies of Rational Choice Theory: A Critique of Applications in Political Science*. New Haven, CT: Yale University Press.

Green, Donald, and Ian Shapiro. 1996. Pathologies Revisited: Reflections on Our Critics. In *The Rational Choice Controversy: Economic Models of Politics Reconsidered*, ed. Jeffrey Friedman. New Haven, CT: Yale University Press, pp. 235–276.

Green, Donald P., Shang E. Ha, and John G. Bullock. 2010. "Enough Already about "Black Box" Experiments: Studying Mediation Is More Difficult than Most Scholars Suppose." *The Annals of the American Academy of Political and Social Science* 628(1):200–208.

Grossman, Herschell I. 1991. "A General Equilibrium Model of Insurrections." *American Economic Review* 81(4):912–921.

Guala, Francesco, and Daniel Steel. 2011. Rationality and Choice. In *The Philosophy of Social Science Reader*, eds. Francesco Guala and Daniel Steel. New York: Routledge, pp. 211–216.

Gurr, Ted Robert. 1970. *Why Men Rebel*. Princeton, NJ: Princeton University Press.

Hacking, Ian. 1983. *Representing and Intervening: Introductory Topics in the Philosophy of Natural Science*. New York: Cambridge University Press.

Hafner-Burton, Emilie M., Stephan Haggard, David A. Lake, and David G. Victor. 2017. "The Behavioral Revolution and International Relations." *International Organization* 71(S1): S1–S31.

Harish, S. P., and Andrew T. Little. 2017. "The Political Violence Cycle." *American Political Science Review* 111(2):237–255.

Hassan, Nasra. 2001. "An Arsenal of Believers." *The New Yorker*, November 12, pp. 36–41.

Healy, Andrew, and Neil Malhotra. 2010. "Random Events, Economic Losses, and Retrospective Voting: Implications for Democratic Competence." *Quarterly Journal of Political Science* 5(2):193–208.

Healy, Andrew J., Neil Malhotra, and Cecilia Hyugjung Mo. 2010. "Irrelevant Events Affect Voters' Evaluations of Government Performance." *Proceedings of the National Academy of Sciences of the USA* 107(29):12804–12809.

Hedström, Peter, and Richard Swedberg. 1998. Social Mechanisms: An Introductory Essay. In *Social Mechanisms: An Analytical Approach to Social Theory*, eds. Peter Hedström and Richard Swedberg. New York: Cambridge University Press, pp. 1–31.

Hibbs, Douglas A. 1996. "The Economy and the 1996 Presidential Election: Why Clinton Will Win with Probability Exceeding 90%." Göteborg University Working Paper.

Holland, Paul W. 1986. "Statistics and Causal Inference." *Journal of the American Statistical Association* 81(396):945–960.

Holmström, Bengt. 1979. "Moral Hazard and Observability." *The Bell Journal of Economics* 10(1):74–91.

Holmström, Bengt. 1984. On the Theory of Delegation. In *Bayesian Models in Economic Theory*, eds. Marcel Boyer and Richard Kihlstrom. New York: North-Holland, pp, 115–141.

Holmström, Bengt. 1999. "Managerial Incentive Problems: A Dynamic Perspective." *The Review of Economic Studies* 66(1):169–182.

Huber, Gregory A., Seth J. Hill, and Gabriel S. Lenz. 2012. "Sources of Bias in Retrospective Decision Making: Experimental Evidence on Voters' Limitations in Controlling Incumbents." *American Political Science Review* 106(4):720–741.

Huber, John. 2013. "Is Theory Getting Lost in the 'Identification Revolution'?" *The Monkey Cage* (blog), http://themonkeycage.org/2013/06/is-theory-getting-lost-in-the-identification-revolution/.

Humphreys, Macartan. 2005. "Natural Resources, Conflict, and Conflict Resolution: Uncovering the Mechanisms." *Journal of Conflict Resolution* 49(4):508–537.

Imai, Kosuke, and In Song Kim. 2019. "When Should We Use Unit Fixed Effects Regression Models for Causal Inference with Longitudinal Data?" *American Journal of Political Science* 63(2):467–490.

Imai, Kosuke, Luke Keele, and Dustin Tingley. 2010. "A General Approach to Causal Mediation Analysis." *Psychological Methods* 15(4):309–334.

Imai, Kosuke, Luke Keele, Dustin Tingley, and Teppei Yamamoto. 2011. "Unpacking the Black Box of Causality: Learning About Causal Mechanisms from Experimental and Observational Studies." *American Political Science Review* 105(4):765–789.

Imbens, Guido W. 2003. "Sensitivity to Exogeneity Assumptions in Program Evaluation." *American Economic Review* 93(2):126–132.

Imbens, Guido W., and Donald B. Rubin. 2015. *Causal Inference in Statistics, Social, and Biomedical Sciences*. New York: Cambridge University Press.

Kahneman, Daniel, and Amos Tversky. 1979. "Prospect Theory: An Analysis of Decision under Risk." *Econometrica* 47(2):263–291.

Kayser, Mark Andreas, and Michael Peress. 2012. "Benchmarking Across Borders: Electoral Accountability and the Necessity of Comparison." *American Political Science Review* 106(3):661–684.

Kinder, Donald R., and David O. Sears. 1985. "Public Opinion and Political Action." *The Handbook of Social Psychology* 2(3):659–661.

Krehbiel, Keith. 1993. "Where's the Party?" *British Journal of Political Science* 23(2):235–266.

Kreps, David M. 1990. *Game Theory and Economic Modelling*. New York: Oxford University Press.

Krueger, Alan B. 2007. *What Makes a Terrorist: Economics and the Roots of Terrorism*. Princeton, NJ: Princeton University Press.

Krueger, Alan B., and Jitka Maleckova. 2003. "Education, Poverty, and Terrorism: Is There a Causal Connection?" *Journal of Economic Perspectives* 17(4):119–144.

LaLonde, Robert J. 1986. "Evaluating the Econometric Evaluations of Training Programs with Experimental Data." *American Economic Review* 76(4):604–620.

Landa, Dimitri. 2006. "Rational Choices as Social Norms." *Journal of Theoretical Politics* 18(4):434–453.

Lawless, Jennifer L. 2015. "Female Candidates and Legislators." *Annual Review of Political Science* 18:349–366.

Lawless, Jennifer L., and Richard L. Fox. 2010. *It Still Takes a Candidate: Why Women Don't Run for Office.* New York: Cambridge University Press.

Lawless, Jennifer L., and Richard L. Fox. 2013. *Girls Just Wanna Not Run: The Gender Gap in Young Americans' Political Ambition.* Washington, DC: Women & Politics Institute.

Lazarus, Jeffrey. 2010. "Giving the People What They Want? The Distribution of Earmarks in the US House of Representatives." *American Journal of Political Science* 54(2):338–353.

Lazarus, Jeffrey, and Amy Steigerwalt. 2018. *Gendered Vulnerability: How Women Work Harder to Stay in Office.* Ann Arbor: University of Michigan Press.

Lee, David S. 2008. "Randomized Experiments from Non-Random Selection in US House Elections." *Journal of Econometrics* 142(2):675–697.

Leigh, Andrew. 2009. "Does the World Economy Swing National Elections?" *Oxford Bulletin of Economics and Statistics* 71(2):163–181.

Lewbel, Arthur. 2019. "The Identification Zoo: Meanings of Identification in Econometrics." *Journal of Economic Literature* 57(4):835–903.

List, Christian, and Philip Pettit. 2011. *Group Agency: The Possibility, Design, and Status of Corporate Agents.* New York: Oxford University Press.

Little, Andrew T., and Thomas Pepinsky. 2016. "Simple and Formal Models in Comparative Politics." *Chinese Political Science Review* 1(3):425–447.

Little, Andrew T., and Thomas Pepinsky. 2019. "Learning from Biased Research Designs." *Journal of Politics.* forthcoming.

Lohmann, Susanne. 1993. "A Signaling Model of Information and Manipulative Political Action." *American Political Science Review* 87(2):319–333.

Lohmann, Susanne. 1994. "The Dynamics of Information Cascades: The Monday Demonstrations in Leipzig, East Germany, 1989–1991." *World Politics* 47(1):42–101.

Lorentzen, Peter, M. Taylor Fravel, and Jack Paine. 2017. "Qualitative Investigation of Theoretical Models: The Value of Process Tracing." *Journal of Theoretical Politics* 29(3):467–491.

Lucas, Robert E. 1987. *Models of Business Cycles.* Oxford: Basil Blackwell.

Lupia, Arthur. 1994. "Shortcuts versus Encyclopedias: Information and Voting Behavior in California Insurance Reform Elections." *American Political Science Review* 88:63–76.

Madestam, Andreas, Daniel Shoag, Stan Veuger, and David Yanagizawa-Drott. 2013. "Do Political Protests Matter? Evidence from the Tea Party Movement." *Quarterly Journal of Economics* 128(4):1633–1685.

Manski, Charles F. 2007. *Identification for Prediction and Decision.* Cambridge, MA: Harvard University Press.

Martin, Jane R. 1969. "Another Look at the Doctrine of Verstehen." *British Journal for the Philosophy of Science* 20(1):53–67.

Maskin, Eric, and Jean Tirole. 2004. "The Politician and the Judge: Accountability in Government." *American Economic Review* 94(4):1034–1054.

McCrary, Justin. 2008. "Manipulation of the Running Variable in the Regression Discontinuity Design: A Density Test." *Journal of Econometrics* 142(2):698–714.

McGrath, Mary C. 2017. "Economic Behavior and the Partisan Perceptual Screen." *Quarterly Journal of Political Science* 11(4):363–83.

Miguel, Edward, Shanker Satyanath, and Ernest Sergenti. 2004. "Economic Shocks and Civil Conflict: An Instrumental Variables Approach." *Journal of Political Economy* 112(4):725–753.

Milgrom, Paul, and Chris Shannon. 1994. "Monotone Comparative Statics." *Econometrica* 62(1):157–180.

Morgan, Mary. 2012. *The World in the Model: How Economists Work and Think*. New York: Cambridge University Press.

Morgan, T. Clifton, and Patrick J. Moriarty. 1995. "State Characteristics and Crisis Outcomes: A Test of the Spatial Model." *Conflict Management and Peace Science* 14(2):197–224.

Morissette, Alanis. 1995. "Ironic." *Jagged Little Pill*, Maverick, Reprise.

Morris, Andrea Michelle. 2020. "Who Wants to Be a Suicide Bomber? Evidence from Islamic State Recruits." *International Studies Quarterly* 64(2):306–315.

Morton, Rebecca B. 1999. *Methods and Models: A Guide to the Empirical Analysis of Formal Models in Political Science*. New York: Cambridge University Press.

Myerson, Roger B. 1991. *Game Theory: Analysis of Conflict*. Cambridge, MA: Harvard University Press.

Olson, Mansur. 1965. *The Logic of Collective Action: Public Goods and the Theory of Groups*. Cambridge, MA: Harvard University Press.

Paine, Jack, and Scott A. Tyson. 2020. Uses and Abuses of Formal Models in Political Science. In *SAGE Handbook of Political Science: A Global Perspective*, eds. Dirk Berg-Schlosser, Bertrand Badie, and Leonardo Morlino. Thousand Oaks, CA: SAGE Publications, pp. 188–202.

Patterson, Samuel C., and Gregory A. Caldeira. 1988. "Party Voting in the United States Congress." *British Journal of Political Science* 18(1):111–131.

Pearl, Judea. 2009. *Causality*, 2nd ed. New York: Cambridge University Press.

Popkin, Samuel L. 1991. *The Reasoning Voter: Communication and Persuasion in Presidential Campaigns*. Chicago: University of Chicago Press.

Powell, Robert. 1999. "The Modeling Enterprise and Security Studies." *International Security* 24(2):97–106.

Powell, Robert. 2002. Game Theory, International Relations Theory, and the Hobbesian Stylization. In *Political Science: The State of the Discipline, Vol. III*, eds. Ira Katznelson and Helen Milner. New York: W. W. Norton, pp. 755–783.

Powell, Robert. 2004. "The Inefficient Use of Power: Costly Conflict with Complete Information." *American Political Science Review* 98(2):231–241.

Prior, Markus, Gaurav Sood, and Kabir Khanna. 2015. "You Cannot Be Serious: The Impact of Accuracy Incentives on Partisan Bias in Reports of Economic Perceptions." *Quarterly Journal of Political Science* 10(4):489–518.

Riker, William H., and Peter C. Ordeshook. 1968. "A Theory of the Calculus of Voting." *American Political Science Review* 62(1):25–42.

Riker, William H., and Peter C. Ordeshook. 1973. *An Introduction to Positive Political Theory*, Vol. 387. Englewood Cliffs, NJ: Prentice-Hall.

Ritter, Emily Hencken, and Cortenay R. Conrad. 2016. "Preventing and Responding to Dissent: The Observational Challenges of Explaining Strategic Repression." *American Political Science Review* 110(1):85–99.

Rohde, David W. 1991. *Parties and Leaders in the Postreform House.* Chicago: University of Chicago Press.

Rohde, David W. 2013. "Reflections on the Practice of Theorizing: Conditional Party Government in the Twenty-First Century." *Journal of Politics* 75(4):849–864.

Rosenbaum, Paul R. 2005. Sensitivity Analysis in Observational Studies. In *Encyclopedia of Statistics in Behavioral Science*, eds. B. S. Everitt and D. C. Howell. New York: John Wiley & Sons, pp. 1809–1814.

Rosenbaum, Paul R. 2010. *Design of Observational Studies.* New York: Springer Science + Business Media.

Samii, Cyrus. 2016. "Causal Empiricism in Quantitative Research." *Journal of Politics* 78(3): 941–955.

Samuelson, Larry. 1984. "Electoral Equilibria with Restricted Strategies." *Public Choice* 43(3):307–327.

Schelling, Thomas C. 2006. *Micromotives and Macrobehavior.* New York: W. W. Norton.

Schnakenberg, Keith E. 2017. "Informational Lobbying and Legislative Voting." *American Journal of Political Science* 61(1):129–145.

Sekhon, Jasjeet S. 2009. "Opiates for the Matches: Matching Methods for Causal Inference." *Annual Review of Political Science* 12:487–508.

Seltzer, Richard A., Jody Newman, and Melissa Voorhees Leighton. 1997. *Sex as a Political Variable: Women as Candidates and Voters in US Elections.* Boulder, CO: Lynne Rienner Publishers.

Sen, Amartya. 2004. "Incompleteness and Reasoned Choice." *Synthese* 140(1/2):43–59.

Shepsle, Kenneth A. 1992. "Congress Is a 'They,' Not an 'It': Legislative Intent as Oxymoron." *International Review of Law and Economics* 12(2):239–256.

Shepsle, Kenneth A., and Barry R. Weingast. 1987. "The Institutional Foundations of Committee Power." *American Political Science Review* 81(1):85–104.

Shields, Donald C., and John F. Cragan. 2007. "The Political Profiling of Elected Democratic Officials: When Rhetorical Vision Participation Runs Amok." *E Pluribus Media* https://journal.epluribusmedia.org/article/political-profiling-elected-democratic-officials.

Shleifer, Andrei, and Robert W. Vishny. 1993. "Corruption." *The Quarterly Journal of Economics* 108(3):599–617.

Shoag, Daniel, Cody Tuttle, and Stan Veuger. 2019. "Rules versus Home Rule: Local Government Responses to Negative Revenue Shocks." *National Tax Journal* 72(3):543–574.

Simmons, Beth A. 2000. "International Law and State Behavior: Commitment and Compliance in International Monetary Affairs." *American Political Science Review* 94(4):819–835.

Simmons, Beth A., and Daniel J. Hopkins. 2005. "The Constraining Power of International Treaties: Theory and Methods." *American Political Science Review* 99(4):623–631.

Simmons, Joseph P., Leif D. Nelson, and Uri Simonsohn. 2011. "False-Positive Psychology: Undisclosed Flexibility in Data Collection and Analysis Allows Presenting Anything as Significant." *Psychological Science* 22(11):1359–1366.

Simon, Herbert A. 1956. "Rational Choice and the Structure of the Environment." *Psychological Review* 63(2):129–138.

Simonsohn, Uri, Joseph P. Simmons, and Leif D. Nelson. 2014. "P-Curve: A Key to the File-Drawer." *Journal of Experimental Psychology* 143(2):534–547.

Sniderman, Paul M., Richard A. Brody, and Phillip E. Tetlock. 1993. *Reasoning and Choice: Explorations in Political Psychology.* New York: Cambridge University Press.

Snyder, James M., and David Strömberg. 2010. "Press Coverage and Political Accountability." *Journal of Political Economy* 118(2):355–408.

Spaniel, William. 2018. "Terrorism, Wealth, and Delegation." *Quarterly Journal of Political Science* 13(2):147–172.

Strömberg, David. 2004. "Radio's Impact on Public Spending." *Quarterly Journal of Economics* 119(1):189–221.

Sun, Liyang, and Sarah Abraham. 2020. "Estimating Dynamic Treatment Effects in Event Studies with Heterogeneous Treatment Effects." *Journal of Econometrics* https://doi.org/10.1016/j.jeconom.2020.09.006.

Tamer, Elie. 2010. "Partial Identification in Econometrics." *Annual Review of Economics* 2(1):167–195.

Tilly, Charles. 2003. *The Politics of Collective Violence.* Cambridge: Cambridge University Press.

Tirole, Jean. 1988. *The Theory of Industrial Organization.* Cambridge: MIT Press.

Volden, Craig, Alan E. Wiseman, and Dana E. Wittmer. 2013. "When Are Women More Effective Lawmakers than Men?" *American Journal of Political Science* 57(2):326–341.

Von Stein, Jana. 2005. "Do Treaties Constrain or Screen? Selection Bias and Treaty Compliance." *American Political Science Review* 99(4):611–622.

Walt, Stephen M. 1999. "Rigor or Rigor Mortis? Rational Choice and Security Studies." *International Security* 23(4):5–48.

Wasow, Omar. 2020. "Agenda Seeding: How 1960s Black Protests Moved Elites, Public Opinion and Voting." *American Political Science Review* 114(3):1–22.

Wasserman, Larry. 2004. *All of Statistics: A Concise Course in Statistical Inference.* New York: Springer Science + Business Media.

Weingast, Barry R., Kenneth A. Shepsle, and Christopher Johnsen. 1981. "The Political Economy of Benefits and Costs: A Neoclassical Approach to Distributive Politics." *Journal of Political Economy* 89(4):642–664.

White, Ismail K., Chryl N. Laird, and Troy D. Allen. 2014. "Selling Out? The Politics of Navigating Conflicts between Racial Group Interest and Self-Interest." *American Political Science Review* 108(4):783–800.

Wolfers, Justin. 2002. "Are Voters Rational? Evidence from Gubernatorial Elections." Stanford Graduate School of Business Research Paper Series No. 1730. http://citeseerx.ist.psu.edu/viewdoc/download?doi=10.1.1.10.8311&rep=rep1&type=pdf.

Wolton, Stephane. 2019. "Are Biased Media Bad for Democracy?" *American Journal of Political Science* 63(3):548–562.

Zaller, John. 1998. Politicians as Prize Fighters: Electoral Selection and Incumbency Advantage. In *Party Politics and Politicians,* ed. John Geer. Baltimore: Johns Hopkins University Press, pp. 125–185.

Zaller, John R. 1992. *The Nature and Origins of Mass Opinion.* New York: Cambridge University Press.

INDEX

Note: Page numbers in italic type accompanied by "f" or "t" refer to figures and tables, respectively.

point identification, 70n

political behavior: and efficacy of protests, 223–32; social pressure's influence on, 192–96. *See also* voter behavior

political parties: influence of, on federal prosecutions, 152–58; influence of, on roll-call votes, 138–41, 188–92, 198

potential outcomes framework, 36, 75 79; difference-in-differences design, 87–95; instrumental variables approach, 101–9; just-controlling design, 81–87, 94; randomized experiments, 80–81; regression discontinuity design, 95–101

potential outcomes function, 36

Powell, Robert, 2–3, 57n5, 65

primitives, 35–36, 38

Prior, Markus, 164

propensity score matching, 121

prospect theory, 54

protests, efficacy of, 223–32

publication bias, 75, 170

racial solidarity, social pressure's influence on, 195–96

randomized experiments, 80–81, *80t*, 108

rational choice tradition, 46–47, 54–55

Ray, Debraj, 61–64

reality: relationship of models to, 2, 12–14, 17, 45, 47; relationship of research designs to, 15; targets of inquiry in, 12

reasoned choice theory, 54

Receive-Accept-Sample model, 13

regression discontinuity research design, 21, 28–29, 95–101, *102*, 108–9, 211–14, 217–23

reinterpreting, 137–50; process of, 137; in study of natural disasters' effect on incumbents' electoral fortunes, 145–49; in study of party influence on roll-call votes, 138–41; in study of terrorist mobilization and recruitment, 141–45; value of, 137

representational features, 13

representative voters, 23, 26, 158–64

research design, 69–132; arguments for, 71, 73–74; assumptions used in construction of, 71, 74; credibility of, 70–71, 73–75, 111, 114–15; difference-in-differences, 87–95, 109–10, 155–56, 178–79, 186–87, 204; estimates generated by, 15; features of, 15; instrumental variables, 101–9; just-controlling, 81–87, 94, 109–10, 128, 130, 216, 232; major examples of, 80–110; randomized experiments, 80–81; regression discontinuity, 95–101, 108–9, 211–14, 217–23; relationship of, to reality, 15; researcher conduct of, 74–75; similarity to world of, 15; statistical procedures vs., 71–72; strategy for, 71–72; what to include in, 67. *See also* elements of research design (ERD); modeling the research design

Riker, William H., 55

risk aversion, 50–51

Robinson, James A., 110

Rohde, David W., 138–41, 188, 191, 198

roll-call votes, party influence on, 138–41, 188–92, 198

Romney, Mitt, 195–96

Rose, Shanna, 199, 201–3, 214–15

Rosenbaum, Paul R., 129

Rubin, Donald B., 13

running variables, 95–100, 108

Samii, Cyrus, 2

sampling variation, 77, 80

Satyanath, Shanker, 204

Schelling, Thomas C., 57

Sekhon, Jasjeet S., 2

selection into treatment, 81–82

selection on observables. *See* omitted confounders

Seltzer, Richard A., 27

Sen, Amartya, 54

Sen, Maya, 52–53

sensitivity analysis, 86, 128–32

Sergenti, Ernest, 204

Shapiro, Ian, 2

A NOTE ON THE TYPE

This book has been composed in Arno, an Old-style serif typeface in the classic Venetian tradition, designed by Robert Slimbach at Adobe.

GPSR Authorized Representative: Easy Access System Europe - Mustamäe tee
50, 10621 Tallinn, Estonia, gpsr.requests@easproject.com

www.ingramcontent.com/pod-product-compliance
Lightning Source LLC
Chambersburg PA
CBHW022304280326
41932CB00010B/983